WHAT THEY ARE SAYING ABOUT LIVING BRAVE

"Living Brave touched my heart and soul. Sharing women's stories and creating a pathway to thriving is a brilliant concept. It does take physical strength, mental clarity and spiritual courage to master life. Thank you for your beautiful, inspirational book."

~ **Eva-Maria Mora**, MBA; Renowned author of *Cosmic Recoding* (R) and other bestselling books with *Random House, Europe*.

"Hilda Villaverde does it again with another ground-breaking book! All about women and their life-changing, inspirational experiences. What a great read! Through the pages of this book, you will find your strength, your resilience, your positivity, and you will win back your life!"

~ **Caroline Sutherland**, *Hay House*; Author of *The Body Knows How To Stay Young*

"Living Brave is a valuable reminder that life and aging is not for sissies. The mini-stories that each woman shares are honest and brave and establish a variety of pathways that are vital to enjoying a healthy and long life.
The chapter 'Nurturing the Inner Garden of Well-Being' is a welcoming breath of fresh air, as an array of outstanding women give their voices with humor, conviction, and personal experiences to welcoming every year as a gift. It's most definitely a must read!"

~ **Karen Drucker**, singer/songwriter; Author of *Let Go Of the Shore*

"Sometimes a powerful story coils around my heart and inextricably entwines me. Here are 29 intimate stories that, through authors Hilda and Mary Beth's questions, pull back a curtain to offer a glimpse into their hearts.
I often tell mentors it isn't the answer you give as much as the questions you ask. Living Brave shows us the value of both - the power of questions to unearth a powerful narrative. Here, the answer is as important as the question.
The collective journey of these brave women is a celebration of our power to create connections that embrace us and welcome us especially when facing unbelievable challenges. I want to hug these women and say 'I hear you. Thank you for sharing yourself.' You remind me that we women are powerful. We are resilient. And we have each other. Living Brave reminds us of that. What a gift."

~ **Lory A Fischler**, Associate Director; Center for Mentoring Excellence; Leadership and mentoring coach and consultant; Co-Author, *Starting Strong: A Mentoring Fable* and *The Mentees' Guide* (both published by *Jossey Bass*)

LIVING BRAVE

WOMEN, STORIES, AND PATHWAYS TO THRIVING

Hilda Villaverde and Mary Beth Stern

Published by Pluma Designs
Phoenix, Arizona
LivingBrave.net

Interior design and production
Jones Media Publishing
YourBookBlueprint.com

Cover design by J Tabor Design
JTaborDesign.com

Interior Line Art by Ron Fusselman,
RJFuss@gmail.com

Cover photography by Lynne Ericksson
Scottsdale, Arizona
lynneericksson@me.com

Printed digitally in the United States of America

ISBN: 978-0-9669607-1-6 paperback

DEDICATION

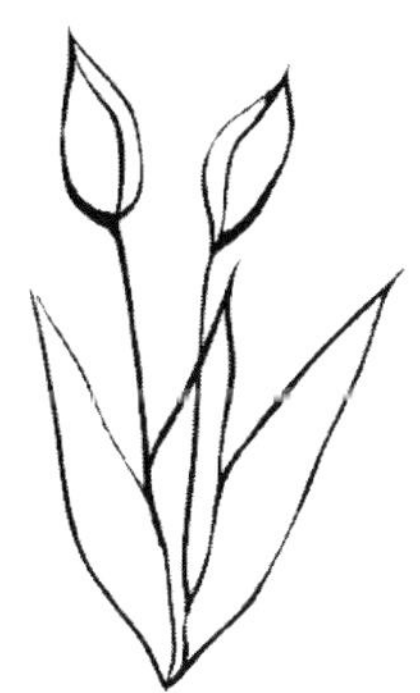

Hilda Villaverde: Dedication

In honor of Don Bewley —July 1, 1952 – October 30, 2015
Founder of Eufora International
For his inspiration, dedication, and passion
for the beauty industry.

Perhaps you find it unusual that a book about women would be dedicated to a man, but Don Bewley was an inspiration to women through his words of encouragement, his commitment to education, and his exceptional view of style and beauty. He shared the stories of his years as a hairdresser with pride and with a vision of hope for all of us. Missed, but never forgotten.

Mary Beth Stern: Dedication

In honor of my mother, Twila, a woman of courage and faith, who was an example of living bravely to her daughters and granddaughters.

To my daughter, Meghan, who is on the journey of living bravely.

To my granddaughter, Skylar, whose story
of living bravely is just beginning.

CONTENTS

PREFACE

Written by Hilda

I have never considered myself to be brave.

As a child and young adult, all of my decisions were made from overwhelming feelings of fear. Whether making personal or professional choices, fear was the motivator and certainly never bravery. Now, well into my sixties, I have come to the realization that bravery is a quality that is cultivated and expands only by the challenge of moving forward into unfamiliar territory. And, although I never felt brave in my early years, I was indeed acting bravely.

Almost twenty years ago, I wrote and published my first book, *Living on the Other Side of Fear*. The essence of the book is based on my life story from my childhood to my early forties. The introduction of that book begins with the sentence *I was born afraid*. The book details my desperate need to rid myself of an anxiety disorder and follows my life journey to the final acceptance that fear is a natural instinct born in all of us to secure our survival. Unfortunately, my survival instinct had been working overtime, and an exaggeration of my fears had permeated my everyday life.

In retrospect, during the writing of my book, I began to understand the importance of having a certain amount of fear and the value of its presence as motivation for a call to action or, at least, to focus on the particular problem at hand. Although I knew this intellectually and could rationalize being motivated by fear, I continued to feel restricted by its hold on me. After the book was published and its popularity threw me into a very public life of speaking, teaching, interviews, and world fame (not really world fame, but it did extend my visibility), I began acting braver and expanding my comfort zone.

Slowly, but surely, with years of counseling and lots of conscious effort to unravel the tight bindings that anxiety held within me, I began to welcome the awareness that, although I was truly "born afraid," I alone could make the decision to change my mind and live an intentionally braver life.

I don't particularly care for the saying, "Fake it until you make it." I prefer to say that I wasn't afraid or embarrassed by my behavior, but I did fake it. I just pushed myself into looking like a more confident person, the one I eventually desired to become. I must confess that it has taken me years to finally feel secure in being the real me. And the real me, of course, continually changes, as it does for all of us, with every year, experience, decade, and relationship that forces me to discover more of my capabilities. But most of the time, the evolution of becoming was not a conscious process, at least not until I was able to look back onto my life and think, "Look who I have become!" By this time in my life,

I can say I am no longer a "passive bystander," as Lewis Richmond says in his book, *Aging as a Spiritual Practice*. At this stage of the journey, I am fully engaged in the creation of my own life.

I love women and their stories.

As an avid reader and an always-striving-to-be-a-better listener, I have read hundreds of books written about and by women, and I have listened for over sixty years to hundreds, if not thousands, of stories by women and about women and have come to believe that there is a beautiful balance of fear and bravery that grows our inner and outer world. It is through this balance of fear and bravery that we become the "real me" of who we are. Arguably, equilibrium of pain and joy must be experienced as we are forced to move away from the pain and toward the joy of life. Over and over again, this is the dance, the balance that is required as we move from fear into bravery and being fully engaged in the creation of our own joyful lives.

One cannot feel brave without having experienced fear. I believe that is the course of becoming and that is what I appreciate most about stories. There is always the beginning of the story, the development of the situation at hand and the introduction of the characters, followed by the problem, infused by fear and more fear and then the solution and the bravery in becoming, followed by the climax, and then the conclusion. Not that each story has a happy ending or, at least, what we personally view as a happy ending, but there is always an ending where the process of becoming stops—at least until the next story begins. And each individual life has a multitude of stories that we, each and every one of us, experience continually in the course of a lifetime. Each and every moment of our lives, we are living and, at times, reliving our stories. We are creating our own lives through the stories we decide to believe.

This book is subtitled *Women, Stories, and Pathways to Thriving*. The idea came about when the thought of losing my ability of being who I have been for over forty years terrified me, and I began to panic. After all, who would I be if at this stage of life if I had to start over again? Thinking back to the times when I had made difficult decisions to change my circumstances, I was much younger, more resilient. I simply had more time to recover or reinvent myself. Also, thinking about the women in my life who had encountered much more serious conditions than what I was facing, I felt a certain guilt for not being more courageous. Many women whose stories I had heard over the years had endured life-threatening illness, the loss of partners or children, faced financial ruin, or suffered through devastating family crises, and they had not only survived but many had been able, once again, to thrive. Hearing their stories had given me hope for my own journey and had made me acutely aware that I was part of a larger story for women destined to thrive. The story I was telling myself in my mind was that I as well deserved to thrive, but the story that I was holding emotionally was overtly fearful.

Nevertheless, the feeling of panic was real to me, and no matter what I said to myself, I worried that a drastic change was coming my way and that I would be unable to handle it.

Here is my story.

MY PHYSICAL BODY CRAVES ACTIVITY. I believe that this is a fortunate characteristic considering my profession as a hairstylist. Developing the stamina for standing all day with arms held up in the air for over ten-hour days, bending, moving, and holding a blow-dryer up to my chest five days a week takes physical strength. Exercising, or movement, has been my preferred life style for all of my adult life. I was a cheerleader in high school, a pom-pom girl marching with the school band on the football field, and a runner in track, and thus began my love affair with physical movement. At twenty-two, just a few months after the birth of my son, I took up the sport of running and ran for almost twenty years. Then, during a half marathon race in San Diego, California, I sustained an injury that required knee surgery. My running days were over.

At the age of forty, I became a gym rat and, along with some gentle aerobic dance, walking, and hiking, started weight lifting. Three to four mornings a week at 5am, I was at the gym in my old, worn out t-shirts and gym pants lifting weights, working the machines, slapping the men's butts (just kidding), and constantly pushing myself to lift the next heavier weight. I thrived in this environment for over twenty years, and my body felt stronger, even though I was now in my sixties.

Then the young man who was my personal weight trainer suggested that we incorporate boxing into my exercise routine. Keeping in mind that I was one month from turning sixty-five, I was very excited to hear his promise that my waist would thin down and my arms would become leaner and stronger. One week later, boxing with new red boxing gloves, the eagerness of Muhammad Ali on his first official fight, and the force of a fairly strong weight lifter, I punched vigorously for a full five minutes. And that is all it took!

The next morning I awoke to both middle fingers so swollen that I could not bend them to dress myself. Although I finally managed to painfully shampoo and blow dry my hair and to dress, it took what seemed an eternity, and by now the fear was beginning to take hold of my thinking. Driving to work with both middle fingers straight up from the steering wheel, I wondered how I would manage a full schedule of clients for the day. And although I had assistants to help with most of the work, I still had to perform the cutting, which requires the fingers to bend or at least not be swollen to three times their normal size.

The first day of work was difficult, but by the second day, the pointer fingers on my hands had joined the middle fingers, both to my relief and dismay. At least while driving I did not appear to be an angry woman signifying my rage to all others on the road. Now I was sporting a double peace sign to all. Nevertheless, the pain was excruciating.

Icing and applying heat gave me some relief, and I made appointments with a physical therapist.

The therapist worked with me for three months as often as I could get on her schedule. Our schedule at the salon was also busy and taking any time off was out of the question. At the end of the second month, she insisted that I see a hand surgeon, which I obediently did. The diagnosis was promising; nothing was broken and no arthritis was present, which he found amazing considering my age and my profession. I did not require surgery, but it would take time to heal as the injury had been severe.

Although I have a very high tolerance for pain, prolonged pain was a new experience to me. And yes! I am one of those: "Do not give me any medication because my body will eventually heal itself." Given enough time and rest (which I was not getting), eventually the body will find its way back to health. But the continuous pain and swelling had begun to have an effect on my thinking.

A couple of months later while I was having dinner with my dear friend Mary Beth and complaining about my hands and swollen fingers, we started talking about women and how they get through painful times. I confessed that the prolonged hurting was beginning to wear me down and that I was feeling much anxiety as to what I would do next if I didn't get better soon. We discussed our friendship, how fortunate we felt to have each other, and how important it is for women to have a safety net, others to depend on when times get tough. We both felt privileged to have had friends and family members who had given us support and an assurance of catching us when we tumbled, but how about the women who don't have safety nets available to them? What becomes of them, and at what age should they begin building their nets? And then there are those amazing women who appear to be flourishing no matter what appears on their path. They emerge solid and stable after a crisis and continue on the other side of adversity. What is their secret, and what pathways have they followed that others could also pursue? The idea of our book was born.

At our next meeting to discuss the process of writing, we decided that we wanted the book to be an inspiration for women of any age to see if we could uncover the thinking and feeling process of caring for oneself. Between the two of us, we knew many women who were consciously participating in creating healthy lives, held an optimistic view of the world, had a vision of hope for their future, and had developed practical skills to live a joyful life. Our list consisted of women whose ages ranged from 20 to 91. Many of these women had survived distressing childhoods, enormous losses and illnesses, and yet they were not only surviving, they were thriving. Others had experienced solid and healthy childhoods and were still living prosperous and healthy lives. We wanted to talk to both groups of women to find the common threads and to share them as an inspiration to others who are rapidly on the same journey to aging. Thank goodness that we all age. It would be so unfair if some did and some not. Age is after all…the great equalizer.

On another note, at this point in our process of outlining the book and assembling the list of women that we would interview, my fear about my injured hands began to subside and was replaced with a feeling of love—love for the subject matter, love for the women, and love for the process of working on a new book with my friend Mary Beth, a multi-talented woman with a bright and confident mind who loves the creative process. It reminded me of a quote that I had read: Make your decisions with love and not fear! So, although I still had the pain, it was a welcome relief to release the anxiety.

As the owner of a hair salon, which I occasionally in jest call my international therapy headquarters and research center, we see thousands of women every year. Some have been clients for more than forty years while others are just beginning their relationship with us, but it's easy to spot the women who, even after seventy or eighty or ninety years of living, still hold passion and courage for their lives. Mary Beth and I knew that each one of these women has a story, many stories that make up their life history. But how would we collect their stories? How could we track the pathways that they had chosen to arrive as women who are apparently thriving both physically and emotionally? It's not easy to write about oneself, especially women who are not used to talking about themselves.

We created a series of fifteen questions divided into three areas of life expression: Physical Strength, Mental Clarity, and Spiritual Courage. We contacted the women and asked if they would consider answering the questions, and if they said yes, we emailed the questionnaire and gave them a date for completion. Afterward, we would arrange to meet with them in person for an interview. In addition, we developed a mission statement that would keep us focused on the desired outcome for the book: to write and publish a book of inspiration by interviewing a diverse and successful group of women willing to share their life stories and experiences of living bravely. The book will focus on creating a vision of hope and on developing practical skills that can inspire and embolden the reader to become the best she can be.

With the exception of four of the women on our list, none of the others had ever written anything that was published. We were unsure as to what to expect from a diverse group who were simply sharing their answers to our questions. Within weeks, as the answers started coming back to us, we were pleased and amazed at the mini-stories that we received through the fifteen questions. We marveled over many of the women whose honesty surprised us, and both Mary Beth and I were already feeling inspired.

These women probably will not have biographies written about them, be recognized by screaming fans and the paparazzi, nor have medals pinned to their chests. Instead, these stories are the spirit of women who have quietly lived courageous and productive lives, becoming the "real me" of who they have become. They have awakened to wanting better, healthier lives for themselves and for those that they love, and they have made a positive difference. Some of the women, as you will read, have expanded their lives and their influence on a larger scale and are boldly affecting the future of many others who need a safety net to renew, encouragement to restore, wisdom to regenerate, and, in some cases, the confidence to reinvent themselves. We have two women who have written about their existing safety nets of friendships that have remained connected during decades of moving forward through the adversities, as well as the joys of life. Yet another woman shares her story of losing her eleven-year-old son to a fatal accident and asks for answers from other women who share her agonizing pain.

Toward the end of the book, we have included a chapter titled "Nurturing the Inner Garden of Well-Being," a reminder that as keepers of our body, mind, and spiritual health, we must nurture within ourselves that which will give us the best chance of living full and productive lives through our life journey. Within that chapter you will read the wise guidance of twelve influential women who have entered the "conscious aging movement," a phrase that Zalman Schachter-Shalomi uses in his book *From Age-Ing to Sage-Ing* to describe the first generation of elders *"to apply the insights of humanistic and transpersonal psychology and contemplative techniques for our spiritual traditions to the aging process itself."* These women, although not consciously aware that they have indeed entered the "conscious aging movement," share their professional experiences and personal pathways of the twelve areas of well-being and living bravely.

Women have long been the keepers of the stories and the gatherers of harmony in our communities. We are hardwired to be kind and generous and to care deeply about those we love. Of course, we have all encountered those who are not kind, generous, and caring, but I am generalizing, and, from my point of view after spending a lifetime with women, the women reading this book care about others! If not, get on board, ladies…it's the only way to live happily ever after!

I firmly believe that what happens to one happens for us all. I learned this principle working with the various Native American Indian tribes in my years of teaching for the wellness programs through the University of Oklahoma outreach programs. The concept is that what happens to one woman not only happens to her but for the benefit of all of us. As we lift one woman up and give her the skills and confidence to become the real deal of herself, others will follow her lead. Ideally, it behooves each one of us to improve our ratio of making good choices for ourselves and for the outcome of our lives. Or as Jen Sincero wrote in her book, *You are a Badass*, "*One of the best things we can do for the world is to improve ourselves.*" She went on to say, "*Set an intention as to how you want to live and go for it!*"

Before you decide to "go for it," here is a reminder: there are aspects of life that are certain. There will always be fear, but there will also be joy. Aging is not for sissies; it is challenging and at times painful, but the on-going progression of living also rewards us with wisdom and, in due course, peace of mind. Loving relationships are vital to our well-being, and love expands when it is shared.

As we bring forth the idea of women lifting other women through sharing their stories of living bravely, we trust that you will benefit from the women who have shared of themselves sincerely and that you will discover at least one tiny practical skill to incorporate daily that brings you peace or a vision of hope for your future, and if you can imagine and feel yourself becoming a healthier and more fulfilled you…then we have accomplished our mission.

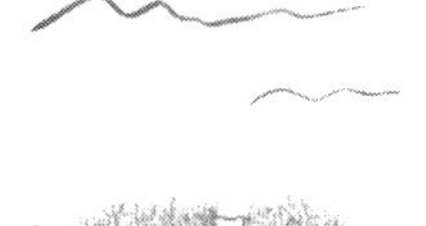

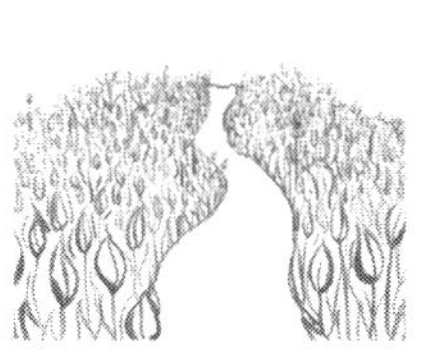

INTRODUCTION

It's as if the flood gates have opened up and released high-quality, reliable, intelligent, enjoyable, generous women who know how to lead and get things done, and they have arrived at our door.

EVERYWHERE WE HAVE BEEN IN the process of writing *Living Brave,* we have had the opportunity to meet, appreciate, and grow relationships with women who have graciously given of themselves to assist in the publication of this book. As the saying goes, "What you think about, you bring about!" Our thoughts have been centered in the reality that good happens and that it can happen to all who share their lives for the betterment of another.

There is a rumor going around that at a certain age women begin to realize that "we need each other" to get the most out of life. We become aware of the parts of us that need nurturing, comforting, and some fun through friendships, mostly with other women, and we begin relating at a deeper level of camaraderie. The reasons for these connections are varied, but they can be as simple as meeting for a glass of wine or a cup of tea to share a story. It could also be that we have been through painful relationships, have experienced loneliness, and have decided to stop the opposition and instead embrace our fellow travelers. This does not exclude our married women who have great partners and solid marriages. They need girl time also. Whether raising their children with other mothers involved in school and extracurricular activities or experiencing the "my children are now gone from home and I have extra time," women benefit from other women.

In her book, *It's Easier Than You Think*, Sylvia Boorstein writes, *"Sharing is a totally natural act." Living Brave* is a work of shared stories written by over thirty women who simply said, "Yes."

We do not want to gloss over how grateful we are to the women who took time out of their busy schedules to answer the fifteen questions, write and rewrite, and dig deep within their lives to dredge up history that had been left behind years ago. They shared their stories honestly, and sometimes we asked for even more excavation into their personal feelings. Sincerely, we appreciate their time and efforts and are grateful for their trust in us.

Our special "thank you" to the twelve women who also opened their busy schedules to contribute to Chapter Sixteen "Nurturing the Inner Garden of Well-Being." You will find these articles written with both humor and wisdom, each imparted with a substantial message from their personal lives and truly a call to action for each one of us to live braver lives.

We are eternally grateful to our patient and loyal friend Sue Jordan whose eye for grammatically correct sentences and a sensitivity to balance and organization kept us moving along and believing that we could tether forty-two distinct women's voices and create an inspiring book. Her sense of humor and enthusiasm held us together like super-glue and we can only hope that she continues to say yes when we call for help again.

My son, Ron Fusselman, who insisted at the age of three that he was an artist and planned to be an artist as an adult, did not listen to me when I insisted that he would go hungry unless he prepared for a "real" career. Well, within the pages of *Living Brave*, you will see what he created for us within a 24-hour space: "Ron, this is your mother, and we need some soft, sweet, and simple artwork for the book...by tomorrow!" Thank you for always loving the art of creating.

Living Brave is organized into four major sections.

Part One on Physical Strength, Part Two on Mental Clarity, and Part Three on Spiritual Courage—each of which contains five of the questions and answers from one or two of the contributors. Three of the women were unable to complete all fifteen questions, but we found their writing to be worthy of sharing. We think you will also. Part Four is a series of short essays by twelve women, each one a personal statement representing her overarching view of—and response to—the pathway that has led her to the uniquely rewarding, thriving life she leads today.

Each of us has her own style of reading.

EITHER WE TAKE ON A book like a hot lover and devour it in one sitting (of course, that can leave you exhausted at a certain age) or we gently read a bit at a time and savor each story like a rich chocolate that requires a slow and systematic approach. We recommend the latter. Take your time and read between the lines; enjoy sharing what is *"a totally natural act."*

PART ONE

PHYSICAL STRENGTH

"The most effective way to do it is to do it." ~ Amelia Earhart

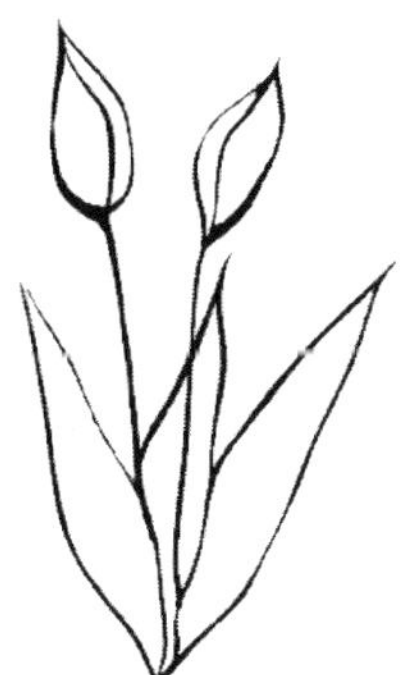

CHAPTER ONE

Overcoming Health Issues

"What we are all doing is, we're all managing gracefully."
~ Sylvia Boorstein, It's Easier Than You Think

KEY QUESTION: WHAT SIGNIFICANT HEALTH ISSUES HAVE YOU HAD TO OVERCOME?

After reading the submitted answers and completing the interviewing process with the *Living Brave* women, we had a strong sense that the majority of the women had resolved the perfectionist tendencies in their lives.

At the very least, they were aware of perfectionist tendencies in their younger years as high expectations and demands on themselves and, ultimately, upon others. But, eventually, with the gathering of time and experiences, they had softened their obsessive inclinations. A feeling of resolve appeared to enter the women after the age of fifty that would not be considered a "giving up" posture but more of a "surrender" or recognition that their life was not about being perfect, but that it had been good enough, and that good enough came as a result of painful and challenging trials turned acceptable from decisions made along their way. In her book, *The Artist's Way*, Julia Cameron wrote about women and their dance with perfectionism. *"Perfectionism is not a quest for the best. It is a pursuit of the worst in ourselves, the part that tells us that nothing we do will ever be good enough—that we should try again."* And try again, the *Living Brave* women have.

Beginning with the fashion industry and the purveyors of beauty products, magazine covers and articles, glamour shots and selfies, not to mention the fascination with Hollywood celebrities, the world is obsessed with the perfect body! Over-exercising, dangerous dieting, and surgical reconstruction have been taken to new heights in our world. A perfect body is not necessarily a healthy body, but if it sells magazines, products, and services (the cover shots of girls with abdominal 6-packs and the perfect perky breasts and big lips) then that becomes the new standard to achieve. The list of new considerations for these higher standards continues to escalate with every passing year, especially for our younger generation. Thank goodness for maturity...wisdom brings us to a deeper search for meaning, and we discover that we have always been good enough.

However, how does a young girl cope with losing the perfect body at the beginning of her teen years and still manage to thrive in a world obsessed with perfection?

Allow me to introduce our first amazingly brave woman, Debra. Debra is not a client of the salon although I would be honored if she permitted me to get my hands on her long, thick, beautiful, blond mane of hair. She is a dear friend of two clients who have known her for many years. They spoke highly of her and suggested strongly that we meet with Debra and cautioned that we would be bowled over by this passionate, bright, and animated woman, who against all odds, is thriving.

But before you read her story, I must describe her to you so that you can have a better visual sense of this remarkable woman. She is tall and slender with a body that makes a healthy and muscular statement. She obviously works out. Debra has beautiful blue eyes and a girl-next-door face with a smile that invites a response. She dresses in bright, fitted, fashionable clothing that enhances her figure, and she wears shoes that give her several extra inches of height. (She may not be as tall as she appears; nevertheless, she's still taller than most.) Overall, as she walked toward us at our first meeting, her dynamic appearance was enhanced by her straight posture and comfortable stride walking with her husband on one side and her black lab Seeing eye dog, Porsche, on the other.

As you read her mini-story, assembled through her answers from our *Living Brave* questions, we trust that you will experience what we see and feel in her presence—courage!

DEBRA, 59

"I am extremely committed to positivity and to the concept that things always turn out for the best."

Debra Cooper acquired her degree in secondary education from Arizona State University. She taught high school for three years in Phoenix, AZ. Subsequently, she worked at *The Arizona Republic* as an advertising copywriter for eight years.

After spending time as a freelance writer, she worked as the promotion coordinator at *Mountain Living* magazine in Flagstaff, AZ and then the senior writer and editor at *The Summit Christian* newspaper. In 2002, she became the staff writer at Remuda Ranch, an inpatient treatment center for eating disorders in AZ. During that time, Debra published a novel, *Behind the Broken Image*.

After eight years, she was hired by Timberline Knolls Residential Treatment Center in Illinois as the communications specialist and has been there for nearly five years. Due to a tragic accident, Debra has been totally blind since the age of fourteen.

Physical Strength

What significant health issue have you had to overcome?

I have been totally blind for 45 years. The use of the word *totally* is absolutely intentional; the vast majority of blind people can see in some regard. The difference between any sight and no sight is similar to being ten pounds overweight and being morbidly obese.

When I was 14, I was at a birthday party. We were just kids, not drinking or doing drugs. It was in a backyard. I was on a swing, as was another girl. Our boyfriends were pushing us. When the swing set fell, I was right under it lying on my back; it broke every bone in my face and knocked out most of my teeth. A former Boy Scout was in attendance. He turned me over, which saved my life, since I was bleeding into my lungs. If it had fallen on my chest, it would have definitely killed me; it would have smashed my ribs in the same way that it did my face. The Boy Scout administered compressions on my back to expel blood from my lungs. If he had not done so, I would have essentially drowned in my own blood. I spent weeks at Yale Medical Center and underwent several surgeries with many more to come in following years.

One day I was a normal teenager excited to soon enter high school—the following day I was disabled for life. The timing was horrific; teenage girls long for cookie-cutter status, in that they want to look and act like everyone else. Suddenly, I wasn't just different, I was shockingly different. By anyone's estimation, it was a tragic situation; actually the reality was far worse than this account would indicate due to the extreme dysfunction in my family.

What part of your body is most important to your health, and why?

I have a profound appreciation for my heart because it keeps me alive. I am thankful for my ears since they must do double-duty. I am so happy to have legs that can walk me around and hands that allow me to work. The truth is that my entire body is important; it is strong and capable. I try to take good care of it. When a person loses something vital, there often remains an inordinate appreciation for what is left.

How has money been a motivating factor in your life?

Money per se has not been a driving force throughout my life for I have always enjoyed a modicum of financial security due to a lawsuit regarding my accident. However, getting paid is incredibly important to me. In our society, money and value are nearly synonymous; therefore, earning a paycheck matters. I provide an important skill and service, and I want to be compensated for it. Although I often write copy free for friends and philanthropic organizations, it is my choice to do so, which makes all the difference.

How have you dealt with the physical changes of aging?

By continuing to do what is positive and healthful. When I was in my 20s, I exercised regularly so that I could do the same in my 50s. I have every confidence that I will be working out in my 80s! I try to eat well and take appropriate vitamins and supplements. I consume FAR too much alcohol—a definite vice. I took up yoga one year ago and have embraced it fully. I am delighted by the fact that I am doing things that I have not done literally in five decades: hand stands, headstands and back bends. Imagine that! I also do many of the standard female strategies to look my best: Botox, filler, and, importantly, appointments with a good hairdresser!

How does your current physical environment bring you joy?

I am fortunate to own two homes; both are very nice. But in my economy, true joy is rarely, if ever, the result of material items or even life events and experiences. While tangible items like clothes and jewelry provide instant gratification and happiness, these emotions are fleeting. Profound and true joy is a gift from God.

My first realization of this concept was 25 years ago when my second husband divorced me. I got my five-year-old son a kitten for Christmas because it had been a very hard year for him as well. One day I was on my bed, lying on my stomach with the kitten playing in front of me below my chest. I had on a diamond necklace and Spike was biting and whacking at it. The necklace was worth probably $15K; the cat had been purchased over the phone for $30. At that moment, not only did I realize that the cat was far more valuable to me than any necklace, but it was the only time that diamond had translated into actual joy because he was playing with it.

Joy in my life is now primarily provided by my two cats. When I pet them, they purr; they delight me with their clever antics. Cats are quintessential joy. My husband and I love them beyond reason; no matter what house we are in, they are there as well. I have never met a bad cat. Thank God, my husband married me or I would have turned into one of those hopeless cat ladies with a million felines!

I also experience joy from birds tweeting outside both of my homes. They delight me with their diverse cheeps and trills; I always wonder what they are gossiping or haggling about!

Mental Clarity

Tell us about a time when you trusted your intuition to make an important decision?

Throughout my life, I believe my strongest skill, regarding intuition, has related to men. Many times I have simply had a sense that something "wasn't right." A man was standing too close or even touching me in a way that, though couched under the guise of helpfulness, was ill-intended.

Perhaps the greatest moment of instantaneous action that didn't seem to come from me at all was in my late 20s. I was struggling with extreme anorexia; the intention was not to live rail-thin, but to die. This is not meant to sound dramatic or theatrical; this is just the truth. Suicidality is rampant in my family. Perhaps the most sorrowful aspect of this predilection, beyond the fact that people are no longer living, is that suicide is then perceived as the obvious, indeed reasonable, method of coping within the family. My life was extremely difficult; I truly thought that if I died, everyone would be better off. So I had gotten on the anorexia train and was absolutely committed to remain on board until it reached the final destination. I am very strong-willed; if I commit to something, I rarely fail to follow through. One day I was in my office at work, feeling ghastly, just so exhausted, and I reached over and picked up the phone; it was as if my hand was acting on its own. There may have been one single second between thought and action. I called a doctor and said I was ready to enter a hospital for help. Obviously, this action saved my life.

What mental skills have you developed over the years to help you navigate the difficult times?

I am extremely committed to positivity and to the concept that things always turn out for the best. I am not obnoxious about it, like some saccharin Mary Sunshine whom you want to shoot on sight; it is merely a personal belief system. For example, my husband and I intended to purchase a home in Flagstaff; it sold 20 minutes before we got to town. Although initially crestfallen, I knew the sale simply meant that we were not supposed to have it. That very day, we found the right home and bought it. Embracing a philosophy of positivity is certainly not always easy since life can be hard. I have many dental issues due to getting hurt; this is the gift that just keeps on giving. When it gets particularly bad, I try to focus on how terribly fortunate I am that I can afford care. How many thousands of people struggle with similar issues but do not have the finances required to get the help they need. I do. I am so thankful for that.

I also believe in the value of speaking positive words. Words are power; I wish people understood that more. If a woman habitually says, "I am stupid," she will believe it to be the case. I think that what you say is what you will ultimately believe. Additionally, I am a huge proponent of gratitude, affirmation, and appreciation. I thank God ALL the time for what is good in my life. I detest negativity and ubiquitous complaining; it is counterproductive and the focus is just all wrong.

At what point did you recognize that you had stepped into your own voice?

I honestly don't know. But it just evolved over time.

Did you have a definitive life plan? If so, how did you stay focused on that plan?

No, I did not. When I was in college, I just wanted to get out so I could work, essentially become a "real" person. I got married the day after graduation and got a teaching job. For some people, a life plan is excellent, but often I think it might be deleterious. When I taught high school, I had students who would state with great conviction "I am going to be a doctor" or "I am going to be a lawyer." This always troubled me because they were too young to truly know what these words even meant; I knew they were simply repeating what their parents had told them.

Who in your family inspired you to be courageous?

My mother. She was brought up in the 30s and 40s in a poor and broken family. She married my father, also from a poor family, and they set their minds on the American dream. My sister became diabetic at the age of five; that was in the early 60s when there was nothing easy about being diabetic. Then I got hurt. No one ever anticipates having a child hurt to such a degree. Coping with that was no walk in the park. And she basically did it alone. My father was there in name only; he was financially successful, so technically, he did do his part. Because he simply could not abide the thought of having a disabled child, he killed himself two years after my accident.

I firmly believe that human beings, at any given time, do the best that they can do. A woman may prostitute herself because she must have money to buy heroin; that is honestly the best she can do at that exact time. My mother made mistakes, but I believe she always did the best that she could do.

Spiritual Courage

What safety nets have you relied on over the years, and how have they served you?

For the first part of my life, I was a card-carrying atheist. If there was a God, which I thought not, I hated him. Due to myriad life events, I became a Jesus-loving, Bible-believing, born-again Christian at the age of 33. This shift literally transpired in about a 24-hour period. My mother thought it was a fad, another phase like my becoming a feminist in my early 20s. Considering that I am still both, a feminist and a Christian, her analysis was clearly wrong.

In my early life, I was my safety net; that did not work out so well. Today, God and my relationship with Him is everything to me. I trust Him 100 percent; I love Him with all my heart. I would be lost without Him. My son and I would have died 24 years ago if not for Him. That is not hyperbole; that is a fact.

What have you loved deeply in your life?

I deeply love God, my husband, son, and cats. I will always love my mother even though we are now estranged. I love to write and read excellent copy. I truly love and value my women friends. I believe God, in his infinite wisdom, provides women with female friends because even He knows that men are strange creatures!

What advice would you give younger people to help them develop a vision of hope for their later years?

Commit to a relationship with God; He is the embodiment of hope. Life can be extremely challenging and difficult. It is hard to do it alone. At Remuda Ranch, I often served as a chapel speaker. Our patient population was highly acute; they were extremely ill. I routinely begged the question: "Can you achieve and maintain recovery without God?" The answer was simple: "Yes." But why would they? Why go it alone when there was a loving, generous God right there with His arms open wide, just waiting to walk alongside each of them and offer support and encouragement? I feel that this concept is applicable to everyone.

Can you describe a time in your life when you moved from surviving to thriving?

Until I met God, I was just surviving, merely getting by. The act of thriving started the minute I committed to Him. Did that mean I no longer had hardship? Of course not. I have experienced a handful of very painful things in my life during the past 25 years, but I know definitively that He was with me. Because of the Lord, my life isn't just good, it is excellent. I believe I am one of THE most blessed people in the world. With the exception of this annoying blindness thing, my life is ridiculously good. I chat with God a lot and pray about many things, but this is mostly concerning other people and their needs. This is not because I am in any way good or noble; it is just that I would have to think about it to come up with something to ask Him for or to change about my life. I have a son and husband, both of whom I adore; I have many smart and lovely friends; I have a good job in which I get to work for an important organization in Chicago yet live in Flagstaff, Arizona; I have the aforementioned homes and no financial woes; and I possess good health. I am beyond blessed.

It is said that bravery comes through taking action. How will you continue to live a brave life?

Simply by taking action! I loathe when people yammer on about what they are going to do. Talk is more than just cheap; it is a waste of time. Stop talking and just do it. Failure is always an option; so is success!

All of us have only one life; that's it. I strongly believe that God did not put us on this earth to do nothing, or worse, to be self-absorbed.

I do not believe in New Year's resolutions because they are a set up to fail. And there is often a high level of grandiosity, as in "I will work out three times a day" or "I will lose a hundred pounds in a week." This is just silly.

Since a new year is a definite marker of time, each year I think about possibilities—things that I might or might not do. Last year, I considered starting yoga and volunteering at the soup kitchen in Flagstaff. Each had an element of trepidation because I am me. I did not know if I could be part of a yoga class, not due to physical inability, but I did not know if I would be able to follow the instruction. Would an instructor be verbal enough so I could reasonably participate, or would I end up looking like an idiot? Regarding the kitchen, I was unsure if I could do what they needed. Could I actually be a help, or would I prove a hindrance. For, as much as I can do in this life, there are many things I simply cannot. Neurosurgery is a fine example!

With both yoga and the kitchen, I just did it. The instructor is verbal enough, and if given a sharp knife, I can chop with the best of them.

A couple of years ago, I made a commitment to never say, "I had a bad day." I can label a day arduous, or challenging, but I will not call it bad. Every single day that each of us has on this earth is a gift from God; therefore, by definition, it cannot be bad. Every day is one more opportunity to use the gifts and talents God gave us. By and large, how good a day becomes is incumbent on us.

Because God works all things together for good, this experience has helped me more fully understand the patient population that I have worked with since 2002.

Debra has given us a vision of her path to thriving.

Her commitment to her faith, her decision to embrace hope, and her giving to charity are clearly principles that she embodies. Her faith is unwavering as she leans in seriously in God's love for her. Her hope continues to grow for herself and her family and for those who she sees in a most positive way, and she currently gives to charity by donating her time at a soup kitchen cutting vegetables for the meals. Yes! She cuts the vegetables. During our interview with her, she had Mary Beth and me laughing out loud describing her techniques in developing a skill set for chopping and dicing veggies.

Live brave.

In their book, *Wise Aging*, Rabbi Rachel Cowan and Dr. Linda Thal, ask the questions:

- What has your body been to you?
- Has it been a source of comfort or discomfort, pleasure or pain, confidence or anxiety?
- When have you related to your body primarily in terms of how it looks, how it works, or how it perceives?
- Has your body been central to your overall sense of identity, or merely a container for who you really are?

Reflecting on my own relationship with my physical body, I could certainly relate to the questions and wondered how my life would have been different had I focused on the health that I possessed instead of giving so much attention to the times that I was challenged, mostly through self-imposed physical and emotional fatigue.

The truth is that most of us take our bodies for granted until we experience discomfort, pain, or anxiety. No one, or at least no one that I have ever met, moves all the way through a human existence without the experience of a physical or emotional break down. Is there something that we can incorporate in our day-to-day activities to engage our bodies into healthier, happier, and more productive living? And if so, would we do it, or as the above question implies, has your body only been "a container for who you really are"?

In Chapter 16 of this book, we write about "Nurturing the Inner Garden of Well-Being." We identify twelve areas of health that can sustain us in living bold lives. Some women are forced to develop courage from the time of their birth and eventually are able to transform its effect to a life of appreciation and courageous living. So if you crave inspiration (I love being inspired by a super-hero woman who is kicking butt and has had to reach far above the ground to do it), then you will love meeting our next *Living Brave* woman, Becky.

How we found our next inspiring brave woman was no coincidence. After moving from northern California to Scottsdale, Arizona, Becky went online to locate a new stylist to care for her hair and found us. I would venture to say that in the Phoenix area there are several thousand hairstylists, most of them with a visible presence on the internet. In our Scottsdale location alone surrounding the city block where our tiny studio salon is located, there are at least 500 stylists. What were the odds of Becky finding our studio salon on the internet?

Becky might have needed a new hairstylist, but after months of pain and physical therapy for my injured hands, I needed inspiration. We had just started the process of writing the book when Becky became a new client. After meeting her and hearing her story, any injury that I had acquired was only a reminder of the remarkable resiliency of the human body and spirit, and I knew that I would eventually arrive on the other side of the injury with a new understanding and appreciation for my health and wellness.

Aside from her physical beauty, Becky is also as beautiful on the inside. Her healthy appearance, outgoing personality, and refined listening skills are but a few of the characteristics that attract people and success to her. Hers is a story of an imperfect body and the way this woman managed to thrive in a world obsessed with perfection.

BECKY, 64

"Because of my disability, I think I have learned to be more in the present moment...to enjoy what I can do physically today."

- Psychologist, Ph.D.
- Newly married to her high school "crush."
- Private practice in Northern California and Scottsdale, Arizona, for adults and couples striving to "live bravely."
- Specialties: Working through trauma, resolving gender differences with couples coping with health issues and mid-life challenges.
- First amputee skier trained at Mammoth Mountain Ski Resort, California, before Mammoth established an amputee ski school.
- Other physical activities: waterskiing, walking, hiking, yoga, pilates, swimming, and weight training.
- Latest physical activity: river rafting down the Colorado River and hiking the Grand Canyon on crutches without a prosthetic.

Physical Strength

What significant health issue have you had to overcome?

I was born missing part of my tibia and fibula with a normal foot—the first in medical history at the time. After five major surgeries at Mayo Clinic, they prepared me for an above-the-knee amputation when I was 13 years old. My mother tells me that before 5 years old, I was in a body cast or the hospital for two-thirds of my life.

What part of your body is most important to your health, and why?

My little leg, as my family calls it, is still the focus as I move into mid-sixties. The normal aging process creates difficulties with the fit of the suction socket that secures the prosthesis to my little leg, and this can inhibit walking.

How has money been a motivating factor in your life?

Like most aging women in our culture, I am constantly surprised at the changes in my physical appearance. Some days I look in the mirror and think, "What the hell happened here?" Other days I feel that a newfound wisdom and calmness offset the aging lines and wrinkles. Because of my disability, I think I have learned to be more in the present moment…to enjoy what I can do physically today. Because the future for me isn't as much about a new wrinkle as the possibility of no longer being able to walk on my own, I am keenly aware and grateful for each day of ambulatory freedom. As my abilities diminish, I focus on physical activities that can still be challenging and contribute to my feeling strong. So, in younger years, I was an avid downhill amputee skier. When my good knee began to complain, I switched to the stationary bike and yoga. Then, with an improved prosthetic, I fell into walking and hiking, which now is supplemented with swimming when the weather is too warm.

How does your current physical environment bring you joy?

I have recently moved to Arizona from Northern California and am still developing an appreciation for the subtle beauty of the desert, the extraordinary sunsets, and the wildlife that live around us. This time of year air conditioning is first on my gratitude list!

Mental Clarity

Tell us about a time when you trusted your intuition to make an important decision?

There have been many times when intuition has pushed through my tendency to over think a situation. Often, I only recognize it as intuition in retrospect. An early example was when I quit an oppressive management job to move to Mammoth Lakes, California, to possibly learn to ski (there were no ski programs for amputees at the time). My plan was to stay for a winter. I left seven years later, having earned my real estate broker's license and having developed proficiency as a skier.

A more recent event was when I reconnected with my current husband at our 40th high school reunion. I had a strong intuition in high school that he was the one for me, but I was way too young and shy to follow that intuition. Imagine, after 40 years, reconnecting with him at a reunion! And when I learned that he was available, I felt terror. So I sent him off for water and flat-out left the reunion before he returned! The next morning at the airport headed home, this little voice inside me would not let me rest. So I trusted that voice and called his office to leave a message apologizing for my fast exit the night before. He called back within minutes—and the rest is history!

What mental skills have you developed over the years to help you navigate the difficult times?

It's second nature for me to see the larger perspective. If I'm having a difficult day with pain, I think about someone who is blind or the people surviving in war-torn countries. It shifts me quickly into feelings of gratitude.

At what point did you recognize that you had stepped into your own voice?

For me it continues to be a process much like the stock market...in my voice, out of my voice.

Did you have a definitive life plan? If so, how did you stay focused on that plan?

I've always been goal-oriented, but the plan or end-goal has shifted over the years. I'm an "experiential learner" which sometimes means "learning through mistakes"...like when I chose to go to law school, which I thought would please my parents. I was 39 years old before I could claim my true calling and begin a Ph.D. program in psychology.

Who in your family inspired you to be courageous?

My entire family inspired me in an indirect and quiet way. My parents are veterans of WWII. They light up when they tell the stories from that time in their life: my father, a

Navy pilot, and my mother, Rosie the Riveter. They chose to raise me with expectations that I could be and do anything that someone with two normal legs could be or do. And my older sister was my constant protector and admirer.

Spiritual Courage

What safety nets have you relied on over the years, and how have they served you?

I was raised in a Christian family; therefore, in my early years, I spent a fair amount of time negotiating with God to grow my little leg. My relationship with a higher power has shifted greatly over the years but continues to be a safety net, especially in times of difficulty. I no longer hold God responsible for my suffering…or even the unfairness of life, but believe instead that *he/she* is always in relationship with me and walking alongside. I feel this presence the most when I am in my private practice sitting with my client or out in the world when a like-spirited person crosses my path.

What have you loved deeply in your life?

I'm not sure how to answer this question as I'm struck with wondering, "Is there any other way to love than deeply?" My family, of course. I have a small but amazing family, not perfect, but easy to love. My husband, Doug, is one who invites a deep connection and love and a basketful of friends to our life. This may sound odd, but I love my clients. Therapy can be such a deeply intimate experience that, when allowed to see the core of someone, it invites deep love. It's why we are trained in developing boundaries, which for me allow those deeper feelings to develop. I suppose a "lesser" loving would be around activities and interests.

What advice would you give younger people to help them develop a vision of hope for their later years?

I would say to him or her that your life is like a play that keeps unfolding. If you're "down a rabbit hole," it's hard to see the light of day. I've experienced numerous rabbit holes in my life and could never have predicted then how my life would turn out at this stage in my mid-60s. Don't struggle alone. Oftentimes, a helping hand can pull you out of that place. For me it was therapy with a loving, trustworthy therapist who helped to reach down into that rabbit hole, and together we worked our way out. For others, it might be a spiritual counselor or an intimate friend.

Can you describe a time in your life when you moved from surviving to thriving?

It was the move to Mammoth Lakes, CA, and the realization that I wanted to learn to ski. Up until that time, I was careful to hide my prosthetic from the public. But because I'm an above-the-knee amputee, I had to remove the prosthetic and ski with outriggers, which exposed my disability to the world. Surviving for me was living behind my defenses (e.g., looking perfect and normal); thriving began when I had the courage to take off my prosthetic for the greater thrill of skiing down that mountain and feeling a freedom that I had never known.

It is said that bravery comes through taking action. How will you continue to live a brave life?

What a great question! I do find that as I age I am more careful. Taking action isn't always easy when we're fighting new fears and anxieties that can arise with aging. The way I move past the fear is by taking baby steps. So if a task or challenge feels too big, I break it down into smaller bits. And then I reward myself greatly…through verbal affirmations and sometimes…potato chips!

A recent example of taking baby steps would be river rafting and hiking in the Grand Canyon without my prosthetic, using only my crutches. The original thought was terrifying, so we broke it down into manageable bits. First, I worked with a wonderful trainer for three months prior to the event who trained me specifically for the Grand Canyon. We also enlisted trusted friends to join the group, and we chose a reputable rafting company. And then we over-prepared for every possible outcome. It's probably the most physically demanding challenge I've attempted in my 60s, as there were times I found myself on a cliff crutching sideways because the rock ledge was only as wide as my foot. My behind still bears scars from scooting across rocks when the path didn't allow a foothold for my crutches. Thriving was realizing that I could reach those magnificent waterfalls with the help and support of many others who made this adventure possible: my husband, friends, and an amazing guide who never left my side. You can bet there were a lot of potato chips at the end of this adventure!

(Organic Olive Oil and Sea Salt Potato chips are a favorite treat at our hair salon, and Becky occasionally brings in a bag for us to share. She is our potato chip gal!)

To know Becky is to love being in her presence.

DESPITE HER LIFE'S STRUGGLES FROM birth to this day, as her body changes, so must she adjust to new ways of reaching for stability to continue walking, an activity most take for granted. Her courage and vision for accomplishment, her sensible approach to life, and her solid ideals of living healthy have been her pathways to thriving, and her optimistic attitude toward her goals is contagious. Having had to redefine her life in a world of perfectionist ideals, she has had to develop a sixth sense of spirited empathy, and when you meet her, you will experience it.

Live brave.

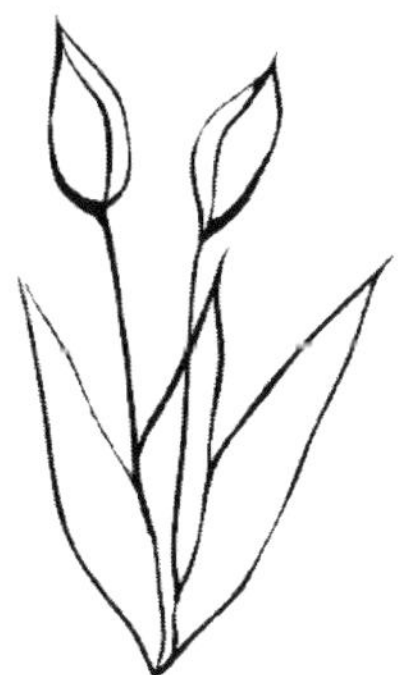

CHAPTER TWO

Focus on Your Body

"Your body hears everything your mind says." ~ *Naomi Judd*

KEY QUESTION: WHAT PART OF YOUR BODY IS MOST IMPORTANT TO YOUR HEALTH, AND WHY?

Mary Beth and I decided that, although not perfect, the questions that formed the *Living Brave* questionnaire must have been divinely guided to us.

We have marveled at how these answers have created mini-life stories and presented a blueprint into the lives and thinking processes of women. We found a pattern to the answer as to which part of the body is most important for their continued health. A healthy mind, emotional centeredness, and a strong heart were looked upon as essential areas of the body for strength, clarity and courage in the aging process.

Taking into consideration that neither Mary Beth nor I have medical degrees, we have been acutely aware and involved with the workings of our physical bodies, and we have both lived long enough to change and advance our own physical and emotional strength. We have also been extremely involved with hundreds of people, including our family and friends, co-workers and business associates, friends of friends, and the list of hundreds quickly expands as we move well into our sixties. This is what we know, at this time, for sure: Pay attention to the voice of your body. It is continually talking and expressing itself to you, the caretaker in charge.

When we met Jolene, we were taken by her calm yet effervescent nature. It doesn't seem as if these two adjectives would merge but in her case, they do. She is young but wise. She is beautiful but appears not to notice her good looks. She is intellectual but can charm a television camera with an innocent smile. She also works with a diverse population of all ages, and because she is an expert in nutrition and fitness, which we now know affect not only the body but mental and emotional well-being, we asked her to share her personal journey of arriving at her current position and her views on health and wellness as women prepare to age and continue to thrive.

Truly, Jolene is an inspiration for our younger generation of women who are determined to live outstanding and vibrant lives…all along the way.

JOLENE, 35

> ***"The enthusiasm and creativity of a younger mind combined with the experience of a more mature mind is a combination that can create and inspire massive change for everyone involved!"***

JOLENE IS A LEADING INTEGRATED health and fitness, holistic nutrition, and natural beauty expert based in Scottsdale, AZ, and the first board-certified holistic nutritionist in Arizona. As a world traveler, she has garnered the best natural health techniques from all over the globe.

She is the nutrition and fitness expert on *Good Morning Arizona*, where she teaches easy and realistic tips to be healthier while having fun! Recently named one of *USA Today's* "America's Premier Fitness Experts," Jolene is a best-selling author and has appeared in international magazines, newspapers, television shows, and fitness videos.

With almost 20 years of experience in the health and fitness industry, Jolene has a Bachelor of Science in geophysics and numerous health, nutrition, and fitness certifications. She loves learning about the latest scientific breakthroughs in the health field.

Jolene also loves speaking at conferences, shooting health videos, being a spokes model, writing, blogging, and traveling (to name just a few of her favorite things to do!)

Physical Strength

What significant health issue have you had to overcome?

I have always had a tough time with body image. In my teenage years and early 20s, I was a model. I achieved a small level of success, but I was not willing to starve myself to be really skinny. My genetics gave me a healthy, fit, curvy figure that is not the traditional model ideal. It created a lasting impact on me to be often told that I was "too big," which to a young girl, translates to "not good enough." Even though I am a normal, healthy weight, I still struggle to this day with loving and celebrating my body as it is. As women in general, we are more predisposed to being hard on ourselves. As I have matured, I've learned to appreciate my strong healthy body just the way it is—but it has been a long road.

What part of your body is most important to your health, and why?

My heart—and by this I mean both energetically and physically. A strong and healthy heart will allow me to stay physically active and enjoy my favorite activities for many more years to come. Energetically, my heart is important because it symbolizes self-love and self-worth. I have studied Traditional Chinese Medicine (TCM), and many health problems start with the heart, so by keeping my heart healthy in all senses, I believe that my health will stay vital.

How has money been a motivating factor in your life?

When I was younger, I decided that I wanted to make lots of money. When I achieved that goal in my mid-20s, I distinctly remember the moment when my thoughts shifted. I was standing on the corner of a city street, wearing head-to-toe designer clothes, carrying a Starbucks coffee and heading back to my high-paying corporate job in the oil and gas industry. I owned a nice condo downtown and drove a Mercedes. I had achieved a level of success that I thought would make me happy, but I remember thinking, "This is it?" I felt empty, and this prompted me on a journey of self-discovery. I realized that money is very nice to have. But it's the freedom that money gives me that really makes me happy. This was a liberating realization to get out of the rat race and focus on what truly made me happy.

How have you dealt with the physical changes of aging?

Age is just a number! It breaks my heart when a new client tells me "Well, now that I'm over 50, there's not much I can do." Wait a minute, there's A LOT you can do regardless of your age!! Some of my clients reach the peak of their health in their 70s once they start working with me! How old you feel is really a matter of mindset, and you can improve on this no matter your age!

How does your current physical environment bring you joy?

When I quit my stable, high-paying job in Canada and moved to Arizona to pursue my passions, I knew that I had found my home. Living in the desert, I feel gratitude every day at my surroundings. The heat feels like a warm hug that is comforting to me. The desert landscape is beautiful, and there are wonderful mountains all around me to hike. Taking joy in these simple pleasures on a daily basis is very special to me.

Mental Clarity

Tell us about a time when you trusted your intuition to make an important decision?

When I left the oil and gas industry, it was a huge decision to give up the comfortable life that I had created for myself. It wasn't my passion, and I wanted to live the rest of my life doing something that I loved. I rented a condo in Arizona for ten days in a place where I knew no one. I spent those days in nature—hiking, biking, enjoying the sun, and really reflecting on what made me happy. I realized that natural health, nutrition, physical fitness, and helping people all made me happy. So I decided to design a new life that focused on creating the most good in the world and doing what I loved.

What mental skills have you developed over the years to help you navigate the difficult times?

I am still learning this skill, but it is extremely powerful. I care less what other people think of me. As long as I am a good person and feel good about my decisions, I am letting go of the power that I allow others' opinions to hold over me. It is truly empowering to base my choices on what is best for ME, as opposed to what I think I should do.

At what point did you recognize that you had stepped into your own voice?

The minute I made the decision to move to Arizona, I knew that it was the right direction. The life that I have designed here is the first time in my life that I feel truly content. Of course, I still have other goals that I want to accomplish, but I am able to live in the moment and enjoy the simple pleasures in life. This is true freedom to me, which is one of my main motivating factors.

Did you have a definitive life plan? If so, how did you stay focused on that plan?

I thought I had a life plan—to be successful in a corporate environment and make lots of money. It's funny that once you achieve a goal, sometimes it feels hollow. I was fortunate to correct my course at such a young age, in my mid-20s. Now that I am following my passion, I don't have a definitive plan except to always stay true to who I am and to keep learning and growing. I like to stay open to new directions!

Who in your family inspired you to be courageous?

I am blessed to have amazing parents! They always told me that I could do anything or be anything. They supported my decisions in life and have always been my rock.

Spiritual Courage

What safety nets have you relied on over the years, and how have they served you?

My family has been my rock throughout my life. I've been blessed to have amazing parents who love and support me in all of my endeavors. Knowing that they believe in me has given me the courage to step outside of the box and try things that I may not have tried otherwise!

I've noticed in many women that I work with that our childhoods often have more impact than we realize on our adult lives. Women who had a positive supportive family usually tend to be able to overcome hurdles a little easier than those who didn't grow up with family support.

However, I've noticed that some of the hardest workers are people who have come from a place that they don't want to go back to—in this case, it is powerful to be able to draw strength from a childhood that may not have been ideal. It's really about switching from the victim to the creator mentality and taking control of your life to be the best that you can be right here right now! An example would be when a doctor tells a person that she is on her way to becoming diabetic. The woman could become a victim and accept that her fate is to be diabetic. Or she could take on more of a creator mentality and decide that she is going to create a new life for herself and educate herself on how to use diet and lifestyle to reverse the condition. It is a switch from being passive and letting things happen to you to being proactive and deciding how you want your life story to be lived!

What have you loved deeply in your life?

New experiences! Different people have different needs that make them happy, but trying new things is a deep love of mine. It may be a new recipe, a new fitness class, or travel to a new country…the sense of discovery and exploring makes me feel alive and happy.

What advice would you give younger people to help them develop a vision of hope for their later years? Working with women over 50, what advice would you give someone to start doing now to live a vibrant life over 50?

I've worked with many women in their 50s, 60s, and 70s. I'm often inspired by them… I've heard many times that life just keeps getting better every year!

There are two things in common that I see in vibrant women over 50:

- They take care of their health, and most started this at a young age. It's true that it is much easier to maintain your health than repair it at a later age. By making sure that we give our body the nutrients that it needs, along with physical activity, our bodies want to be healthy.

- Positivity! Having a positive outlook on life translates to a healthier body and a glow from within. The women that I work with have all faced adversity in life, but the ones who come out smiling are the ones who are able to find the good in almost every situation.

It is said that bravery comes through taking action. How will you continue to live a brave life?

By being true to myself. In the end, it doesn't matter what others think of you. It matters what you think of yourself. I will continue to seize new opportunities and live in the moment. I want to learn as much as I can and keep helping others to live their best lives. Above all, I want to continue to appreciate the simple things in life. For me, daily gratitude equals happiness. One of my favorite things to do is to inspire others by speaking and writing. This is my true calling in life, and I consider this a brave life to follow my passion!

Considering your young age and your work with more mature women, what do you know at this time that is helping you get results with this demographic?

One thing that is really powerful when working with women of all ages is the ability to share decades of experience. I love connecting with the energy and wisdom of women who have lived a full life and who have stories to tell. Sharing my passion and purpose with others, I'm often told that I infuse inspiration and hope into the lives of those around me, both professionally and personally. Having friendships and business relationships that span the decades allows everyone to get the best of both worlds. The enthusiasm and creativity of a younger mind combined with the experience of a more mature mind is a combination that can create and inspire massive change and great results for everyone involved!

I especially love to speak at women's conferences; having a room full of women who are there to be empowered and learn from each other is a very special dynamic to me. As women, no matter the age, we need to embrace each other, boost each other up, and help each other achieve our dreams!

We met Jolene when we came across her Monday Fit Tip weekly newsletters posted on the Internet.

THE CONTENT IS ALWAYS UP-BEAT, informative, and relative to the time of year, seasons, holidays, etc. Anyone can benefit from her insights, recipes, and inspiration. Here is a sample of one newsletter that we found inspiring.

Monday Fit Tip by Jolene

Please decide . . .

If you're like most people then reading this subject line was a little uncomfortable and you may have even experienced a bit of anxiety.

Make a decision? Do I have to?

We are forced to make decisions every day, but that doesn't make it any easier.

When you stop to think about it, your life is the sum total of all the decisions that you have ever made…up to this point. Your health, your mindset, your finances are all an outcome of the decisions you've made. Some decisions are so small that they seem insignificant—and other decisions weigh on you for days because you know that the outcome will change the course of your life.

You'll wade through a myriad of trivial decisions today—ranging from the flavor of your coffee, to the gas you put into your car, to the food you put into your body. It's easy to be fooled into believing that these have no real impact on the big picture—but they do. You'll shift over to automatic while making your habitual decisions today—these no longer require a second thought since your preferences are defaulted.

The time you wake up each morning, the way you take your eggs, the frequency in which you exercise. Your habitual decisions play a huge part in determining major factors in your life, and these aren't always easy to modify once the habit is in place.

We're always making decisions.

Big ones like "Should you marry him/her," "Should you have another child," "Should you stick it out another year at that job?" Life-changing decisions are forks in the road that demand your full attention and analysis.

There's a famous quote from General Norman Schwarzkopf: "A bad decision is better than no decision" which makes sense when you realize that indecision is a decision. It's best to simply bite the bullet, choose a side, and stick with it (unless you realize you made the wrong decision LOL).

You make a life-changing decision when you choose to get fit.

I want to help you with that...

I want to help you reach your goal in a big way.

And the fastest way I know for reaching a fitness goal is to begin a challenging and consistent exercise program like the ones that I offer to my clients. And that leads us to the decision that I want you to make today.

No matter your age, no matter the physical condition of your body, there is always room for improvement.

THIS IS THE MESSAGE THAT comes from Jolene in every one of her newsletters, and it is truly her life mission to assist others to accomplish optimal health and well-being. The pathway to creating a meaningful and committed relationship for the health of the physical body pays great dividends all the way through to the end.

Live brave.

QUESTION: WHAT PART OF YOUR BODY IS MOST IMPORTANT TO YOUR HEALTH, AND WHY?

Many years ago I had the opportunity to hear our next *Living Brave* woman present a talk on "Getting Your Ask in Gear" to a group of eager professionals.

AT THE TIME I WAS very new to the idea of asking for what I wanted, either professionally or personally. Consequently, both areas of my life were suffering because I wasn't getting what I needed to thrive. As you may have already surmised, Connie's message is that if you don't ask for what you want, then don't expect to get it!

That one presentation by Connie changed my perception of asking, not as a demand for something that I wanted but as a request for information, information that would aid me in helping others get what they want. I don't consider myself a sales person; instead I am educating a client who wants the best results possible for herself. If I truly believe that I have a service and product that will benefit the client, I am providing her with what she wants. Nevertheless, I didn't mean go on a tangent on asking, but when several women answered the question, "What part of your body is most important to your health?" and they answered "my mind," I immediately thought of Connie.

Connie's mind is unstoppable! She devours books, attends educational seminars, classes, and Toastmasters, delivers unique presentations, hosts online webinars, owns a business, coaches professionals, and turns every rock over to see if there is anything under it that she can uncover and discover. I appreciate her sincere, positive mindset toward every situation that comes her way. And I marvel at her honesty. After all, how many women would confess to having liposuction and call it a very positive experience in a book that is expected to sell worldwide?

CONNIE, 57

"My deep sense of a spiritual world keeps me from spinning out of control."

Connie is the president of Exceptional Sales Performance, an international sales training and coaching practice. She is a recognized expert in identifying and eliminating "Sales Call Reluctance." Connie has a proven track record in diverse industries. Because of her expertise in overcoming "Sales Call Reluctance," Connie earned a solo article in the *Wall Street Journal*. Thanks to a cold call, she was paid to do a radio commercial for American Express. She has been interviewed by *Investor's Business Daily, Bloomberg Business Week* and *Inc*. magazine. Companies throughout the United States and Canada rely on Connie to assess salespeople prior to hiring them to assure that they are most likely to succeed. Connie helps people get their "ask" in gear.

Physical Strength

What significant health issue have you had to overcome?

As a teenager and a young adult, I experienced a moderate case of bulimia. I began psychological counseling after a man I was dating confronted me. The psychologist scared me by telling me I was going to be a very sick old woman with rotten teeth, ugly skin, sick stomach and intestines, and dull eyes. Then someone loaned me an audiotape by Marianne Williamson, *A Course in Miracles* teacher, who also had an eating disorder. She said that people who experienced bulimia were able to take in the world but not able to digest it. That helped me get a grip on what was causing the bulimia, and I have been free for over thirty-plus years from any eating disorder.

What part of your body is most important to your health, and why?

My brain is most important. I want to jump out of bed every day with zeal and enthusiasm and have a concentrated, focused, crystal-clear mind that is intelligent and discriminating.

At age 29, I had liposuction on my lateral hips. Very positive experience and I would do it again in a heartbeat. All the exercise in the world was not going to get rid of my genetic lateral hips!

How has money been a motivating factor in your life?

Money has always been a motivator. At age five, I sold poppies on Veterans Day for the Veterans of Foreign Wars nonprofit. I loved the experience more than playing with my Pekingese puppy. My mom secured her children a big newspaper route that required not only delivering papers, but collecting. From the time I was eight, I always had a job. I sold newspaper advertising before I had a driver's license and made $45 commission in one sales call that lasted around seven minutes. Out of high school, I chose a career of court reporting just for the money, and it was extremely difficult–so money is not everything–I have to enjoy making the money.

How have you dealt with the physical changes of aging?

One morning I got out of bed and was stiff. It was a real heads up. I wondered what in the world . . . if I am stiff at age 54. . . what is it going to be like when I am 84? Adjusting food intake that excluded gluten has made all the difference in the world. I am determined to be prescription free throughout my entire life. I have chosen a vegan lifestyle with daily exercise of either biking, hiking, or walking. Part of my vision is that I take impeccable care of myself, including impeccable dental care.

How does your current physical environment bring you joy?

We have had a Feng Shui expert in our home three times. Because of that experience, we have a non-cluttered, beautiful, eclectic, clean, and organized home that is peaceful. My husband is super clean. I love cleaning our home and keeping it organized. Every 3-4 months, I haul stuff away that is no longer giving joy. We have two sweet dogs that bring us joy. We have original artwork and beautiful plants that add to the home.

Mental Clarity

Tell us about a time when you trusted your intuition to make an important decision?

I trusted my intuition when I married my husband, and that was 29 years ago. He is a prize! I know what it feels like to be loved and appreciated. When I started my business, I had no business plan, never have had one to this day. A business consultant tried to get me to do research on my competition, and I couldn't stand it. I used intuition to pursue contract work in Trinidad, West Indies, and traveled there over 26 times to facilitate training with organizations like British Gas, Canadian Embassy, and Glenmark Pharmaceuticals.

What mental skills have you developed over the years to help you navigate the difficult times?

Having a Doctorate of Divinity from Ageless Wisdom University, I have worked on knowing and choosing what I identify with and what to focus on. Having a deep sense of a world beyond the physical world, when I start spinning, I can usually remind myself within a few hours what is real and what is not real.

At what point did you recognize that you had stepped into your own voice?

I have always had a voice, thanks to my mother. She encouraged speaking up and sharing opinions. But other opportunities have strengthened it. In 1992 I accompanied my husband on a business appointment and the gentleman we met with communicated with elegance. His sentences were concise, precise, and organized. I asked Bill how he had learned to speak so eloquently. He replied, "Toastmasters." That day I found a Toastmasters Club, the international organization for people to learn to communicate before any group effectively. At the first meeting, I was ready to slide under the table when they asked me to introduce myself. By living brave, I joined that evening and was assigned a mentor, a former grade school teacher, Liz Bebo, who helped me construct my first three speeches, and I won "best speaker" for each speech. I read a Dale Carnegie quote, "The royal road to self-confidence is through public speaking." When we can stand before a group and communicate persuasively and convincingly in a supportive environment, we develop solid skills that transform fear. Currently, I am president of Biltmore Toastmasters. I appreciate each member because they are all deliciously different and diverse and because they grapple with fear speaking before a group; they also practice and welcome feedback to implement ideas, which allows their confidence to soar.

My only regret is that I didn't start audio and video recording my presentations earlier. This takes *Living Brave* to watch the re-run and be constructive and not too critical.

This feedback also affirmed that what I had to say was valuable. When I started my training company, I was willing to be bold and challenge people. Early in my business as a sales trainer, I got harsh feedback that it sounded like I was scolding people. That hurt! However, it made me so aware of my motive and tone while speaking. At age 57, I do believe I am speaking more from the heart than the head. It took a long time. I see my audiences and clients as people who are intelligent, gifted, and talented and also who feel vulnerable in some areas of their lives. I love teaching classes in telephone and communication skills to younger audiences because I can integrate solid spiritual concepts that are masked as human relations skills. My internal voice is more gentle, loving, kind, and considerate toward self and others. It is so much fun to witness the unfolding.

Did you have a definitive life plan? If so, how did you stay focused on that plan?

I do not believe I have had a definitive life plan, maybe intuitively because I am so drawn to the spiritual world. However, my spiritual teacher was also very cognizant of living on earth, prospering, and being of service. My plan on a daily basis includes forward movement activities, always being proactive.

I have relied on consultants and coaches who have been extremely effective in helping me keep focused and moving forward. It seems that when I have a question or inquiry, the answer is in a book, a YouTube video, a blog, someone sharing—something shows up pretty quickly.

Who in your family inspired you to be courageous?

I was blessed by having a cheerful mother. She would come into my room every morning and open the curtains and say "Rise and shine!" My dad super-believed in me. There was no doubt in my mind that I was loved as a child. My dad loved my mom and that was the strength of the family. My mom listened to Earl Nightingale as we delivered newspapers. Earl was a great motivational speaker who was dubbed the "Dean of Personal Development," saying you can do anything you think you can. I remember listening to him every afternoon. I have only had one professional person actually tell me that I was not that great. It did rattle me, but my core belief system didn't buy into the negativity longer than a good cry one afternoon. It is still there though because I remember it.

Spiritual Courage

What safety nets have you relied on over the years, and how have they served you?

My deep sense of a spiritual world keeps me from spinning out of control. My husband is a solid rock who doesn't read any books or try to improve himself. He is simply a good, solid, sensible person.

What have you loved deeply in your life?

I love ageless wisdom teachings which are based on virtues and love. I love my family. I love life and the opportunities that it brings. I love travel and the experiences of life. I love people who are kind to others. I love people who celebrate other people's success and want people to be happy and healthy. I love people who are disciplined and joyful.

What advice would you give a younger person to help them develop a vision of hope for their later years?

Do not drink alcohol or take drugs; they rob you of your will and your life. Not even a sip of wine. It is liquid fire that is toxic to every organ in the body and the brain. It also stunts emotional maturity. When confronted with life challenges, people who reach for alcohol and drugs numb the experience and do not emotionally mature. At 58 they have the emotional maturity of a 16 year old or less. Alcohol destroys families, communities, and nations. When people use alcohol and drugs, they lose their connection to their all-knowing and wise spiritual body.

Can you describe a time in your life when you moved from surviving to thriving?

When I was in court reporting school, I was dating a "bad" boy, and my mom came to visit. She said "Connie, he makes my skin crawl." I believe my mom was bold and courageous to tell me how she felt. I woke up and broke up with the "bad" boy. So many mothers think that their children won't or don't listen to them. However, I believe that children will listen to their parents. I hunkered down and cleaned up and then met my Real Man who my mom and dad respected! We married two years later.

It is said that bravery comes through taking action. How will you continue to live a brave life?

By jumping out of bed each morning saying "I sizzle with zeal and enthusiasm as I move forth in mighty faith to do that which ought to be done by me." This is a Charles Fillmore quote, and I love it.

When life challenges come or family members pass on, I have the inner core of strength, believing that there is an invisible power that breathes me and is alive within me that helps me sort out challenges. I am able to recognize that this is just an experience and do my best to emotionally detach. I am still a work in progress on learning the lesson and being compassionate. I will continue to be brave by not imposing on anyone else, by recognizing that we are all here to seek mastery in our lives, and by that deep sense of knowing that keeps me into the adventure but out of the fray. Honoring others and minding my own business is how I will build my courage to live my life's purpose.

After reading Connie's answers to our questions on living bravely, we could clearly see that her childhood path led her to create a strong self-image of belonging and worthiness all along the way.

ONE ANSWER STOOD OUT THAT led us to undoubtedly recognize the influence of good parenting. Her answer to the question "Who in your family inspired you to be courageous?" was her parents, who were her greatest motivators and inspiration. Her mother, who she felt blessed having, and her father, who "super-believed in me," both gave her the mental skills and emotional confidence that a child needs to flourish.

In her book, *Daring Greatly*, Brene Brown, says this: *"I have no doubt, however, that when it comes to our sense of love, belonging, and worthiness, we are most radically shaped by our families of origin—what we hear, what we are told, and, perhaps most importantly, how we observe our parents engaging with the world."*

Right now is always the best time to begin any new venture and to parent ourselves through the challenges that are likely to arrive during our reinvention. Whether it is embarking on a healthier lifestyle, releasing toxic people or harmful habits from our lives, beginning a new career, or simply living a braver, more expansive life, it is possible to parent ourselves with reverence and encouragement and become the best we can be in our later years.

Live brave.

CHAPTER THREE

Motivated by Money

"Everyone has inside of her a piece of good news. The good news is that you don't know how great you can be, how much you can love, what you can accomplish, and what your potential is." ~ Anne Frank

KEY QUESTION: HOW HAS MONEY BEEN A MOTIVATING FACTOR IN YOUR LIFE?

In his 2002 book, *Thou Shall Prosper: Ten Commandments for Making Money*, Rabbi Daniel Lapin states that money is spiritual!

LET'S BEGIN WITH THE WORD *spiritual*: Of, relating to, consisting of, or having the nature of spirit; not tangible or material. Of, concerned with, or affecting the soul.

In Part Three of *Living Brave*, we will be asking questions concerning Spiritual Courage. They are not physically tangible nor material, meaning not actually visible, as in creating safety nets, loving deeply, providing advice for the future, moving from surviving to thriving and living bravely, and, for many, they require courage. But all are indeed visible when accomplished. Visible is the safety net that we can tumble into, whether that safety net be our parents, partners, friends, or money. Visible is a deeply loving relationship that will hold us close, no matter the circumstances. And advice that redirects us into favorable outcomes and supports us in escaping surviving to a new life of thriving produces visible and tangible results that we can see and touch.

Rabbi Lapin continues in *Thou Shall Prosper*: "*Money is a numeric analog for how you run your life and what you have done for others. Money is a metaphor for the strength of your human relationships. Unlike a swamp or a forest, money ceases to exist in the absence of people. Money is a combination of a claim and a promise. Money is intangible. It is only as good as the invisible network of trust that links vast number of humans into a loose kind of unity. It is a claim against other people for the goods and services you need, and it is a promise on their part to supply those goods and services to you.*"

When I read the above quote that money is a metaphor for the strength of your human relationships, it confirmed my belief that money is energy, a spiritual energy. Some people radiate a sense of confidence and trustworthiness. Their ability to develop strong human relationships will benefit them, and they will be paid for that invisible energy that animates from their being. Two examples are Nordstrom and Apple. Although you can see the store, products, and services that they distribute, the energies of confidence and trustworthiness are unmistakably present. Those who shop either or both of these establishments know that reliability and the promise to deliver goods and services are a priority to their success. Both have reached a high level of financial success. A man in a rain coat who runs up to you and, upon opening his coat, shows an assortment of watches and jewelry for you to purchase…not so much!

In the introduction to this book, I wrote that, ideally, it behooves each one of us to improve our ratio of making good choices for ourselves and for the outcome of our lives. Or as Jen Sincero wrote in her book, *You are a Badass*, *"One of the best things we can do for the world is to improve ourselves."* In chapter 16 of this book, in her article "Be Attractive," Silver Rose writes, "You attract more of what you focus on, and it's important to focus on your own beauty in every stage of life—your inner beauty, your energy, and your hard-won wisdom. I challenge you. What would happen if you were to 'Be Attractive' on purpose? What if you were to flip any negative focus you have to a positive one? What would your life be like if, with that simple switch, you could attract what you've always wanted?"

For most women, safety and security are uppermost in their needs and wants. Although money does not purchase health or happiness, it can provide financial security and some safety for making good choices for ourselves to improve our lives greatly. Nothing can protect us completely from illness, loss, and disasters, but we can be prepared without adding the stress of financial burdens. But what stops women from depending on their own talents and influence to reach their financial goals?

Most women shun their personal success and rarely talk about money. In her book, *Lean In: Women, Work, and the Will to Lead*, Sheryl Sandberg writes of the inequality of women's successes compared to men in the same industries and often in the same management positions. She presents a strong argument that women still care too much about being liked by others and that this can hold them back. She wrote: *"Less than six months after I started at Facebook, Mark and I sat down for my first formal review. One of the things he told me was that my desire to be liked by everyone would hold me back. He said that when you want to change things, you can't please everyone. If you do please everyone, you aren't making enough progress. Mark was right."*

I don't believe that anyone has to be a bad person or as a woman might be called, a bitch, to get ahead, but it is important to lean in and be attractive in our own energy. Become, as Jen Sincero says, a "Badass" in a good way. Set goals and accomplish them, establish boundaries while holding them as we raise our vision of living fully. Recognize our strengths and build upon them to flourish in our careers. Become valuable in word and action to either the employer or to the clients who are dependent on us for their success. Surround ourselves with those who bring out the best in us, people who are ahead and willing to mentor our talents. Focus and save for a future that includes health and happiness. It certainly makes it much easier to live bravely.

Allow me to introduce an artistically talented *Living Brave* woman that I have had the pleasure of knowing for many years.

SHE IS AN AUTHOR, TALENTED artist, and so much more. She is also an enjoyable and optimistic woman with a full and diverse pallet of activities, including spending time with family, writing books, painting colorful and vibrant watercolors, public speaking, and volunteering.

MARILYN, 77

"Look at you! You've come a long way." If he could see me now, would he be surprised!

I WAS BORN IN WILLIAMSPORT, Pennsylvania, but when I was six my family moved to Brooklyn, New York. Brooklyn was bustling, and that's when I became an introvert for the next forty years. I graduated high school at sixteen and at eighteen, while I was attending Hunter College in the heart of Manhattan, my father died and it deeply impacted by life. I commuted from home to college and had a double major: early childhood education and fine arts.

I was married at twenty-one and moved to Charlotte, North Carolina, where I taught first grade for three years, became pregnant with my first child, and became a stay-at-home mother. We lived there for nine years and had two sons. Then my husband had an offer to work in Mexico City. We sold our house and moved lock, stock, and kids, ages three and five to Mexico. I had to learn a whole new language and how to live in a foreign country. Our daughter was born in Mexico. I am now fluent in Spanish and so are all of my children. We left Mexico after seven years and moved back to North Carolina. A few years after returning home, my husband and I were divorced and, for the first time, I learned to live alone.

During that time, I spent two years as a temp, and that was the worst type of job I have ever had. I felt invisible. Next I became a realtor for about four years but decided that wasn't for me either. I also taught Spanish and art in a little private school in Phoenix, Arizona, for three years and then in Charlotte, I spent one year as a substitute in junior high teaching Spanish. During that year I had my first and only panic attack and swore I would never teach junior high again.

Three years after the divorce, I decided to start a new chapter in another city and chose to move to Scottsdale, Arizona. A few years after arriving, I went back to school to earn a Master's Degree in Counseling Psychology. A week after graduation, I met my present husband and we married two years later

I took a theme from an idea for a thesis and expanded it into my first book, *The Relationship Trap*. Since then I have written another book, *When Angels Call Your Name*, and am about to publish a third book. At the same time, I have been writing my memoir. I am an author and a professional watercolor artist. I have been painting on and off since I graduated from college. I love painting even more than writing, and I love writing. I find writing comes very easy for me.

I am very spiritual and led a meditation study group for eighteen years.

Physical Strength

What significant health issue have you had to overcome?

I've had to overcome health issues all my adult life, and each time I came out a victor. I experienced a miscarriage before giving birth to my first son and, shortly after his birth, gall bladder surgery. At twenty-eight, I had another son, and at thirty-five, my daughter was born in Mexico City. After my daughter was born, I had a hysterectomy. In 2006 I had a routine mammogram where they discovered a lump that was later determined to be cancer. A lumpectomy was performed. The lymph nodes were clear, and I had radiation by one of the best radiologists in the country and no chemo. It's ten years later, and I am a survivor!!!

How has money been a motivating factor in your life?

Before I told my husband that I wanted a divorce, I decided I needed to build a nest egg. I had heard too many horror stories about divorced women who were in dire straits because they didn't have any money. I was not going to be one of them. Therefore, since I had taken a job as a substitute teacher that year, I began putting away my salary.

I asked my mother to open an account in both our names, and I sent her as much as I could. I was able to put away $20,000, enough, I felt, to pay for an attorney and to help me make a fresh start. If I hadn't had that nest egg, I might have been too afraid to go through a divorce.

Another example is that every time my husband and I saved enough money, my husband invested the savings in a new business. Several businesses went down the drain, along with the savings. We were never able to get ahead. After the divorce, I was determined to save money and carefully began investing it. The market was kind to me, and my nest egg grew until today I am financially independent and able to enjoy painting and writing in my retirement. On the other hand, my ex-husband died broke 15 years ago. If I were still married to him, I would be working, unable to stop working, and desperately trying to make ends meet.

How does your current physical environment bring you joy?

Thirteen years ago I remarried, and we now have two homes and go back and forth from Scottsdale to Sedona. In Sedona I find the physical environment both peaceful and inspiring. Both of our homes are filled with colors brought in through the paintings that adorn our walls, a good number of which I have painted, but we also collect originals from other artists. We have added texture and design to our homes and feel grateful to be living in the welcoming warmth of the Arizona desert.

Mental Clarity

Tell us about a time when you trusted your intuition to make an important decision.

About three years after my divorce, I had a sense that a chapter of my life was over, and it was time to move from Charlotte, NC, to a new city and start a new life. I didn't want to be known as someone's ex-wife. I just wanted to be me. Therefore, I began investigating other cities. Eventually, someone recommended I talk to a lady named Barbara who was moving to Scottsdale, Arizona, also to start a new life. We met at a restaurant, and she arrived with an armful of reading material about Arizona. After talking to her, I decided to spend a few days in Scottsdale and flew down on July 4th weekend. It was 112 degrees the day I landed. After touring the town for two days, I fell in love with the beautiful city and decided that, if I could stand 112 degrees, the winters would be delightful. I made up my mind...and selected Scottsdale. I didn't know anyone in Scottsdale except Barbara, and she didn't want me hanging on her coattails, so to speak. I didn't know my way around town. I didn't have a job, and yet, my intuition told me it was the right move. I had lived in Mexico City for seven years and was fluent in Spanish. The white houses with their red roofs reminded me of Mexico, and I felt at home the day I arrived. I never felt lonely and never regretted the move. My intuition was right. I always trust my intuition.

At what point did you recognize that you had stepped into your own voice?

After my divorce and the first time I spoke to a group about my new book.

Earlier, I mentioned that, at the age of six after our family moved to Brooklyn, I became an introvert for the next forty years. When I was a child, my mother decided everything for me, from what dress to wear to how I should think. She was a very strong and controlling woman, my biggest critic. When I married my husband as a young woman and left home to live with him, he simply took over my mother's role of controlling me and I became a poster child for codependency.

After my divorce, I began to come into my own voice. Also, as a writer and published author, I was able to give voice again to what I felt inside of me. Speaking to groups about my thoughts and feelings forced me out of the comfort zone, which was small, and required me to develop myself and to speak up.

Did you have a definitive life plan?

At this stage in my life, I am enjoying every moment that I am in good health and that I can paint, write, travel, and enjoy visiting my children and grandchildren.

I have several more books that are waiting for me to finish. One is at the printers, as I write. I am also in the process of writing a sequel to my book *When Angels Call Your Name*. After reading the book, a number of people told me, "I could have been in your book. I have a story…" and so I began the sequel. I am almost finished with that.

Who in your family inspired you to be courageous?

My brother inspired me. When I was going through the divorce, he was there for me. He had been through a divorce and was now remarried. I remember once when my husband was trying to get me to start over again with him and not go through the divorce. I'll never forget what my brother said to me. "Do you want to go through this all over again five years down the road?" Those were such strong words. My answer was no, definitely not! He kept me going. Once, when he called, I said I was in bed because I was tired. The divorce was taking its toll. He said, "Get out of bed and get on your exercise bike...now!" I got out of bed, and he made me promise to ride that bike every day. He knew how exercise would help create a healthy state of mind. He is a doctor, and although he lived at the other end of the country from me, he was always there for me.

Spiritual Courage

What safety nets have you relied on over the years, and how have they served you?

While going through the divorce, I joined a divorce support group. It proved to be an invaluable safety net. I am still in contact with two of the women in the group. We became close friends for a number of years and provided support for one another whenever needed. Each of us has moved on. Two of us are happily remarried. A third is happily living in a retirement community and has a steady boyfriend there. We have all found peace and contentment, but we all needed that safety net in the beginning. My nest egg has also proven to be my other safety net. With money, I gained security.

WHAT HAVE YOU LOVED DEEPLY IN YOUR LIFE?

Besides loving my husband, my children, and grandchildren, I have loved painting deeply. I have painted watercolors all my life, and now I have the leisure time to paint. I sit in front of the window in Sedona with a blank sheet of paper in front of me, my palate on one side, a glass of water, and a jar filled with brushes on the other side... and I paint. The time flies by, and there is such joy in seeing the painting come to life in front of me. Although I am an author and love to write, nothing gives me as much pleasure as painting...except, perhaps, eating chocolate.

WHAT ADVICE WOULD YOU GIVE YOUNGER PEOPLE TO HELP THEM DEVELOP A VISION OF HOPE FOR THEIR LATER YEARS?

First of all, even if you are an introvert, know that you have a voice and that you can use it. Get in touch with your true, inner feelings and get to know yourself well and what brings you joy. Don't let anyone tell you what you need to feel, especially if you don't feel that way. In my book *The Relationship Trap*, I write about women who don't speak up, even when the red flags are flying for everyone to see in a relationship that is unhealthy. Don't hold back and give voice to what you truly want and deserve for your life...after all, it is your life! Second, I would highly encourage every woman to have her own money. Build yourself a nest egg, or you can call it a safety net. But don't be left vulnerable for someone else to decide what is going to happen to your life. After all, it is your life!

Can you describe a time in your life when you moved from surviving to thriving?

The closest I came to moving from the surviving to thriving mode was the day after my husband moved out. We were living in the same house while going through the divorce, and after four months of surviving one day at a time, I finally breathed a sigh of relief when he moved out. The next day he called asking how I was. "Fine," I answered although I was far from fine. I was determined to survive on my own, to regain my self-esteem, and to develop my independence. I decided I would take one day at a time and survive one day at a time. I thrived in the glow of my new independence.

It is said that bravery comes through taking action. How will you continue to live a brave life?

I sometimes wonder where I got the courage to divorce my husband. I am so outgoing now, strong and independent, but I was so different then. I remember one time when I asked my husband, "How do you check into a hotel?" Because of a job I had, I had to go to a conference in Columbia, SC, but I was so afraid of traveling by myself and had never checked into a hotel.

I used to wait in the car while my husband checked into a motel and then we would drive around to the room and park the car there. If you dropped me in the middle of Paris and came back a week later, I would still be in the same place. I was fearful and unsure of myself thanks to the put-downs by my husband. He once told me something like this: "If you open your mouth in a group, you will make a fool of yourself." I believed him and never volunteered an opinion when in a group. Now I enjoy speaking in front of groups and often think, "Look at you! You've come a long way." If he could see me now, would he be surprised!

I began a spiritual practice because I wanted to be less afraid.

IN SEARCHING FOR THE PEACE of mind that I required to be less afraid, I found that financial security was one of the four spiritual pillars necessary for vanishing away my fears. Aside from a healthy physical body, a clear and uncluttered mind, and a solid belief in a higher power, a financial base for shelter, food, and the necessities of everyday life filled me with the confidence to rest in my spiritual practice and enjoy the process of thriving. As Marilyn states in her answer for having a safety net, "My nest egg has also proven to be my other safety net. With money, I gained security."

Live brave.

CHAPTER FOUR

Physical Changes of Aging

"The women whom I love and admire for their strength and grace did not get that way because shit worked out. They got that way because shit went wrong and they handled it. They handled it in a thousand different ways on a thousand different days, but they handled it. Those women are my superheroes."
~ Elizabeth Gilbert

KEY QUESTION: HOW HAVE YOU DEALT WITH THE PHYSICAL CHANGES OF AGING?

As I mentioned in the introduction, choosing a few "brave women" to highlight in our book was a difficult task.

But I must admit that when Gandolfa's name was placed on the list, it brought a smile to both our faces, and we were sure that this everyday hero deserved recognition.

Remarkably, one would never guess her age by her straight posture, her ability to move around a room and her flexibility, her clear eyes and terrific smile (it must be the yoga and strength training classes that she attends regularly) and her bright and youthful spirit. When she enters a room, one feels the wave of her optimistic vitality.

In their book, *From Age-Ing to Sage-Ing*, authors Shalomi and Miller, write: *"Across our country, people are casting off the negative images and expectations that sentence older adults to the junk heap as social outcasts. In its place, they are hoisting the banner of what gerontologists call 'successful aging,' an activity-oriented approach that promises increased physical vigor, continued intellectual growth, and meaningful work during the elder years."*

Gandolfa is activity-oriented in her approach to her physical health and continues to grow intellectually as a student of life and people. Her work is her life, for when she shows up, we are learning.

GANDOLFA, 83

"Oh, my! Surviving has been a thread weaving its way through my entire life."

Born on February 1, 1932, my handmade birth announcements were created by my mom and had hearts in red on golden vines. I was number three in an eventual line-up of seven children. The family faith was Roman Catholic, so I was schooled in parochial institutions through high school graduation.

In 1940 my mom passed away from cancer. My dad hired several housekeepers, none of whom stayed very long. After several years, the housekeeping fell to the three young girls in our family, ages sixteen to eleven.

When I graduated from high school, I was employed by an international shoe company until my older sister, Barbara, who was working as secretary in my dad's CPA office, entered the convent. Because I was next in line, I was expected to leave my employer and work for my dad. I fulfilled those responsibilities until I married at twenty-two.

My life changed dramatically at that point. My husband, Gene, was a newly commissioned ensign in the U.S. Navy and his ship was stationed at Pearl Harbor. When his ship left for five months of sea duty, I moved in with the ship engineer's wife in naval housing near Pearl Harbor. My days were filled with Navy protocol and advantages until his military duty was over in December, 1955. Afterwards, we returned to St. Louis and lived with Gene's mom, Angela, for six months while we each found employment and an apartment.

In 1959, having been married five years with no sign of a pregnancy, we placed our name on a list with Catholic Charities, planning to adopt an infant. Before we could do that, Gene was transferred to GM's central office, and thanks to a colleague of my obstetrician, we were able to adopt Lisa at three weeks of age. Once again we placed our name with Catholic Charities and adopted Mike at three weeks of age also. We eventually moved to Arizona, but prior to moving, I became pregnant. Juli was born three weeks after we arrived in Scottsdale. Six years later, Laura was born, and she completed our family.

When Laura was an infant, I began classes at Scottsdale Community College and received my AA in 1979. I was employed as secretary to the Dean of Continuing Education at SCC and from there became secretary to the State Board for Community Colleges and its executive director, the position from which I retired nine years later.

In 2002, just after my 70th birthday, I graduated with a BS in communications from Prescott College, located in northern Arizona. Prior to my graduation, I created a group for women to share the ways each had found to foster her personal development. After a few years, I partnered with a psychologist friend in writing a program for middle school girls, mentoring them in life skills.

After 54-plus years of marriage, Gene passed away in 2009 from metastatic cancer, and I have been living singly since that time, enjoying traveling and keeping in touch with my many women friends.

Physical Strength

What significant health issues have you had to overcome?

I dealt with significant depression following the births of my two daughters. Because I was hospitalized the first time and in therapy for some time following, I had learned more about myself, so my second experience with depression was not as serious.

What part of your body is most important to your health, and why?

My heart, as it was discovered over the years that I have atrial fibrillation.

How has money been a motivating factor in your life?

Because of the humble history of my family, security in the form of money has been a need. I was fortunate to marry a very solid and successful man who provided this security.

How have you dealt with the physical changes of aging?

I am striving to be graceful with the changes which occur with age—minimized metabolism, which for me means weight gain, wrinkles, minimized energy, and A-fib, the medication for which creates edema and, I suspect, shortness of breath.

How does our current physical environment bring you joy?

It brings me joy to live alone. If you mean physical activity, I enroll in nearly year-round yoga and strength training classes that keep me in good physical condition. I also have a need for adventure. I travel often; it brings me joy to be in new environments.

Mental Clarity

Tell us about a time when you trusted your intuition to make an important decision.

After forty years of marriage, I separated from my husband, having no knowledge of the path I had stepped out on. I was petrified. We came back together again with some definite changes in place and worked on our relationship.

What mental skills have you developed over the years to help you navigate the difficult times?

When there is a mental issue that requires clear thinking, I use two methods for clarification. To avoid mental obsession, I visualize the issue as a brightly wrapped package that sits on a shelf for now. This method and the frequent repetition of the visualization allow clear thinking to come through. For stickier issues, I use *The Welcoming Prayer, which is a beautiful practice for accepting and, yes, even welcoming, obsessive thoughts.

At what point did you recognize that you had stepped into your own voice?

My own voice! My awareness of it began in my 40s when therapy helped me to learn that I had the right to make choices that resulted in feelings. My voice has grown through the years, so that at 83, I trust my voice.

Did you have a definitive life plan? If so, how did you stay focused on that plan?

A definitive life plan? No. My generation of women mostly allowed LIFE to happen to them.

Who in your family inspired you to be courageous?

After concentrated therapy, I was able to forgive my father's behavior and could honor his courage.

Spiritual Courage

What safety nets have you relied on over the years, and how have they served you?

I learned to count on myself, and when I can not give myself satisfactory information, I talk with my "living brave" women friends until I am satisfied.

What have you loved deeply in your life?

My children and my friends.

What advice would you give younger people to help them develop a vision of hope for their later years?

Learn to listen to your inner voice.

Can you describe a time in your life when you moved from surviving to thriving?

Oh my! Surviving has been a thread weaving its way through my entire life. At eight years of age, my mom died of cancer, leaving seven children. There were three girls, and I am in the middle. For four years we had a housekeeper, but when she left, my sisters and I were expected to take over all household duties and discipline of three younger brothers and ourselves. Just before my teens, my dad violated me, as he did my sisters. I did not know until many years later how that impacted my psyche. I worked through that trauma over many years, strengthening myself in the process.

I was in a loving and secure marriage that was threatened by my husband's eventual alcoholism after thirty years. With therapy, Al-Anon, and AA, we survived.

Just this summer, my eldest daughter died at age 56 from prolonged use of morphine. Lisa was adopted at three weeks of age, and as is so prevalent in adoptees, she was unable to learn about and work through her abandonment issues to the point that, in the end, she abandoned herself.

It is said that bravery comes through taking actions. How will you continue to live a brave life?

I smile as I read this final question. It is my hope that I will be able to continue counting on myself and the beautiful souls who are my family and friends. I also have moved into a quiet spirituality that must be anchored in the many years I spent practicing Catholicism. I no longer practice an organized religion and feel certain that is my path.

My sweet sister, Carmela, took her life at age 23. Today, as I respond to these questions on September 12, I am aware that this is her birthday.

When we asked Gandolfa what spiritual practice brought her the most inner peace and stability, she gave us The Welcoming Prayer.

WE WERE SURE THAT IT was worth sharing with our readers.

The Welcoming Prayer: The history of the Welcoming Prayer is a little surprising. It's not an ancient practice, though it's an ancient idea. Mary Mrozowski of Brooklyn, New York, one of the first leaders of **centering prayer**, developed the method. She was inspired by **Abandonment to Divine Providence**, an early 18th century spiritual work by Jesuit priest and spiritual director, Father Jean Pierre de Caussade. Father Thomas Keating and others saw the value of her little method, so over the years it has been supported, fine-tuned, and expanded within the community of people who practice centering prayer and beyond.

If you are struggling with a bad feeling, this method offers a structured way to embrace and accept it, allowing you to release it and move on. There are three phases to the Welcoming Prayer. You might go directly from one to the next in a single, relatively formulaic, prayer sequence. Or you might find yourself staying in one phase as it does its interior work. Using Rev. Cynthia Bourgeault's labels, the three parts are:

Focus.

Welcome.

Let go.

Focus: Bring your attention to the emotion that carries the most charge for you in this moment or is the repeating emotion from some incident—identify the emotion, such as anger, sadness, fear, anxiety, etc. Focus on the feeling of it, considering the location in your body, the shape, any color that you associate with it, how much it would weigh, and any other descriptor that would bring you into the feeling of it. Take 3 to 5 minutes to do this or more if needed.

Repeat 3 times: **Welcome** (name the feeling)

Then repeat 5 times or more:

I let go of my desire for safety and security. Welcome.

I let go of my desire for affection and esteem. Welcome.

I let go of my desire for power and control. Welcome.

I let go of my desire to change the situation as it is. Welcome

If the emotion continues, repeat the whole process, bringing yourself deeply into the feeling. This is counterintuitive; what we usually do is to avoid the feeling or try to control it. This practice can appear to be miraculous in its ability to quiet our intense feelings without losing them.

If I were to fashion a story around Gandolfa's life, it would be of adventure and enjoyment.

IN HIS BOOK, *The Power of I Am*, Joel Osteen writes, *"Don't endure your life; enjoy your life!"* And this is the woman that I witness when I am with her. Not that she has not endured her share of heartbreaks or been wounded and lost, but she has been the bravest because on the path that she still walks, she endeavors to love again.

Live brave.

I met Linda almost twenty years ago when I was looking for a miracle to save my marriage.

THE THOUGHT OF A THIRD divorce was incomprehensible to me. But that is exactly what my thoughts were when I made my first appointment with her.

In the years that followed, through her advice, encouragement, teachings, and leadership directives, I have been able to carve out a life filled with peace with myself, gratitude for my childhood, and a heck of a lot of hope for my future.

Linda is an intuitive teacher. Her thinking process is uncanny and right on target, and her words are decisive and accurate when she leads you to discover your own potential to make good decisions for yourself.

When I speak of Linda, I describe her as an authentic woman of her word, an intelligent woman who sees the good and God in everyone she meets.

It is my true pleasure to introduce you to my dear friend, coach, and *Living Brave* woman, Linda.

LINDA, 69

"Make peace with your body at the earliest age possible, and then you can appreciate every stage of your development."

Linda is an international workshop leader, professional life coach, and co-author of the book *Full Heart, Satisfied Belly*. She is a certified Enneagram teacher and has been using the Enneagram as a primary tool in her work for over 25 years.

Linda has over 35 years' experience working with individuals, businesses, and the government to enhance life and increase productivity. Her professional training is in Transpersonal Psychology and Imagery. She has been in private practice in Colorado, Maryland, and, currently, in Scottsdale, Arizona. In addition, she was a professional speaker on the national speaking circuit for ten years. Her primary message is the importance of recognizing the connection between the mind, emotions, and success.

For the past eleven years, she has been under contract with Maricopa County Superior Court in Phoenix, AZ, where she facilitates executive coaching and judicial observation with Superior Court judicial officers.

Physical Strength

What significant health issue have you had to overcome?

When I was a child I had very poor vision, but I didn't know that I wasn't seeing well. It was just the way I saw the world. My feet tripped over themselves, I couldn't catch a ball, and the black board at school was a complete blur. For some unknown reason, my parents didn't put the clues together that would have told them that my eyesight was severely compromised. I struggled in the first four years of school and was, at best, a mediocre student and terribly shy.

When I was 10, in the 5th grade, my school began to have all the students' eyes tested. My results were alarming, and my parents were told I needed to immediately see an optometrist! There were no specialists in my small town of Salida, Colorado, in 1956, so we went to the much larger city of Colorado Springs, Colorado. I will never forget that day at the optometrist. After checking my eyes, the doctor read out loud a list of symptoms of poor eyesight in a child, such as walking late, frequent falls, being clumsy, shy, not being able to spell, etc. My mother answered yes, that I exhibited all those symptoms.

The doctor actually said to her "Pat, what were you thinking?" I had never heard an adult say anything critical to my mother before. She was stunned and ashamed and apologized to me and the doctor. Then the doctor put the lenses before my eyes! It was like the scene in the *Wizard of Oz* when Dorothy and her friends saw the Emerald City for the first time! I entered a new world. I didn't know there were leaves on trees! I didn't know there were lines on the road! There were patterns everywhere, and I was delighted and amazed!

My mother was cautioned by the doctor that I might not want to wear my glasses, but the opposite was true. I didn't want to take them off! I wore them in the bath tub and asked if I could wear them to bed!

The good news is that because of that intervention and many more visits to the eye doctor, I began to fully recover my eyesight. My grades immediately improved, and I became much more confident and outgoing.

Unfortunately, there were some side effects that remained due to lack of brain development in the first ten years. I still can't tell right and left without really thinking about it. I have never been able to spell, and my ability to visually remember directions is dismal. I have some learning disabilities that are similar to dyslexia. Through the years, I have learned to compensate for all of these aspects and have been successful at hiring people to work for me whose strong suits are what I lack.

Mental Clarity

Tell us about a time when you trusted your intuition to make an important decision?

There was a major benefit that has served me well from the first ten years of my life being nearly legally blind. Not being able to see heightened my ability to listen, and my intuition became the guiding light that compensated for my lack of visual acuity. My intuition has made it possible for me to work with individuals and groups of people in a way that would not be the same without drawing easily and naturally on that sixth sense. Because of that ability, which I believe we all have, I can help individuals recognize and eliminate their own hidden blocks and patterns that hold them hostage and then guide them to their highest potential.

While speaking before a large group of people in Pennsylvania, I intuited that I should change the ending I had prepared for my workshop. I spoke very personally, and as I walked off the stage, I felt very vulnerable and was wondering, "Why did I do that?" Immediately, a man in the audience ran over to me crying and said "I was sitting here broken hearted for the last two days, but what you just said as you ended has given me exactly what I need to keep my heart open to my teenage daughter!"

We all have whispers of intuitive knowing in our ears. I believe the first ten years of my life with very little eyesight prepared me to listen and trust those whispers and led me to my life work. I am grateful every day for that gift.

Spiritual Courage

What advice would you give to a younger person to help them develop a vision of hope for their later years?

Growing older is not a curse; it is a privilege!

I think one of the biggest secrets to enjoying your life at every age is being present wherever you are with whatever your body looks like at the time.

As we age, we often look back at pictures of ourselves when we were younger and are amazed at how attractive we were then. At the time the picture was taken, all we could think of was how fat we were or how we didn't look good in what we were wearing! Make peace with your body at the earliest age possible, and then you can appreciate every stage of your development.

You can tell a woman who has been present in her life as she lived it through the good times or the bad. There is a depth in her soul and a sparkle in her eye that is undeniable!

Challenge and defeat the bad habit of comparing yourself to others. There will always be people who you think are more attractive or accomplished than you are: admire them, learn from them, and be grateful for their good example.

Throughout our lives, there are times of pain, fear, or anger that never get thoroughly processed or released. They can accumulate and create what I call emotional land mines that create overreactions when they get triggered. Some people outwardly express and others take all that energy inward. In either case, exploding land mines are not fun. Whether anyone can see them or not, they are not good for our overall wellness. They can cause unrest in relationships and at work. If you immediately know what I am talking about, get some help to deactivate your personal land mines. You will be much happier currently, and your later years will be much more peaceful and satisfying.

Learn how to get connected to your essence. In the ideal world, we would stay deeply anchored to our essence, not just our egos, while living our lives, having relationships, raising children, and working at a job or building a career. That is easier said than done! It takes consistent focus on personal and spiritual growth throughout a lifetime to understand what essence is and how to access it on a regular basis. We have to consistently learn how to carve out time for ourselves to connect with our own essence and learn how to enjoy silence and the beautiful experience of "being," not doing, without guilt.

Being in touch with your essence has nothing to do with physical exercise or looking your best or even being your ideal weight. Those aspects of taking care of yourself are important, but not as critical as being in touch with your essence because all of those physical aspects will eventually deteriorate, and then what do you have?

Acknowledging that you are a spiritual being and really living from that place makes all the difference when it comes to facing life's challenges. It doesn't stop the challenges from happening or stop the physical or emotional pain, but it does provide a sense that ultimately you will be all right. Your ego will say you have to be wealthy or have a great house and a great love to be all right. Your essence knows you can be okay anywhere with very little by yourself.

The good news is that it is never too late to get in touch with your essence because it has never left you. IT came with you as you were born, has remained with you throughout your life, and will be there for you when you die.

In summary, being present, giving up the habit of comparing yourself to others, accepting and loving your body, staying in touch with your essence, and eliminating painful land mines from your past not only gives you a vision of hope for your later years but paves the road for your journey now.

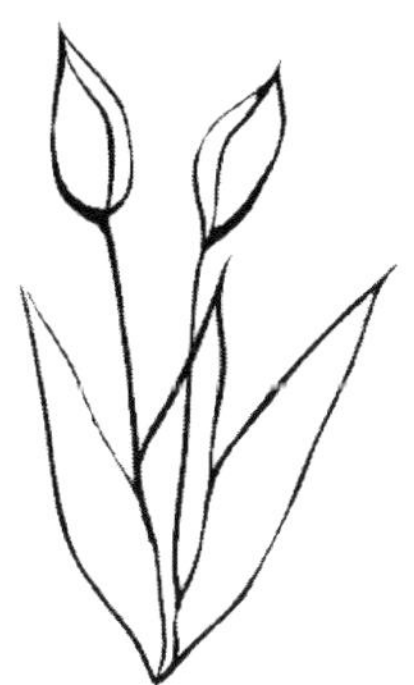

CHAPTER FIVE

The Joy of Environment

"My mission in life is not merely to survive, but to thrive; and to do so with some passion, some compassion, some humor, and some style." ~ Maya Angelout

KEY QUESTION: HOW DOES YOUR CURRENT PHYSICAL ENVIRONMENT BRING YOU JOY?

Bless the women in our lives who, like the oars on a boat, gently push the water aside and keep us moving forward in a straight line.

My relationship with Sydney began over thirty years ago when she became a salon client. Her daughters had just started pre-school, and they also became clients. Vividly, I recall them getting their haircuts sitting on my counter tops at the salon because they were too small to sit in a salon chair. Both had thick and curly hair, but the oldest had the thickest and the most kinky, curly hair ever. What a chore it was for her to keep it under control. During their regular appointments, I watched them grow into bright and beautiful young women. Even after they left for California to attend college, they would still come in for their cuts when they came home. They shared their stories with me, and we talked about most everything, including school, boys, and stuff, and only once did I totally screw up when one shared that she had had a body piercing…how was I to know that her mother wasn't supposed to know? Boy, did we all get in trouble for that!

Just a few years ago, both the girls asked if I would officiate their wedding ceremonies. The youngest first and, a year later, the oldest walked down the aisle toward me. It was my sincere pleasure and delight to witness the years of nurturing a relationship with a family whose values and consideration for one another had inspired me and filled me with hope for the future of humanity. Currently, during the writing of this book, both the girls are pregnant and their father, Jim, Sydney's husband, passed away just last week. We are mourning an immense loss and yet anticipating the joyous arrival and celebration of their first babies.

My comment at the beginning of Sydney's introduction, like the oars on a boat gently push the water aside and keep us moving forward in a straight line, is the vision that I see when I think of her. Throughout our years together, I have come to rely on her superb book recommendations (she is an avid reader with only the very best subject matter), been encouraged by her counsel on practical matters, and thoroughly enjoyed her commentary on her global travels and political views. Sydney has a natural calming presence. Her voice is tender, and her appearance is always cheerful. She is indeed one of the gentlest spirits that I have had the pleasure of knowing both as a client and a dear friend. As a mentor and inspiration in my life for over thirty years, her dedication to her marriage, family, and community has expanded my view of healthy living and living bravely. It is my pleasure to introduce you to our next *Living Brave* woman.

SYDNEY, 67

"Surround yourself with friends and love. Look for the joy in life."

I WAS BORN AND RAISED in Los Angeles. I have been married to my husband, Jim, for thirty-eight years. We have two married daughters, Whitney and Stephanie. I have lived in Arizona for almost thirty-five years.

I knew from a very early age that I wanted to be a teacher. I retired from the Scottsdale Unified School District after teaching forty years, and for the past thirteen years, I have taught at Kiva Elementary in Scottsdale.

Volunteerism is an important part of who I am. I am a sustaining member of the Junior League of Phoenix, and in my retirement, I like to spend my time volunteering at the Assistance League of Phoenix. Currently, I am co-chair of the Birthday Book Corner Program that supplies new books in nine Title 1 schools. The mission of the program is to give every child in the school a new book for his/her birthday. I am passionate about getting books into the hands of children because I believe that literacy is their future.

Physical Strength

What significant health issue have you had to overcome?

I was born without a hip socket, a condition known as congenital dysplasia. I loved playing sports but couldn't run very fast. I didn't let that bother me and have had two hip replacements in my adulthood, my first hip replacement at the age of thirty-four.

What part of your body is most important to your health, and why?

My brain is most important to me. I feel that I can overcome most difficulties by thinking them through. I also feel that if a person has a positive mental outlook it will aid one's overall general health.

How has money been a motivating factor in your life?

While I have been blessed and live very comfortably, money has never been a motivating factor in the choices that I have made. Obviously, teachers don't get rich on their salaries. My first teaching assignment (1973) was in a parochial school that paid me $400 a month. I was thrilled to be able to practice my profession, so the money wasn't a big factor.

How have you dealt with the physical changes of aging?

I feel that I am proactive. I try to do some form of exercise every day.

I have yearly checkups with my doctors, and I keep a positive attitude. I now have the time to focus on me and try to do things that bring me joy and nourish me. Many friends aren't doing well physically due to underlying conditions. I am lucky to be healthy and able to have a routine of exercising. Moving is key, as is strength training. If the body is active, so goes the mind.

How does your current physical environment bring you joy?

I am fortunate to live in Scottsdale. I live on a lake, which is very important to me. Looking out at the lake brings me solace. I love being around water, which I think came from having been raised near the Pacific Ocean. Some of my cherished vacations are those spent on the beach. My home is also important. When we were house hunting, we walked into this house and knew immediately that it was our home. We have lived here for 35 years.

Mental Clarity

Tell us about a time when you trusted your intuition to make an important decision?

When I met my husband, we both trusted our intuition. We had not known each other for very long. I was thirty years old, and he was thirty-one. Neither of us had been married before. We met in October and were married the following February. We just had a sense of being right for one another, and we have been married for 38 years.

What mental skills have you developed over the years to help you navigate the difficult times?

During my first hip replacement at the age of thirty-four, my daughters were very young. The mental skill that I developed was not to dwell on myself. I never thought that the surgery was going to go anyway but well. I have never been a worrier, and I wasn't going to start now. I try to stay positive and upbeat. I also rely on my faith to sustain me in difficult times. Prayer keeps me strong mentally.

At what point did you recognize that you had stepped into your own voice?

I think this happened when my husband and I moved to Arizona. I had never lived away from my family. I was very close to my parents and grandmother, so it was very difficult. I learned to rely on my own judgment and grew as a person. I came into myself and heard my voice.

Did you have a definitive life plan? If so, how did you stay focused on that plan?

Ever since I was in fourth grade, I knew I wanted to teach and work with children. I spent summer jobs working at camps and nursery schools. I attended college with the goal of getting my teaching certificate. My profession has always brought me joy. I always wanted to be a mom and was blessed with two wonderful children.

Who in your family inspired you to be courageous?

My mother inspired me. The way she lived her life was my model. She valued her friends, loved her family, and her grandchildren. She showed me how to live with grace and confidence.

Spiritual Courage

What safety nets have you relied on over the years, and how have they served you?

My friends and family are my safety net. I have one particular friend that I have walked with every morning for the past 25+ years. She is 85 years old. We share our joys, frustrations, sorrows, and happiness. I am a firm believer in connecting with others and sharing these experiences. It makes me happier, and it helps to be able to vent. I am also blessed with dear friends that I have known for years. Several of them live far away, so each year I make a point to visit with them. My husband encourages me to spend this time with them as he realized early on in our marriage that for me to be happy and healthy I need to nurture these relationships. I know how important it is to have these connections to others and not to isolate myself.

What have you loved deeply in your life?

I love my husband and children, naturally. I also love to spend time in nature. I find that being in beautiful places can be very spiritual. I feel closer to God when I experience the beauty of the world around me. I have also loved reading because it transports me and opens the world of possibilities to me.

What advice would you give a younger person to help them develop a vision of hope for their later years?

Surround yourself with friends and love. Look for the joy in life.

Can you describe a time in your life when you moved from surviving to thriving?

The death of my mother and father was very difficult for me. I went through a period of mourning and loss. There isn't a day that I don't think about them and miss them. With the support of my family, friends, and faith, I was able to move forward.

It is said that bravery comes through taking action. How will you continue to live a brave life?

I will strive to be involved in things that I am passionate about. I will also speak up on issues of injustice. I will continue to surround myself with positive people and shun or avoid those who are always negative and complaining.

I share my waiting with Sydney. As she awaits the birth of two babies that will certainly change her life again, I anticipate the birth of still another book, *Living Brave*, that will certainly change my life again. All of us walk the pathways of change and wait to arrive once again. Here we must embrace the present moments and celebrate them while they are alive in us. And then we will wait again.

Live brave.

PART TWO

MENTAL CLARITY

"I attended a mindful meditation class and learned a new skill; when talking too much, this is called Unskilled Speech. Because it is a skill, we can learn to change it. It is a choice."
~ Gandolfa, Salon Client

CHAPTER SIX

Trusting Your Intuition

Mary, who works with us at Pluma, being kidded about a new outfit she was wearing (she is more daring than the rest of us) answered:

"You have to practice being a little brave every day!"

KEY QUESTION: TELL US ABOUT A TIME WHEN YOU TRUSTED YOUR INTUITION TO MAKE AN IMPORTANT DECISION?

These days I find it difficult to guess the age of a woman.

I WOULD NEVER HAVE GUESSED Linda's age by her appearance and her pace.

She moves quickly and is as agile as a much younger person, and she always dresses impeccably, including makeup and freshly coiffed hair. In the years that we have known each other, she has always held a positive attitude toward everything. We have discussed religion, children, politics, health and family matters, eating well, and exercise, and her position on everything has continued to be upbeat and optimistic.

"Where does that optimistic outlook toward life come from?" I would think to myself after being with her. Although I suspected that it was because of her childhood and the nurturing of her spirit and self-worth by her parents, I wanted to share her with others to confirm what love can do for one's life.

I believe that it takes a brave woman to run a full and wholehearted life of marriage, managing a home, participating in her husband's work, volunteering, being an active grandmother, and keeping a busy social schedule with friends and family while still maintaining the appearance of a youthful person. When I asked her if she would share her life with us and answer the *Living Brave* questions, she didn't hesitate. "Absolutely! When would you like it sent to you?" She is an inspiration to me and my team at the salon.

LINDA, 77

"Keeping cool, calm, and collected and trying to always have a positive attitude and to stay strong, no matter what!"

I WAS BORN IN BAKERSFIELD, California, raised in San Francisco and moved to Pasadena, California. Attended

Arizona State University—Poly Science major, Business minor.

Worked in San Francisco at Crown Zellerbach and then moved to New York for thirteen years. Worked at NBC TV as a production assistant on news and game shows where I met my husband, Ed. Together we had a son and daughter.

I became heavily involved with politics and the local school until Ed transferred to Los Angeles where he worked with ABC TV.

I then worked as an office manager for a private school for twelve years. We moved to Arizona in 1992 and I spent twelve years doing medical market research and working for the Miss Universe organization, where I was paid to travel the world. I was also heavily involved with the Italian community in Phoenix and Scottsdale.

Currently, I help my husband in his work as the executive director of the Biltmore Area Partnership—a large, upscale shopping center in Phoenix.

I am also an active grandmother of four granddaughters.

Physical Strength

What significant health issue have you had to overcome?

No serious health issues. I have good genes.

What part of your body is most important to your health, and why?

My mind is most important to me. I believe that you can deal with most anything if you can function mentally. You have to have a good attitude and look around to see those who really have it hard where there is no good outcome for them. If you know your name and you can walk, it's going to be a good day.

How has money been a motivating factor in your life?

Only to the extent that I would think of health and education expenses.

How have you dealt with the physical changes of aging?

By keeping a positive attitude and trying to keep my body in good condition. I would rather age and have problems than not age at all. A person needs to always take pride in her appearance and herself—not for vanity, but for pride, which is important. Get to know your body and what looks good on it. Dress to your good qualities. Working for Miss Universe, which required a lot of physical labor as well as mental, I realized the busier I was, the more energy I had. The lesson I learned was that keeping your mind and body busy will keep you younger and in better health.

How does your current physical environment bring you joy?

Living in a sunny environment gives a person a more positive way of looking at things. It is a more relaxed lifestyle, and you have the opportunity to exercise most of the year. Live in gloom and you tend to have a gloomy attitude.

Mental Clarity

Tell us about a time when you trusted your intuition to make an important decision?

While recently dealing with my husband's health problems and in the past managing health problems for my parents, I followed my intuition when talking to the doctors and in making medical decisions. And most of the time, I have been right to do so.

What mental skills have you developed over the years to help you navigate the difficult times?

Keeping cool, calm, and collected and trying to always have a positive attitude and to stay strong, no matter what. During the time that I lived California and worked for a school, we had to prepare the children and ourselves for earthquakes. We had to make sure that we stayed aware, in charge, and able to handle anything that occurred, yet remain calm...always remain calm and never panic. I think this experience has stayed with me through my difficult times.

At what point did you recognize that you had stepped into your own voice?

I have always been my own person and felt as if I had my own voice. Also, all of the experiences of having children, being involved in politics, and working for Miss Universe taught me that I had a lot to give and to contribute. Working for Miss Universe taught me how much could be learned about other cultures and an appreciation for others' beliefs, which resulted in making me more understanding of others. Also, all the traveling with the pageant and dealing with these cultures made me realize that no matter what problem came up, if I kept a cool head, I could handle it. And because there was always something that came up, when I was able to handle it, I realized I had learned a good lesson by staying calm and listening to what others were saying.

Did you have a definitive life plan? If so, how did you stay focused on that plan?

No, I did not have a life plan. I felt I should always be ready for changes and to accept changes. I learned this when I worked for Miss Universe and was involved in politics. In politics, I was a co-chair of a women's committee for a mayoral candidate in a big city in Westchester County in New York. When we moved from New York to California, I was listed in the top 500 women in that particular political party. I learned that I needed to listen carefully to what people said and to be very careful of what I said. By the way, our candidate won and went on to serve several terms.

Who in your family inspired you to be courageous?

My father did. He was ahead of his time in that he felt women were capable of doing what they wanted, and he always instilled in me that I could do what I wanted to do and that I needed to be self-reliant. Not sure if *courageous* is the right word, as I would use the word *strong*. I was always loved and supported by my parents. I always knew that they would be there for me no matter what and I, in turn, would always be there for them.

Spiritual Courage

What safety nets have you relied on over the years, and how have they served you?

Be optimistic and keep calm and try to stay in control. Be self-reliant as there is a plan for everything and usually things—good or bad—happen for a reason.

What have you loved deeply in your life?

I love my four granddaughters, including a set of triplets, as they are the future, and they will contribute to the future. I think that I must have done something right in raising my own children as they have become great parents.

What advice would you give younger people to help them develop a vision of hope for their later years?

Always be proud of yourselves. Always accept change as it can lead you into a wonderful new world. Know what is happening around you in the world and the reasons why these things are happening. Keep your mind and body active. Never stop learning and enjoying life. Get on your computer and get more knowledge. There is still so much to know.

Can you describe a time in your life when you moved from surviving to thriving?

Because of my father, I have always been a thriver. He taught me to think, look at the situation, and weigh my options. There are always options.

It is said that bravery comes through taking action. How will you continue to live a brave life?

Always looking at the positive, keeping active, and taking pride in myself; staying healthy and enjoying life and always having good friends. If your family is not nearby, there is nothing like the strength you get from good friends.

There is also one more thing: one must be ready to give back. I will continue to give back wherever I can.

Although this was just a small peek at Linda's optimistic and stay-calm attitude, it is obvious that her path to developing self-confidence and living a wholehearted life came about through the encouragement that she received from her father.

He instilled in her the promise that she could do whatever she wanted to do and that she needed to be self-reliant, and indeed she did, and she is.

One more bit of Linda that I treasure her saying: "Take pride in you…for goodness sake!"

Live brave.

Some people are natural givers.

THEY INVEST IN OTHERS FOR the sheer pleasure of giving. The openhandedness of a giver is an expanded energy that creates a ripple effect capable of touching many lives in its wake with the possibility of flowing endlessly. My friend Arlene says this about the energy of giving: "Try the ripple effect; be a ripple across the pond of the lives of others, gently changing them for the better." Her words brought to mind this *Living Brave* woman, Michelle.

Although we have only recently met Michelle, our salon stylists have been donating their hairstyling services to her organization, Mother's Grace, for several years. We learned about the organization through one of their board members who is a client at our salon. We are happy to donate our time, services, and products to an organization dedicated to improving the lives of women by helping them create a vision of hope for their future and that of their families.

When tragedy strikes a family, most turn away from the situation because they're unsure as to what they can actually do or say. But Michelle's group of women engages in the process of lending a hand during the adversity and stays on to help rebuild and revitalize the women, their families, and, eventually, through the ripple effect, their communities.

Michelle has created a safety net for women. Her boundless energy and passion for supporting women in "healing the world one mother at a time" is a call to action for her organization. And a universal reminder of the importance for women that what happens to one woman happens for us all…to learn, to grow, and to support each other to be the best we can become. The question then for all of us is this…How can we give?

MICHELLE, 50

"Just when I think I need to grab hold and try to fix an 'outcome,' I breathe in and let go and what comes next is grace."

I AM A 50-YEAR-OLD MOM of three boys, the founder of Mother's Grace Charity, and the Vice President of Business Development for LabCorp. I love to travel, hang out with my boys, and explore the world.

Eight years ago, the day after Mother's Day, I had a double mastectomy. I had just been diagnosed with a very aggressive form of breast cancer at the age of 42. Prior to that month, my life was going great. I had three beautiful boys, a twenty-year marriage to my college sweetheart, fabulous friends, and a flourishing career. My husband and I were not wealthy, but we were doing very well and had built a strong savings. We had a good life. Life changes on a dime! I was diagnosed with breast cancer, had surgery, received a questionable prognosis, and three weeks later, my middle son Brooks, age seven, was rushed to the hospital, the night before my first round of chemo was to start, and diagnosed with juvenile diabetes.

I was sitting in the ER with my son and my husband, holding our son's hand, thinking, "WHAT THE HELL! I am supposed to be starting chemotherapy tomorrow like it's just another day, pick up my son from ball camp in Tucson, and then go to work, and now I am in the hospital with my son who is also fighting for his life." That was then, and two years later, I felt broken, unwell, depressed, close to losing our home, and, on top of everything else, I was FAT due to my hormones being cut off!

I went through five surgeries and one full year of chemo, all the while teaching our seven year old how to be insulin dependent. I thought I could hold it together, keep my job, and manage my family! I worked for a year this way, but it was exhausting, overwhelming, and physically horrific for my health.

One day I was driving from work after leaving a meeting in 100 degrees of sweltering heat in our Arizona desert. I was wearing a suit and high heels and was to lead a ten million dollar acquisition call for the company I was working for in about fifteen minutes. I was not feeling well at all. I had left the previous meeting in a hurry, was out of breath, and had developed a horrible headache. Right before I was to dial in to lead the call for the acquisition, my car ran out of gas. I hadn't been paying attention. I pulled over and could see no gas station in sight, so I got out of my car and sat on the curb to call my husband for help. I was so overwrought that I missed the time of the kickoff call by ten minutes and had left several high-level executives waiting for my call—while I had a nervous breakdown! Thirty minutes later, I called my boss and quit my job! I decided that I had to take care of myself for the next year to heal from the intense cancer treatments, to heal my heart and soul, and to start working on the great passion that I held within me…creating a safety net for women: Mother's Grace.

Physical Strength

What significant health issue have you had to overcome?

I had aggressive breast cancer in 2008, a double mastectomy, five surgeries, one year of chemo, and they also took my ovaries for premature and instant menopause, which was worse than chemo.

What part of your body is most important to your health, and why?

I would say my heart and my lungs. Without a healthy heart and lungs, you cannot do anything physical.

How has money been a motivating factor in your life?

It is huge, and since I have always been the breadwinner for our family, money motivates me more as a security thing vs. needing things. It is not that I don't love to shop and have material goods, but that is not my point. What motivates me more is the need to be secure and not in another tragic situation. While going through so many things in my life, I have found that money does not make me happier; however, it is just easier to have some when you are dealing with "tough stuff"—hence, Mother's Grace.

How have you dealt with the physical changes of aging?

I pray a lot! Exercise, meditate, practice hot yoga, get lots of sleep, eat good food, and have joy. I also try to expand my horizons each year and push my limits. Last year I hiked Mount Kilimanjaro with two of my sons, my uncle, and a dear friend. It changed my perspective, got me out of a rut, and encouraged me to continue to have physical goals.

How does your current physical environment bring you joy?

I love the wilderness and exploring new places. I hiked both the Grand Canyon and Mount Kilimanjaro this past year, and it was so great to be in nature, yet to have a respect for boundaries within nature. I like being able to see outside wherever I go, and it brings me peace to look upon nature. No matter what, I like a cozy, comfy home with plant life all around me. My grandmother taught me about making a home and not needing to have a mansion to create an amazing space. She always had the most amazing food cooking with good smells all around and a tidy clean environment. It could be that because I felt so much love in her home it has driven me to try and emulate that feeling my whole life.

Mental Clarity

Tell us about a time when you trusted your intuition to make an important decision?

I have really come to depend on my intuition which I believe is God guiding me. Instead of trying to control anything whatsoever, I have learned to breathe and let go and I am always divinely guided to the most appropriate answer for me. Just when I think I need to grab hold and try to fix an "outcome," I breathe in and let go and what comes next is grace.

What mental skills have you developed over the years to help you navigate the difficult times?

FAITH, FAITH, FAITH! Put it all in God's hands, and then let it go. Also, plowing forward and finding solutions. I have experienced many obstacles in my life, but I always feel like there is a solution. When I have a particularly tough day and get bad news of some sort, I take a deep breath and remind myself to try a few things and then let go. Tomorrow is always a better day.

At what point did you recognize that you had stepped into your own voice?

I think over the last three years (49-51) after cancer, after healing, and starting a foundation. Knowing I would not work so hard to control outcomes but would allow myself to be led divinely.

Did you have a definitive life plan? If so, how did you stay focused on that plan?

NO! Not really, I just keep moving. I am a live-in-the-moment gal and have as much fun and love as possible. I also fly by the seat of my pants on many things.

I do not make a plan. I go with a gut intuition and figure it out as I go. I try not to pontificate or let any barriers hold me back. I just keep pushing in the moment.

Who in your family inspired you to be courageous?

Definitely, my mom, who passed away at the age of 27, inspired me to be courageous. She was a force to be reckoned with, and everyone said I was just like her. Also, my two grandmothers who were there for me after her passing...unconditionally...and always. I had and have a fierce love for them. They helped raise me after the death of my mom and were there for me until they both died in their 90s. I would add my son Brooks as well, who at age 7 became insulin dependent and doesn't let a day go by without living out loud. He does not let his disease hold him back!

Spiritual Courage

What safety nets have you relied on over the years, and how have they served you?

My faith and Mother Mary have been my safety nets. Without my mom I look to the Virgin Mary as a link to my own mom. Neither my faith nor she has failed me yet.

I can't fail to include amazing girlfriends whom I chose deliberately. They are all very strong, fun loving, and honest gals. I have some great ones! Being with my friends feels like the truest thing to my heart. We have similar faith ideals and can speak honestly about it. It feels like I have been in and lived in every one of their situations. Intuitively, I know how they feel, what they need, and, without judgment, how to get it done. They also know that they can let down their walls, strength, and masks with me and be real!

What have you loved deeply in your life?

My boys, husband, family, sisters, friends, God, and nature…not to mention a love affair with shoes!

What advice would you give younger people to help them develop a vision of hope for their later years?

Establish a faith based life, work on it from every angle, and teach your children that same discipline. It is the only thing that won't fail you.

Can you describe a time in your life when you moved from surviving to thriving?

After cancer, post five years, I got back in shape and took my life back. I went back to work in a job that felt good, worked on my female friendships, and really put my energy into my foundation.

It is said that bravery comes through taking action. How will you continue to live a brave life?

I will continue to ask myself if this action brings me peace or more stress. How can I simplify? Is this healthy for me and my family? I will continue to live deliberately with respect to faith, exercise, nutrition, and friendships.

Here is some information about Mother's Grace.

Their mission statement: Mother's Grace Foundation is dedicated to the support of mothers and children who have endured life tragedies. By providing financial support and guidance, Mother's Grace empowers these women to reach their goals of making a difference in their communities by helping others inflicted with similar circumstances.

How they do it: Mother's Grace remains committed to healing the world one mother at a time. Our goal is to create the opportunity and secure funding streams for these specific endeavors. We wish to empower these mothers to take leadership roles and support their desire to heal, rebuild, and revitalize their communities.

Here is one example of how Mother's Grace supported and revitalized a woman in desperate need:

The husband of Lori, an elementary school administrator with two children, one with Asperger syndrome, got laid off work and went to NOLA to find labor work. He fell in love with another woman and left Lori and the children without any financial help. When she went up to the attic to pack the rest of his things, she fell through the roof and broke her back. She was hospitalized for a month and had to build herself up until she could walk with a cane. During this time, she was unable to work. Then right before she did go back to work, she found out that she had breast cancer. Bam! Bam! Bam!

I invited her over, and we really talked. I shared all of my past, and she shared hers. We were no longer strangers, and there was no agenda; we are just connecting. We got Mother's Grace to supply the cleaning service for her home, including steam cleaning carpets and furniture. We arranged meals, grocery gift cards, and we paid her mortgage and utilities for over three months so that she could get back on her feet. I spoke with her frequently about her treatment and gave her empathy and love. When she was finally back to work, we invited her to our Mother's Grace Brunch, and in front of three hundred women, we introduced her and let everyone know her story and how far she had come back. Her hair is growing back, and she is feeling better. We also assisted in getting her son into community college with a scholarship. We do this to illustrate the powerful influence of women supporting women. With these women, all demographics and socioeconomic and religious/political measurements are invisible, and we are one and that is how our conversations go. From minute one of meeting with every one of them, we are simply connecting and assessing their needs. Since inception, Mother's Grace has supported over 1000 moms with financial assistance in the way of monthly bills, medications, meals, housekeeping, childcare, and ancillary services. In addition, Mother's Grace has given grants to over 25-501c (nonprofit) organizations run by moms, either through fiscal sponsorship, mentorship, and/or strategic partnership.

It is obvious that Michelle's path to healing her body opened the door to her giving.

MANY TIMES, WHEN A WOMAN struggles with a physical or emotional issue, the beginning of the healing process will start when she decides to do something exceptional for someone else.

Besides Mother's Grace, we donate our products and services to other organizations as well that are uplifting women and children in our communities. "Heal and empower the women and the world will heal and thrive" is a belief that I hold closely to my heart.

Another commendable organization that we assist is Hope Women's Center, a Christian non-profit organization that has served vulnerable women and teen girls in the communities for over thirty years. Thousands of women, teens, and their families have received free services and care through education, mentoring, pregnancy support, and material resource programs. Their current CEO, Tammy, has been my very special hair client for over thirty years. She continues to bless my life as I have watched her grow since she was just entering college when we first met.

Another organization is Assistance League of Phoenix that makes sure children receive reading materials and clothing to prepare them for school. Along with Eufora International, our preferred salon products, we also give our time and services to Child Help for the prevention of child abuse.

I continue to firmly believe that what happens to one of us happens for us all.

Live brave.

CHAPTER SEVEN

Navigating through Difficult Times

"I love the person I've become because I fought to become her."
~ Kaci Diane

KEY QUESTION: WHAT MENTAL SKILLS HAVE YOU DEVELOPED OVER THE YEARS TO HELP YOU NAVIGATE THE DIFFICULT TIMES?

We've all heard the phrase—there is something special about that person.

AND THAT IS PRECISELY HOW I will introduce Jennifer to you. There is something special about her. When she is present with you, she is *with* you. When she speaks with you and when she looks at you, she *speaks* and *looks* at you. Her conversation is honest, her manner is gentle, and her voice is easy and exudes a sincere caring temperament. There is always a smile that fills her face. She has a lightness about her that is warm and inviting, and her style is down-home and relaxed.

Raising six children with her husband, working outside the home in her husband's business, staying busy with the last child still living at home, juggling time with her grandchildren and children, and being a good daughter to her own mother, Jennifer's life is full of activity.

When asked if she would share with our readers an experience that helped her create her strong mental and spiritual skills to navigate the difficult times, she wrote the following:

JENNIFER R., 59

"I share this story often. I think it is important to be available to other women who may be suffering through the same trials. I had someone to encourage me along the way."

One year into college on a double blind date, I met a young man who made me laugh. I was instantly smitten, and one year later, we started our life together as one. He taught me to enjoy life and to have a sense of adventure. With a vow to never say the word *divorce,* we began our family: 6 children, 11 grandchildren, and 37 years later, we have had that vow tested many times and, thereby, strengthened. Our journey through the world of drug addiction with one of our children stretched us beyond our capabilities, and yet through this, God taught us many lessons of unconditional love, boundaries, and peace, in spite of circumstances.

Our goal to raise well-adjusted, happy children was one of our strongest desires as we began our journey as Mr. and Mrs. A big family, love of God, prayer, home-school, lots of love, hard work, and adventure–surely that was the recipe for children who would never wander and who would sport such a strong sense of self that would never allow them to be pulled away.

When our second son (child number 4 of 6) was born, we rejoiced. Curly, blond, full of energy, and constant mischief, he was certainly a challenge and loved the more for it. We worked hard to keep him focused, engaged, and aware that all things have consequences, a lesson he didn't seem to easily hear. He knew the drill, "Son, think of the...Yes, you are right...consequences!"

As junior high approached, he was more and more disruptive at home, so we enrolled him in a Christian school. There he smoked his first pot. He never looked back. That was 16 years ago. The struggles have been equal to a roller coaster ride, extreme highs and crippling lows. As a young man, the issues were many: running away, breaking curfew, lying, drugs and alcohol, sneaking around and running away from home. Later, when he left our home, the problems were bigger, much bigger: extreme drug abuse of heroin and meth, homelessness, jail, lies, divorce, missing in action...all things that break a momma's heart. This took an enormous toll on our family. I was heartbroken and found it hard to give the other kids the attention they needed at times. If things were not right with my son, then things were not right in my world.

The problem is that these same things break a daddy's heart, too, but in a different way. Our marriage, which had suffered through some significant financial trials and become the stronger for it, now struggled. My husband saw through the lies. His concern was for our son's maturity and for his ability to function as an adult, to be a decent human being and a law-abiding citizen. I couldn't seem to get past the emotional hurt my son was suffering. I sometimes tried to protect him from consequences, smoothing situations over; it was as if someone had literally pulled the wool over my eyes. I was a pawn in my son's games of smoke and mirrors. My actions made the situation worse, and we both did and said things we would later regret. Crazy making leads to more crazy making!

My husband and I couldn't see from each other's point of view. It caused arguing and hurt we had not experienced before. At one point, my husband looked at me and said, "I have taken the light out of your eyes." It was close to that point in time that we realized that we needed each other in this one. I needed him to help me understand that our son needed to mature. He needed me to help him understand the emotional needs of our son. It took us both to get through this; it took us a lot of years to figure out how to trust each other as our viewpoints were so different.

Many days I was in such emotional pain that I could hardly breathe. I kept a set of verses on a ring, and I found comfort in reading God's assurances of His love for me and

His love for our son. The wisdom and comfort of His words and the assurance that He heard my prayers held me tight as I prayed Psalm 27:13 *"I would have lost heart unless I had believed that I would see the goodness of the Lord in the land of the living."*

God answered this mother's prayer, preserving our son's life through many dangerous situations. He is doing better now, but he still struggles. We have learned to be thankful for each day and each victory, no matter how small. Life is a blessing, and we have to choose to look for those blessings even in hard times.

I share this story often. I think it is important to be available to other women who may be suffering through the same trials. I had someone to encourage me along the way. She taught me to love my husband and love my children. Why does someone need to be taught these things? It is because we are human. And at times the battle is hard. It is easy to want to give up. It is easy to become focused on ourselves and our own problems and to look for relief through a seemingly easy way out.

Preserving marriage is tremendously valuable and worth fighting for. It starts with realizing that true love is more than a feeling. It is choosing to love, no matter the circumstances. It is important to remember our vows to love our husband in spite of sickness or poverty or trials.

I encourage others to maintain a respect for their husbands even if they aren't handling life as we would want them to. Men and women are different in so many ways, and it can be a challenge to remember that first love. For moms of wayward children, it is crucial to know that indeed love is sometimes tough.

Often we make decisions in an effort for relief more than basing it on what the child needs. This is not love. The very thing our children need from us is truth, spoken in love, and the prayers of people who love them unconditionally. The key to preservation of our families is God's love… now abide faith, hope, and love…the greatest of these is love (1 Corinthians 13:13)

A very special thank you goes to Jennifer who opened her heart and her family life to us to share their story.

THEIR PATH TO PRESERVING THEIR family, marriage, and hope is because of their strong and steadfast faith in God.

Live brave.

CHAPTER EIGHT

Stepping into Your Voice

When asked how she travels alone at 88: "I just play that old lady card and ask for help. It works every time."
~ Nancy, Salon Client

KEY QUESTION: AT WHAT POINT DID YOU RECOGNIZE THAT YOU STEPPED INTO YOUR OWN VOICE?

Admittedly, I am a late bloomer.

IF THE STATEMENT MEANS THAT it took me too long to learn from my mistakes, I resemble that statement. After all, married three times and divorced the same amount of times, really!

The day I found my voice was an unforgettable moment. I was working in a salon, Gossip. Yes! Gossip was the name of the salon. I did not like the name, but the location was perfect, and the woman who owned the salon promised me more money than I had ever made in my twenty-five years of hairdressing. I was a nervous wreck in that particular salon. The owner was a sharp gal, a manicurist. She was a hard worker who placed her large manicuring station at the front of the salon so that she could greet everyone who walked in the front door. The salon was exquisitely decorated with a modern design and was furnished with only the very best equipment and décor. The colors were bright, and the walls and artwork were dazzling and fancy. Actually, other than me, everyone who worked at Gossip was dazzling! The girls dressed as if they were out on the town after work, including high heels and jewelry, neither of which I had ever worn to work.

Although I thought that I felt confident in my appearance wearing my usual, more traditional clothing, there was a part of me that felt insecure walking in the salon. The owner, whom I truly respected, liked and, to this day, appreciate for the effort that she made to keep the salon in such stellar conditions, always commented as I walked in the front door, "We're going to have to dress you…Bling you out! Make you sparkle!" I would walk by, smile at her and the clients sitting at her manicuring station and the other clients in the salon, and take my place at my station toward the back of the salon. No matter what I was wearing for the day, I felt rather frumpy or, at the very least, that I had no sparkle!

One day at work, I heard someone laughing with lots of enjoyment. I quickly looked around, and to my surprise, I discovered that the laughter was coming from me. I know that this statement sounds ridiculous and naïve, but I shall always remember that day as long as I have my memory. Of course, I was talking with my clients about something funny said between us, but in general the salon circumstances were anything but conducive to feelings of cheerfulness and enjoyment. I was indeed harboring some resentment about the statements being thrown at me, but the laughing just poured out of me. Laughter and my voice staked its claim. The next week I resigned my position.

My point is that a person never knows when the voice of the "real you" will come pouring out to claim the real you.

Live brave.

More than a dozen years ago when I first met Arlene, I would have described her as an unassuming, apprehensive, nice woman with lots of potential. Now, however, she has blossomed into a mighty confident woman, knowledgeable in a wide spectrum of subjects, mostly the imperceptible matters of life that affect every human being through the energies of the planets, moon, and sun. Of course, I am speaking of astrology and the cosmos and the quantum physics of the universe, to name only a few of her favorite subjects. Arlene is a woman of great substance who has come to understand clearly how the universe works and how we function within its cycles, forces, and energy. Her work with her clients is motivating and specifically researched to each individual, using a wide spectrum of resources. I personally enjoy her weekly email messages that inspire me to stay centered and connected to every person in the world because, after all, we are all part of the larger story of life.

I am delighted to introduce you to my friend Arlene.

ARLENE, 68

"The interesting thing is that when I found my true voice, I felt less of a need to shout and make noise."

My personal and professional life has been an eclectic array of careers and experiences. My first jobs were in the food industry, and then one day when I was 31, I decided I wanted to be in banking. I found the human resources office, and for three months straight, I went to that office every Friday. I had no experience in banking, but after persisting, the bank hired me, and within six months, I was promoted to teller supervisor. When I left the bank, they wanted to make me vice president of the branch. However, I went on to get my Bachelor of Arts in organizational management from George Fox University and began working in an academic environment. My primary accomplishment is that when I wanted a job, I found a way to get it. And whatever job I got, I always excelled and was easily promoted. I have honed my skills as an entertainer and have become a very good stand-up comedian. Currently, I am an entertainer, writer, and personal growth coach.

Physical Strength

What significant health issue have you had to overcome?

Being overweight for most of my life has led to numerous digestive issues.

What part of your body is most important to your health, and why?

My digestive tract is the key to my health and well-being.

How has money been a motivating factor in your life?

While I enjoy money, I believe the motivating factor in my life is making a difference in the lives of others and helping others believe in themselves. Money's role in my life has been as a teacher, for when I become anxious about money, I know that a new lesson of trust is about to unfold.

How have you dealt with the physical changes of aging?

I have learned that aging is part of life's journey. My way of dealing with the changes of aging is to maintain a positive outlook on life and learn to trust and focus on the positive aspects of aging. I also believe that one of the best ways to deal with the natural aging process is to keep learning and avoid the kind of thinking that will lead to rigidness and stagnation.

How does your current physical environment bring you joy?

I have a wonderful work space that nurtures me and reflects the things that bring me joy, peace, and contentment. As I have opened up to being more authentic in my life, I have found that having visual reminders of my values and principles in the form of cards and collages help me to remember who I am.

Mental Clarity

Tell us about a time when you trusted your intuition to make an important decision?

There are so many times I have trusted my intuition to make important decisions. In fact, those are some of the best and most positive decisions I have made. When we moved to Arizona, I was guided by my intuition to move here, even though logically it would have been better to stay in Oregon. The decision to move to Arizona has resulted in more resources and positive connections than I had in any other time in my life. As I have matured, I have come to realize that both intuition and logic have a place in the decision-making process. The key is to find the optimal balance.

What mental skills have you developed over the years to help you navigate the difficult times?

The body scan meditation by Stephen Cope and creating inspirational cards keep my mind focused on a positive approach to any problem.

At what point did you recognize that you had stepped into your own voice?

It became the most evident when I turned 60, and yet it continues to grow within me more and more. One of the benefits of aging is a sense of what is really important. As a result, I see myself feeling less attached to what others think I should be or do and more connected to what I know is right for me. The interesting thing is that when I found my true voice, I felt less of a need to shout and make noise. I have developed a calm inner confidence that allows me to speak when necessary and to remain silent when necessary.

Did you have a definitive life plan? If so, how did you stay focused on that plan?

No, I did not have a definitive life plan, but I have always set intentions and stayed open to whatever came next. I wanted to go back to school, but it did not look feasible; however, because I knew it was the right thing to do, I made it happen. The older I get, the more I realize that having a life plan takes way more energy than just developing an inner confidence that allows me to adjust my plans and be open to what comes my way, which leads to less striving and more thriving.

Who in your family inspired you to be courageous?

It was my second husband with his loving support who gave me the courage to pursue my dreams. His unconditional love has helped me to grow beyond difficult beginnings. While the women in my family exhibited a different kind of courage, I now believe that my mother and sister wanted me to be prepared for difficult times in my life. Women in my family had to be strong for they often had to be the breadwinners or the strength of their families. This prepared me for a time when I was left alone with three small children to raise.

Spiritual Courage

What safety nets have you relied on over the years, and how have they served you?

My spiritual path has always been a safety net for me since I was a child. I truly believe I am guided by a loving force that leads me to my highest good. The face of that loving presence has changed for me over time, but only because I have changed in the way I see God.

What have you loved deeply in your life?

I have loved writing, inspiring, and entertaining others for my entire life. I have been blessed with a wonderful loving marriage partner that I love deeply. My children have been a deep source of joy and pride in my life. I see the strength in my daughter, and I know that my growth has paved the way for her to live brave in her life.

What advice would you give younger people to help them develop a vision of hope for their later years?

No matter what happens, know yourself, cultivate your highest qualities, and trust yourself. Seek to flow with life instead of trying to control it.

Can you describe a time in your life when you moved from surviving to thriving?

I began my journey from surviving to thriving when I started studying self-discovery through astrology, the Enneagram, psychology, and the Taoist way of life.

In my studies, I have learned that our openness to examining our beliefs and philosophies and how well they are working happens in 12 year cycles. At age 60 I experienced one of these internal shifts that helped me to see that I could let go of trying so hard to change myself in order to fit in and to simply accept that everything I need to be is available to me right inside my heart. For years I struggled with a constant low grade anxiety that colored everything I did.

Once I was able to begin trusting that my life is unfolding just as it is meant to, I could relax and thriving came naturally. It has not been a onetime experience, but a constant renewal of faith and hope in Spirit.

It is said that bravery comes through taking action. How will you continue to live a brave life?

My experience has taught me that the bravest life we can live is to be 100% ourselves at all times. To have the courage to stand out, live with abandon, and stop worrying about whether others will like me or even get me.

In that context, bravery for me, as demonstrated numerous times in my life, is knowing clearly what I want and what I want to accomplish, creating a clear image of it in my mind, which for me often involves a collage (a physical visual image), and then refusing to settle for anything less than what my confident self says is possible.

I will laugh more, take more risks, and, for sure, I will stop saying I am too old to do anything.

I think MaryAnn Radmacher's words say it best. These words currently hang framed in a room in my home.

> **Live with intention**
>
> **Walk to the edge**
>
> **Listen hard**
>
> **Practice wellness**
>
> **Play with abandon**
>
> **Laugh**
>
> **Choose with no regret**
>
> **Appreciate your friends**
>
> **Continue to learn**
>
> **Do what you love**
>
> **Live as if this is all there is**
>
> **And finally, stop waiting for someday**

Arlene's path encompasses a multitude of clients who trust her wise counsel and star readings. She is a straight shooter with no castle-in-the-sky promises who relies on the science behind the cosmos of the universe that influences our human bodies. And just for fun, she is also a stand-up comedian and entertainer...a diva of sorts!

Live brave.

Key Question: At what point did you recognize that you had stepped into your own voice?

> **Throughout the years if someone had asked me to make a list of people whom I admired, Sherry would always be on that list.**

But our relationship did not begin in that most splendid way. We met over forty years ago at the very first Fiesta Bowl Parade in Phoenix, Arizona, when I was twenty one years old and pregnant. At that time she was a volunteer, helping to handle the details for the bowl parade and half-time events. I was in my eighth month of pregnancy and had managed to gain fifty pounds (not all of this weight was baby, of course). My husband and Sherry had been working the parade and half-time preparations together for several months, and they were both the same age, fifteen years older than I was.

This was before cell phones were invented so all calls came to our home phone since my husband's office was in our home. While my husband traveled extensively for his job, Sherry and I had many conversations by phone as she called with vital information that he needed to have on his return. Months of these conversations were beginning to get on my nerves. She was always so cheery and nice and happy to talk with me. Some of the calls were details about the Fiesta Bowl contenders vying for queen for the bowl. As my waist had gotten to 54 inches, I resented that these adorable, young, and slender ASU students with nineteen-inch waists were being considered. My imagination ran away with me as all I could think about was what Sherry would think of me and my very large size. She would probably think I had been careless in gaining so much weight, so, on and on, my thoughts rummaged in my mind. After all, she is very bright, resourceful, articulate, beautiful, blonde with blue eyes, thin as a rail with great slender legs, and everyone loved her at the Fiesta Bowl, which is exactly the way my husband described her every time he spoke of her. Honest to goodness, I thought to myself, she can't be all that! Ridiculous as it now sounds, I decided that I was not going to like this cheery Sherry woman with whom my husband was so involved. Also, I thought that he probably has a bit of a crush on her.

On the day of the parade, I dressed as nicely and as warmly as I could, which meant that I wore several layers of clothing, only making me look more like a refrigerator. I just knew she wouldn't like me. All the same, my best friend, Dee, would be attending the parade with me because I so needed the support. I had been whining to her for several months about the upcoming event where I would finally meet the perfect woman in my husband's life, and we had both decided that, no matter what Sherry was like, neither one of us would like her. Well, the moment we shook hands, talked, and visited with Sherry about the parade and the excitement surrounding the upcoming game and halftime, both Dee and I could not help but love her...I mean it, we loved her!

At Sherry's insistence, Dee went on to volunteer for the Fiesta Bowl and, eventually, worked for Sherry in the hospitality industry for several years. To this day, they are best of friends, and I am still Sherry's hairstylist. She embodies all of the characteristics that my former husband used to describe her, and she is much, much more. I love this woman.

SHERRY, 80

"When I was in my twenties, as an attractive young woman, I believed I was perceived as 'arm candy.' I fell into the trap of living people's perception of me by playing that role. I woke up one day and realized that I needed to live my life authentically."

Raised by "a village"...working mom, grandmother, aunts, uncles, and cousins in a two-bedroom, one bath, low middle-class home...a very happy place with always room for one more to stay for dinner. Married young, had a beautiful daughter, the light of my life. Attended St. Louis University but did not graduate.

Started a career as a travel agent and tour operator. Career path best described as "generalist." From travel agent/tour operator to husband's medical practice manager and public relations. Advertising for land developer, hospitality/tourism for 30 years... started as Director of Sales & Marketing at an independent resort hotel, became assistant general manager and then general manager... upward mobility to VP of management company where we developed other hotels, president of my own hospitality management company, Fiesta Bowl manager and Director of the Arizona Tourism Alliance...appointed by Governor Jan Brewer to join her cabinet as Director of the Arizona Office of Tours (6 + years); also worked for Governor Doug Ducey in the same role. Currently, back in the hospitality business as Director of Sales for the Prescott Resort.

Community involvement has been a huge part of my life from entertaining nursing home residents to the Fiesta Bowl, volunteering for 35 years, which allowed me the opportunity to chair the Parade, be elected to the Board of Directors and, ultimately, become Chairman of the Board. Chosen to lead tourism associations in the metro Phoenix area and the state of Arizona.

Proud of accomplishments:

First woman to be elected to the Fiesta Bowl Board

First woman to be elected chair of the board

First woman to be elected to any major bowl

Created the Tempe Tourism Office, served as president for the first three years and, subsequently, served on the board for 20 years

Founded the Fiesta Bowl Block Party and chaired it for three years; it was voted by *USA Today* as one of the top ten places in the country to celebrate New Year's Eve

Guided the Arizona Tourism Alliance and the Arizona Lodging & Tourism Association through consolidation to become the Arizona Lodging &Tourism Association

As Director of the Office of Tourism, led the agency through the challenge of the recession without losing market share and visibility for the state

Physical Strength

What significant health issue have you had to overcome?

I am very fortunate to have never had any serious health issues other than a skin condition that requires me to stay out of the sun and use lots of sun screen.

What part of your body is most important to your health, and why?

For me it is my legs that are important to my health. With healthy legs, I can still do most anything: walking, running, dancing, golf, tennis, biking, gardening, and hiking...an endless list of physical activities, including tap dancing for the past ten years.

How has money been a motivation factor in your life?

I am proud that money has never been a motivating factor in my life. I am fortunate that I have always had the opportunity to work hard, learn, try new paths, embrace change, and the money has followed...different levels; loved all I did for different reasons.

How have you dealt with the physical changes of aging?

Physical aging...hmmmm...I've kept a sense of humor, used lots of wrinkle creams, plus Spanx! I never think about the aging process. I am the same person I was 50 years ago and feel blessed that I was able to maintain good health. I count those blessings every day, even with the wrinkles! Age is a number, but it does not define who I am.

How does your current physical environment bring you joy?

I love my new "doll house." I just downsized into a tri-level townhouse half the size of my previous home, yet I was still able to stuff ten pounds of treasures, mine and my mother's, into a five pound bag. I love coming home and being surrounded by collections and photos, all of which evoke wonderful memories...there is truly joy in that every day.

Mental Clarity

Tell us a time when you trusted your intuition to make an important decision?

My not-at-the-time husband was walking across Arizona and New Mexico to raise money for charity. He did not ask me, but I took the initiative to follow my instincts and my heart and fly to California to meet him as a surprise and to share in his accomplishment and celebration. Two months later, we were married!

What mental skills have you developed over the years to help you navigate the difficult times?

My mental skills stem from being blessed with a happy, positive personality that I embrace every day as the gift I believe it to be. I focus on staying positive and counting those blessings. I try to always embrace change and live every day focused on seeing only opportunities when challenges, disappointments, and sadness confront me. I also depend upon the love of my family and loved ones.

At what point did you recognize that you had stepped into your own voice?

When I was in my twenties as an attractive young woman, I believe I was perceived as "arm candy." I fell into the trap of living people's perception of me by playing that role. I woke up one day and realized that I needed to live my life authentically, not as people perceived me. I had found my authentic voice.

As a young woman blessed with a pretty face and figure, I was able to earn money modeling for a ladies clothing manufacturer. I was recently divorced with a three-year-old daughter and out of necessity living with my mother and stepfather, who was an alcoholic and borderline child molester (I never shared that with my mom—a story for another time). Into my naïve life walked "Prince Charming," a tall, handsome, wealthy gentleman who, for whatever reason, fell madly in love with ME! Unfortunately, I think he fell in love with the exterior package without exploring the internal, and I was not savvy or experienced enough to grasp that at the time. It was easy to return his feelings as he offered safety and comfort and literally convinced me to marry him by emphasizing that he would cherish and take care of me and my daughter.

Upon becoming his wife, a whole new sophisticated world opened, full of security for me and my daughter, a new home, an escape from the living environment of my mother's house, money, country club membership, exotic trips, beautiful clothes, parties, and amazingly cultured and educated people. Obviously, I was dazzled, and looking back, I was willing to play whatever role necessary–or so I thought. I was the youngest woman in the entire social circle (husband was older), and he proudly "displayed" me. I let him, and his friends followed his lead. I never voiced an opinion as it was never asked. and even when we built a new home of his design, I had no participation. Within a few years the role playing "Arm Candy" became more difficult–partly because I was becoming more educated and confident–and partly because I was not being true to myself, a value my mother had instilled in me at a very young age. Thanks to an outside friendship I developed, I began to realize that I was living a sham, and, frankly, it was not only not fair to me, but it was likewise not fair to this lovely man who had in many ways helped me to mature. Once that realization sunk in, I told him the truth that it was unfair to him, and although I cared for him deeply, I did not truly love him to the degree that he deserved…so I left…a new enlightened person. I took only my beautiful daughter, one car, and my piano! I left everything else behind. I did not ask for a settlement or alimony since it was, in the end, more my fault than his.

He went on to remarry, have two children, and enjoy an abundantly full and happy life. We always remained friends, and until his recent death, we communicated as friends throughout the years.

I will always be grateful for my time with him and the experience, and I still cherish many of those memories. The biggest lesson I learned was to always be true to yourself, be honest, listen to God and the universe, and follow your heart.

Did you have a definitive life plan? If so, how did you stay focused on that plan?

I have never had a definitive life plan other than to stay focused on each chapter with passion, commitment, and joy.

Who in your family inspired you to be courageous?

My mom always inspired me to be courageous. She has always been my best cheerleader and supported me through all the chapters of my life. I was inspired by her even as a child who watched her work long, odd hours and still find time to make costumes for her only child and to celebrate Christmas and holidays at all hours with enthusiasm and joy. From her I learned the importance of a solid work ethic and of experiencing every day to the fullest.

Spiritual Courage

What safety nets have you relied on over the years, and how have they served you?

I never think about safety nets. If it is not illegal or immoral, I have always followed my heart and intuition and taken the leap!

What have you loved deeply in your life?

I have loved so many people and experiences deeply that it would fill volumes, starting with my daughter, of course. My husband Mick, who passed away way too young, my previous husband who also died way too young, my family and extended family, and friends, I cherish and hold close to my heart. I have a deep love for God and thank Him every day for my many blessings, and I love life–every day deeply!

What advice would you give younger people to help them develop a vision of hope for their later years?

I have never been one to give advice; however, if asked for recommendations, I would start with follow your heart and your dreams; set high expectations, as that delivers high rewards; focus on positivity and keep it top of mind; whatever job you have at the moment, give it all of your passion, energy, and creativity; hold onto the premise that everyone is innately good until proven otherwise; embrace change; and, if you cannot say something nice about someone, say nothing. Also, avoid gossip, be kind to yourself, and listen,

listen—listen to your heart and to others! If you can create a vision, you can make it a reality.

CAN YOU DESCRIBE A TIME IN YOUR LIFE WHEN YOU MOVED FROM SURVIVING TO THRIVING?

I feel that I am always thriving–every day.

IT IS SAID THAT BRAVERY COMES THROUGH TAKING ACTION. HOW WILL YOU CONTINUE TO LIVE A BRAVE LIFE?

I will continue to live a brave life the way that I have always lived my life—with passion, joy, positivity, and appreciation of each day, each loved one, each experience. As corny as it sounds, I still believe in the value of living The Golden Rule every day.

I realize that I spent much time introducing Sherry and describing the story of how we met when I was in my early twenties, pregnant, and very unsure of myself.

MY REASON FOR THIS IS because each and every one of us begins the life journey with the insecurities of what others will be thinking of us. Finally, as we grow and experience relationships and their complexities, we win a few and lose a few, we get through our insecurities, and we feel free when we arrive at a most wonderful time in our lives. We comprehend that we have always been the best me at every age that we were in. No matter the pathway that we choose to arrive at our destination, or the voice that we were using, it was who we were at that time.

No one could say it better than Elizabeth Gilbert in her book, *Big Magic*, when she writes about a time in her life in her insecure twenties when she met a clever, independent, creative, and powerful woman in her seventies who offered her a superb piece of life wisdom: She said, "*We all spend our twenties and thirties trying to be perfect because we are so worried of what people will think of us. Then we get into our forties and fifties and finally start to be free because we decide we don't give a damn what anyone thinks of us. But you won't be completely free until you reach your sixties and seventies when you finally realize this liberating truth—nobody was thinking of you anyhow!*"

Years later, Sherry has been a true friend to me, a confidant, and a most valuable mentor. Our paths crossed, and we kept our friendship alive by being authentic with each other.

Live brave.

CHAPTER NINE

Making a Plan

"We must be willing to let go of the life we have planned so as to have the life we have waiting for us." ~ Joseph Campbell

KEY QUESTION: DID YOU HAVE A DEFINITIVE LIFE PLAN? IF SO, HOW DID YOU STAY FOCUSED ON THAT PLAN?

When Mary Beth and I came up with this question, we realized that neither one of us had a life plan of our own.

ALSO, HAD WE HAD A plan, we don't think we would have stayed the course. As you will see with the majority of our brave women's answers, most did not consciously decide to stick with a particular plan but instead made adjustments as life came their way.

This reminds me of a story of a couple that I had the opportunity of meeting several years ago for a very short time but who made a big impact in my view of life. I assisted them in making a dramatic adjustment to their short life plan.

It was Thursday afternoon at the salon when a phone call came in and my assistant announced that the caller insisted on talking with me. She would not take no for an answer and said it was an urgent matter. The woman on the phone said that she and I had not met, but she had acquired my name and number from her neighbor, who was indeed one of our long-time favorite clients. She knew that I was not only a hairstylist but also a minister and that I could perform a wedding ceremony. She wanted to know if I would be available the coming Saturday, just two days away, for an afternoon ceremony. It was for her brother and his girlfriend who were in town for just a few days. They had already purchased their marriage license and wanted a small ceremony in the back yard of her home with just a few members of the family and some close friends.

Looking over my salon schedule, I would be available, so without any hesitation, I answered, "Yes! I would be delighted to officiate the wedding for your brother and his girlfriend." Of course, I was curious about this couple and their dilemma of such an abrupt marriage. Besides, I do believe in fate. For some unusual reason, my schedule was open on Saturday. This rarely happens. It felt like a door had opened, and my curiosity called me to step into it...to wherever it took me. A small adventure, but none the less, an adventure.

After work on that same day, I headed to the caller's home, which was near the salon, to meet the soon-to-be bride and groom. After all, with only one evening, Friday, to write and prepare a personalized ceremony, it was necessary to meet with my couple as soon as possible. Of course, on the drive to their home, I imagined a young couple, the girl pregnant and the young man nervous, both possibly still in college, neither with a plan for a baby coming along.

To my surprise, after being greeted at the front door by the caller, a woman in her late forties with a charming and gentle manner, not at all as demanding as she had seemed on the phone, I met the couple. The man was in his early to mid-fifties, tall and very, very thin with a bald head and markings for beam radiation treatments directed specifically to the left side of his head. (I assumed that the tattoo markings were for radiation treatments because I could not imagine that they were there for any other reason). The girlfriend, approximately the same age, was tall, tanned, trim and slim with an athletic figure, sporting a well-cut short style on a thick head of dark, wavy hair. (Of course, I notice hair on everyone).

They both greeted me warmly and led me into the spacious living room filled with old world furniture. Soft and full sofas were piled with large colorful pillows, and heavy Italian rugs covered the wooden floors, filling the room with the ambiance of warmth and good taste. The couple sat on a small love seat sofa very close to each other, holding hands, as I sat in a beautifully upholstered chair facing them. "Well," I said, "So this must be one of those shotgun weddings." We all laughed, and the ice broke around us, opening the space for them to tell their story.

They had met working at a large technology corporation many years earlier. They were both engineers and had both been married and divorced. They had dated for over ten years and had never planned to marry. There was no mention of either having children, so I didn't ask. Together they had traveled the world, exploring the climate and cultures of every country available to them. Life had been an exciting adventure for them where they had learned to play and live in the moment, and they loved each other intensely. But his cancer had reappeared. Their plan had changed. They wanted to be married more than anything else, and they could hardly wait until Saturday.

I arrived Saturday morning at ten to a very festive and beautifully decorated back yard. Flowers and ribbons and balloons lined the patio and a wooden bridge spanned a small pond filled with water. The sky was clear and the weather could not have been more perfect. Greeting the family, his sister and her husband and their children, I was also introduced to the groom's mother, who appeared to be in her eighties, and the rest of the friends and family who had gathered. The couple was nowhere to be seen, most likely waiting inside to make a cheerful entrance. Everyone stood in a semi-circle at the entry of the bridge except for the elderly mother who sat in a patio chair at the very front of those standing.

I took just two steps on the narrow bridge, turned to face the attendees, and asked for the couple to come forward.

From a side door of the house, they appeared together. The groom, dressed casually in a floral Tommy Bahama-style shirt, was as excited as he had been two days before when I had first met them. Eagerly, he held the arm of his bride, dressed in a beautiful off-white, lacy sundress and strappy sandals, as jointly they stood facing me, ready to repeat the vows that I had prepared.

As I began with the traditional, "We are gathered here in the presence of God, family and friends to grant the wishes of"... he leaned in toward her lips and tried to kiss her. "Oh, no, you don't," I said to him firmly. "You have to wait until you are married for that kiss!" And everyone broke into laughter, a welcome sound that relaxed everyone, including his mother, who had appeared a bit anxious.

One more time as I was having them repeat their vows to each other, he tried to kiss her, but I chided him to wait. Again the laughter broke loose and a joyful cloud of happiness filled the space.

Finally, I pronounced them husband and wife and they kissed...respectfully, of course, in front of his mother. But it was unmistakably a kiss that alluded to a million reasons why they were married to each other that day, none the least, that they profoundly loved each other.

Less than four months later, I received the call from the bride. The groom had made his transition, and she asked if I would conduct the memorial service. He had requested my presence at his service.

Recently, I read the quote, "A life plan is an imagined future." It offered me several thoughts to ponder. The majority of the women who answered the question, "Did you have a definitive life plan?" had answered a profound no! And, as I admitted earlier, neither Mary Beth nor I had ever written out an extensive, definitive life plan. But have we imagined and prepared for a future? Have we set goals? Do I still carry my goals for the year written on a piece of paper in my wallet and place yet another paper with my goals by my bed side that I read nightly? Yes! We all make plans in our thoughts and organize our activities around a preferred outcome in our future. Making plans is yet another pathway to thriving in our lives. The thrill of anticipation of arriving to the expected plan is just as satisfying as arriving. Plan and then adjust your plan…it's called life.

The couple above had lived their plan. They fell in love. They traveled and saw the world with each other, and then, they changed their plan and married.

Live brave.

One of our brave women, Caroline, did have a plan from the beginning of her childhood.

As you read her answers, you will see that making a plan served her well. Although she made adjustment along the way, she eventually did indeed reach her goal to be financially independent.

KEY QUESTION: DID YOU HAVE A DEFINITIVE LIFE PLAN? IF SO, HOW DID YOU STAY FOCUSED ON THAT PLAN?

A salon client and now a personal friend, Caroline is fun, fascinating, talented, and, most definitely, an out-of- the-box thinker.

SHE IS A SOLID WOMAN who takes great pride in everything she endeavors to accomplish, who is devoted to her faith, home, health, and dogs and who has a highly educated view of the world. Unlike most women that we interviewed for our book, when asked the question, "Did you have a definitive life plan?" she answered, "Yes." Well, not a complete "Yes." She said, "Yes...and...no." But as you will read, she did make choices that kept her on track moving on a plan for financial freedom so that she could "smile at her future."

CAROLINE, 65

"Do not waste time being bitter; do not complain. Jealousy and whining are not only unattractive, they make friends disappear."

CAROLINE WANTED TO BE A veterinarian. Instead, to please her musician father, she pursued a career as a classical cellist and soprano. She earned multiple scholarships for undergraduate and graduate study and appeared as soloist in multiple venues across the United States. She married, divorced, and moved on to life in the corporate world where she spent thirteen years in trust and probate administration.

She retired early to care for her mother. After her mother's death, Caroline resurrected her musical efforts, spent a decade accomplishing some bucket list performances, and is now contentedly retired. She reads, enjoys close friends, does jigsaw puzzles, tends her pets and garden, and volunteers at a local nursing home. Her next project will be to research, design, and build a chicken coop, and then to learn how to raise chickens in a sustainable urban garden.

You ask if I had a life plan to make financial security happen. That answer would be, "Yes…and…no."

Oprah and her cadre of self-determiners might say my life today is what I made it. I am not so sure. Well, maybe a little bit sure.

I believe my comfortable situation today is partly due to stupid luck, partly due to great planning. I cannot take credit for all the decisions that turned out to be great; some were made consciously while some were thrust upon me by others. And some, I believe, were the result of otherworldly actions—heavenly intervention or fate or Karma, if you will.

From an early age, the most powerful influences on my attitude about money, saving, and financial security were twofold: my parents and my discovery at age ten of the book of Proverbs in the Holy Bible.

My depression-era parents taught by example: make do, use, reuse, do without. Never pay retail. Impulse purchases will not make you happy; sometimes they will make you very sad. Pay off credit card balances in full every month. The only acceptable debt is a house mortgage. Double up monthly payments and pay down mortgage principal early.

To acquire objects of desire: sweat, wait, save, and earn them—the old-fashioned way. Sometimes our best efforts come to nothing. Move on, try again. The universe owes us nothing. Do not waste time being bitter, do not complain. Jealousy and whining are not only unattractive—they make friends disappear.

My parents married in December, 1933, in a small midwestern town. Pop put himself through college during the Great Depression by mopping hospital floors at night and playing piano in dance bands. He met my mother at his first post-graduate job, teaching music in the little town's only high school. Mother played clarinet in his concert band. As soon as she graduated at the ripe old age of 18, they married.

I was the surprise baby who came along ten years after they gave up trying to have a sibling for my brother. We were living in Arizona; Pop was still teaching music in high school. Money was tight. Among my early memories are packing up the car and driving to Kansas to spend summers with the grandparents because my father had no income when school was out.

Clothes and shoes were purchased on sale or not at all. As a family member, I was expected to "do my share." I did not receive an allowance. The things I needed were provided in moderation, and the things I wanted were given sparingly. Any luxury that was a "want" and not a "need" was something very special indeed, and to this day I remember every special thing my parents saved up for and gave me, and on which Christmas or birthday that happened. I learned to iron and sew at an early age and made many of my clothes. As a young married woman, I shopped sales, canned seasonal foods, and made do, or did without.

Unfortunately, I married a man who had poor impulse control, who considered a credit card in hand the equivalent of money in the bank and debt a mere inconvenience. The marriage did not last. Once free of marital debt, I never looked back. The only debt I shouldered was a mortgage. I made sure to pay down the principal balance as fast as I could save the money. I also saved "for a rainy day." Now that I am retired, those rainy day savings cover my needs, such as they are.

Where does the Book of Proverbs come into the mix? As an impressionable ten year old, the wisdom of Proverbs became not just a lifeline, but the line of my life. Consider Prov. 31:25-27: *"Strength and dignity are her clothing, and she smiles at the future. She opens her mouth in wisdom, and the teaching of kindness are on her tongue. She looks well to the ways of her household, and does not eat of the bread of idleness."* Just three sentences that address mental, physical, emotional, and spiritual health. Other proverbs teach us how to deal with criticism, work, gossip, diet, exercise—the whole gamut of human experience. The 31 chapters of the Book of Proverbs together guide us to optimal physical, mental, emotional, social, financial, and spiritual health. Through the years I have read many self-help books, but none equals the Proverbs' profound wisdom.

Now that I am an old woman, I continue to look to Proverbs for guidance. All those years of planning and saving, added to sheer dumb luck, have turned out well for me. I am so grateful. That doesn't mean I have a clue how to behave now. I recently remodeled my house, for which I planned and saved six years and, yes, paid cash. Even so, writing those big checks sent me into shock! More typically, I go on a spending spree at Costco to buy small practical things that I or others will use. I still give the pretty $80 earrings a pass. But I will buy a $15 sweater and feel very fancy. This is a new chapter in my life. I am learning to buy what I want—a challenge for me since my lifelong habit is to simply not want. As I figure out what I want, the one thing I know for sure I *do* want, however it all works out, is to smile at the future.

Although Caroline describes herself as an old woman now, she looks anything but an old woman.

SHE IS SHARP AS A whip with her money, and her home décor is artistically vibrant with color and style. She works out with weights with a trainer, no messing with that girl, and she is a sought-after actress in the community. Her singing voice is mesmerizing! Her path in the art world has served her well.

Live brave.

Key Question:

Did you have a definitive life plan? If so, how did you stay focused on that plan?

As a business owner for many years, it is easy for me to recognize that there is a rhythm to the ups and downs of business. My friend Arlene would make the connection to the moon, sun, and stars being in alignment or not. And indeed the moon, stars, and sun have been shining on me with this beautiful group of women that I have currently working with me at our salon.

Allow me to introduce you to one of the shining stars. Nicolette was just out of cosmetology school when we invited her to join our team at Pluma Designs. It was an intuitive feeling that we had about her ability to meet the high standards that we promote in our small and very active salon. Professionalism, continuing education, and a high standard for customer service are required from the team. She has met and exceeded any expectations that we had for her. I tell each one of the women working with me that she is my favorite, and they all joke about it. They are, indeed, all my favorites. It is my pleasure to introduce you to one of my favorites, the up-and-coming Nicolette.

NICOLETTE, 20

"I want to be the kind of woman who is honest, courageous, diligent, and intelligent, and thus far, the

development of all of these qualities has led me to fulfilling goals outlined in my plan."

Nicolette is a twenty-year-old hairstylist, originally from Laguna Beach, California. In 2006 she moved to Litchfield Park, Arizona, with her mom, stepdad, and twin sisters. She graduated high school with honors and went on to complete beauty school in less than nine months. Although her strengths include detail, analysis, and schedule management, she has always been drawn to the beauty industry for its overwhelming composition of independent women in business ownership. At the young age of 18, she began her work at Pluma Designs and soon moved into a small condo by herself in Phoenix to accommodate the commute to Scottsdale. She maintains strong relationships with close friends and family and, much to her delight, spends most of her time at work.

Physical Strength

What significant health issue have you had to overcome?

At the age of fifteen, I was diagnosed with a hormonal imbalance that significantly affected my mood and caused almost nonstop menstruation and pain. I was prescribed hormone supplements and the issue resolved promptly.

Three years later after graduating from high school, I developed anxiety disorder that triggered minor asthmatic episodes, but I had never considered my body significantly compromised until the summer of 2015. It started in June with flu-like symptoms: severe sore throat, swollen glands, nausea, fatigue, congestion, and fever. The initial symptoms that were too debilitating to allow me to go to work were resolved within a few weeks, but for the next two months, I would have periods when the fatigue returned and my fever would spike to 103. Within a few days, it would go away and I could return to work. I saw several doctors during this time, all of whom assumed I had a recurring cold, but it was nothing that some rest and vitamins couldn't knock out of my system.

Towards the end of August, one doctor finally prescribed antibiotics, which I was anxious to finish, thinking I had a lingering sinus infection that was causing the other symptoms. Seven days later, a rash (imagine the pictures of children with measles you've seen in textbooks) broke out on my entire body from head to toe.

Keep in mind that I was only nineteen and living entirely on my own in Phoenix, so from the period of June to August, despite the fevers, constant vomiting, and fatigue, I was still working and trying to deal with it the best I could.

It was at this point though that I panicked and thought something must be severely wrong, so I went to live with my parents. My stay with my parents lasted a month, during which time I was diagnosed with a severe case of mono, hospitalized for a day, prescribed OxyContin and steroids, and became a regular in my ENT's office.

Although I was back at work by October, my final battle with mono did not end until December when my ENT made the decision to remove my tonsils and adenoids, a horribly painful surgery as an adult, but which, much to my relief, finally put me on the path to total recovery and wellness.

Although mono is not the worst case scenario in any viral regard, it certainly gave me a new respect for my body and taught me to listen to it, to ask for help, and to trust that it will get better.

What part of your body is most important to your health, and why?

My mind is and always has been the most important part of my health. Beyond the cliché of "mind over matter" and "attitude is everything," I have always considered my mind to be an extraordinary part of my body. I graduated high school with a 4.25 GPA and can honestly say that I very rarely struggled, even in my AP classes. I took part in musical theater and memorized plays the weekend before rehearsal started. I've never missed a due date or been tardy, but I didn't truly start to appreciate my mind until I began working in a salon environment under someone who recognized and encouraged my talents, and now I often think what life would be like if I were not capable of deep analysis, quick numerical calculations, and especially time and financial management. Everything we do stems from our brain, and there's no greater way to honor that than to use it for a greater purpose than just functioning at a minimal level.

How has money been a motivating factor in your life?

I was born in a wheelchair while my mother was being pushed to the delivery room. Her doctor told her, "Reach down and catch," and thus my life began. Even in the womb, I was ready and rushing to whatever came next, and I have always been anxious to get to the next stage of my life. As a teenager, I meticulously calculated the career path, standard of living, monthly income, and future I would need to acquire in order to make it on my own. Obviously, money is a big factor in that equation. I have never lacked in work ethic although I was fortunate enough to have my father buy me a vehicle of my own when I turned 16. I promised him I would pay for the insurance, repairs, gas, and maintenance, and within a week of looking, I obtained a job to do just that. I respected and loved that car, which I lovingly named Rebecca after my favorite novel. My little Honda Civic represented a future to me. She represented work and freedom and responsibility, and that was the first stepping stone to my independence. Just before my nineteenth birthday, I moved out of my parents' home in Litchfield Park into my very own studio condo where I have lived all by myself for almost two years, loving every minute of it.

How have you dealt with the physical changes of aging?

Although I can hardly consider myself aging at the baby age of twenty, with each passing year I've really grown into my own voice and confidence. Much of that comes from working in an environment where I'm surrounded and encouraged by strong, intelligent women all day long, but I'd like to think my own wisdom and wit has brought me to this conclusion as well. Age represents responsibility to me, not to societal standards or even to the standards and desires of my parents but to myself. I have set very high goals and expectations for myself, most of which are connected to age, and I hold myself accountable for their accomplishment or their failure. I have learned to accept and be at peace with either, although my daily battle with perfectionism steers me to the former.

How does your current physical environment bring you joy?

I have never loved a home so much as the home I've created for myself. In 500 square feet of space, you have to be creative. It's not much, but it's mine. I've earned it; I've nourished it; I've decorated and respected and loved it, and that brings me joy each time I walk through the door.

Mental Clarity

Tell us about a time when you trusted your intuition to make an important decision?

The story of divorce is so common that I won't bore you with the details of the very ugly relationship I witnessed, beginning at the age of three. It lasted through most of my childhood although I was fortunate that my mother remarried when I was five to a wonderful man who volunteered to raise three little girls after his own two were just beginning their journey into adulthood. That being said, I don't think you should give young children the option of choosing which parent they like best. We were constantly involved in custody and child support battles, which only got worse when my mother and stepdad decided to uproot us from our tiny home in Laguna Beach, California, in order to have a better life in Arizona. I was eleven years old at this point and requested to live with my dad in California, which launched a yearlong custody battle. Obviously, I am still in Arizona, so you can probably guess the end result is that I changed my mind. Twelve year olds shouldn't be given enough power to devastate their parents in order to follow their intuition, but I was. After a year of petitioning with the courts, thousands of dollars in attorney fees, and an emotional tug of war, I finally got what I wanted...only it wasn't. Throw any child into a completely foreign situation, and they'll instinctually cling to the familiar, especially with my very structured and organized personality. After living in Arizona with my mother and stepfather for a year, I knew it was best for me, particularly as I entered my teen years. At such a young age, I barely understood what intuition was, let alone how to follow it, but I had to make a choice, and I chose to stay. I knew living with my dad would probably be more fun, but even at that age, I knew I needed structure, and staying was for the best. Needless to say, this was devastating for both sides of the family, particularly my dad, who never had the opportunity to live with his children after the age of five. I dwelled in so much shame and tortured myself with guilt over the agony I had put my family through, but in the end, I was right. I learned the wrong way, but it was the right thing to do.

WHAT MENTAL SKILLS HAVE YOU DEVELOPED OVER THE YEARS TO HELP YOU NAVIGATE THE DIFFICULT TIMES?

I am a planner. I plan everything. My entire life is organized into a series of lists and schedules. I understand this is not a system that works for everyone, and many people have encouraged me to give myself more freedom… so I schedule free time. Ultimately, I live a very privileged life being an American born into an educated and hardworking family. I know there's nothing in life, apart from injury or death, of course, that won't work itself out. I make pro-con lists, prepare for the worst, panic for about ten seconds, and then give it to God and have faith that it will be okay. When we overanalyze difficulties, we exacerbate the problem, and I'm learning not to do that.

AT WHAT POINT DID YOU RECOGNIZE THAT YOU HAD STEPPED INTO YOUR OWN VOICE?

As I mentioned earlier, being given the power at twelve years old to decide my future gave me a voice that was probably premature but which allowed me a newfound value in my decisiveness. Although causing that monumental family distress opened the door for a lot of shame, I learned early that my voice did, in fact, give me power and control over my own future, as well that of others, and I've worked very hard to be aware of that at all times. Words are powerful. They can speak life and joy and encouragement or just the opposite, and I'm constantly striving to establish the merit and effects I'd like my voice to have.

Did you have a definitive life plan? If so, how did you stay focused on that plan?

Of course I had a life plan. I'm acutely aware that much of life is entirely out of my control and that my plan will be forever changing, molding, and shifting, but at its core, my plan is more about the kind of person I want to be rather than the exact accomplishments I'm able to achieve. I want to be the kind of woman who is honest, courageous, diligent, and intelligent, and thus far, the development of all of these qualities has led me to fulfilling goals outlined in my plan. I have become the kind of young woman who's dedicated, industrious, and dependable, and it has brought me a very comfortable life supporting myself at the age of twenty. Onward and upward from here.

Who in your family inspired you to be courageous?

In spite of all the things my parents did to inspire me as a child, my favorite story of courage will always be that of my grandparents. They fell in love in a small town in Italy when my grandmother was just fourteen and my grandfather was seventeen. Although their love wasn't encouraged at first, they courted each other for four years until my grandmother moved to America with her father. My grandfather, who was already slender and tall, lost ten pounds and became so ill and forlorn without her that he packed his things, followed her to America, and proposed. Last year they celebrated fifty years of courageous love, and that is the kind of love I hope to find.

Spiritual Courage

What safety nets have you relied on over the years, and how have they served you?

Being a planner, I've set up a series of safety nets to rely on in my life. For example, last year, I set enough emergency money aside to be able to support myself through five months of on-and-off work during my battle with mono. Most of my plans have baby plans...and those baby plans have back-up plans. I know it sounds neurotic, but I really do love and embrace that side of myself. Besides my family, whom I can always count on, I have learned to be very self-reliant, and it has served me well.

What have you loved deeply in your life?

I'm fairly new to life, so I can't say I've experienced every facet of deep love, but at this point, I have deeply loved my sisters and myself. I would venture to say most young women don't love themselves, and I probably didn't either... until I lived alone.

Living alone with only your own thoughts and habits is so important, and I would recommend it to every young woman. When there's no food in my fridge, it's my own fault. When the bathroom's messy, it's my mess. When my bank account doesn't reflect the number I want it to, I have no one to account for that but myself. There are no distractions, no one else to blame, and I think recognizing the way you live and treat yourself is an essential part of knowing and loving yourself.

As for my sisters, they are some of the few people in my life I've had a consistent friendship with. I have twin sisters, who are two and a half years my senior. They do everything together. They live together, they went to college for the same major in education, they work in the same school, and they teach the same subject, but their personalities could not be more opposite.

During our childhood, I often felt left out, not having a twin of my own, but now I've grown to love and admire them as individuals.

Although they're older, I have always looked out for them. I am assertive and stubborn, and I am always behind them, pushing them never to settle.

I can recall a time when Brigitte, the younger of the two, was being degraded and bullied by a so-called friend in school. She was a sophomore, and I was in the eighth grade and had never even met any of her friends. Now I recognize that this poor boy was probably just being a typical obnoxious teenager, but when I had the chance to meet him at her track and field banquet, I immediately introduced myself with the preface, "I know who you are, and I don't like you."

You can imagine that a tiny 5 foot 2 eighth grader standing up to some sixteen-year-old boy was probably not the most intimidating gesture, but that was and is just the kind of relationship I have with my sisters. I will probably always be the yappy little Chihuahua, standing in front of and defending my sweet golden retriever sisters.

What advice would you give younger people to help them develop a vision of hope for their later years?

The advice I would give to my peers is to stop defining all the faults of their personalities as disabilities and do something about them. Unfortunately, I was born into the tea cup generation of entitlement and expectation.

I have met many diligent and motivated young people like myself, but too many of my peers rely on what I call the "Whatever Mentality." This "Whatever Mentality" is the response to a formidable situation with apathy and ignorance. It's when the bills don't get paid, and you say "Whatever, I'm sure it'll be fine." Although I can admire and occasionally envy the nonchalant personality it takes to be able to look at a situation that would strike immediate panic in me and not flinch, I don't think it's generally conducive to a productive adulthood. In fact, I've found, more often than not, young people do this, not because they've developed coping mechanisms to calm their anxieties and face the world with an "it'll be okay attitude," but more so because they aren't equipped with the tools they need to look at a situation realistically and take action.

Things don't work themselves out when you don't work on yourself. Life doesn't just fall into place, and it's not enough just to recognize that your vice is laziness, apprehension, or disorganization. You have to actually do something about it.

Can you describe a time in your life when you moved from surviving to thriving?

I can honestly say that this very moment, this phase of life I'm currently in, has been the most I have ever thrived. Especially after having an illness that knocked me out of all of my norms and habits for five months, I am finally feeling amazing. Appreciation for my body and health has increased dramatically; I'm completely settled into my living situation; I've focused more of my energy on myself and not my outside relationships, and I'm working with more confidence and joy than I ever have before. I've never felt that cosmetology is the career best suited to my personality. I'd probably be a much better accountant or librarian, and not necessarily for lack of skill or talent, but because I fear and loath the spontaneous. Very little in my life has been done without a premeditated plan, but this industry just doesn't work that way. I am finally starting to accept and embrace the unpredictability in this industry and how truly wonderful it can be when you allow it to be.

It is said that bravery comes through taking action. How will you continue to live a brave life?

I know it makes me sound delicate and fragile, but I feel brave every time I overcome the daily anxieties of learning things on my own for the first time. My parents always said their job was not to be my maid, friend, or personal assistant, but to teach me how to be a self-sufficient adult and productive member of society, and that's exactly what I'm doing. Living by myself for the first time has opened up all sorts of possible scenarios I have to plan and be prepared for, but I'm doing it. Complacency is not in my nature and probably never will be. As long as I'm consistently living a life that displays honesty, diligence, faith, reliability, and love, I can say I am living bravely.

Optimism is the feeling I get when I am around this vibrant, beautiful and intelligent young woman.

SHE REPRESENTS HOPE FOR OUR world that there are many others like her who see the world with self-responsibility and the willingness to work for what they want in life.

Live brave.

CHAPTER TEN

Inspired by Courage

"Courage is not something you have or don't, like your height, but something you can develop." ~ Rabbi Daniel Lapinl

KEY QUESTION: WHO IN YOUR FAMILY INSPIRED YOU TO BE COURAGEOUS?

Sabra and Lou are both women, married to each other, and they are in love.

WE HAVE KNOWN ONE ANOTHER for several years, but just recently, they became clients of the salon. They are equally intelligent and sensitive women who are actively and purposely living life to its fullest. They travel the world, host meditation groups in their home, and volunteer their extra time. Lou is retired while Sabra still works her career as a psychotherapist, and they have a diverse and fun group of friends. I found this out attending gatherings in their beautiful, colorful, and inviting home.

When I asked them if they would share their life in *Living Brave*, they didn't hesitate to say yes. For years I have admired them and have been curious about their life as a couple. They represent a way of life that is foreign to me and many others but is quickly becoming a new standard for many women.

It is my pleasure to introduce my friends Sabra and Lou.

SABRA, 73

"One of the bravest things we now do every day is to tell people who we are: 'She's my partner' or 'She's my wife.'"

I AM A GRADUTE OF Smith College. I was an English teacher first and then became a psychotherapist. It has been my joy to help so many people with the traumas of their past, as well as the chaos and conflict in their present, and to teach them tools to deal with the future.

I spent my first 10 years as a therapist in Michigan and the last 24 years in Arizona. One of my accomplishments was moving out West and setting up a private practice when I knew nothing about logos, licenses, trademarks, or marketing.

Another proud accomplishment is the writing of "*Who's Walking Around in Your Head with Muddy Boots?*" a self-help book based on my therapeutic experiences.

LOU, 64

"I was just growing old, much older than my chronological age. When Sabra and I came together, I started living!"

I WAS IN CORPORATE MANAGEMENT and was much loved and respected by my team. I created teams that had little in common but were able to work toward and achieve a common goal. But my more important personal accomplishment came after retirement—as a hospice volunteer and as a Reiki practitioner in a cancer center. I also wrote a children's book entitled *Freeda's Fancy Feet*, which has the lesson for children that they are perfect exactly as they are.

Sabra and Lou

For the last 15 years, we have been in a wonderful relationship with each other, and we married when same-sex marriages became legal.

One of the bravest things we now do every day is to tell people who we are: "She's my partner" or "She's my wife!"

We hope to provide others with a better understanding of what a healthy, same-sex relationship looks like, and we hope to reduce prejudice in that area.

And, we both touch people's lives with our minds, our bodies, and our spirit.

Physical Strength

What significant health issue have you had to overcome?

Lou: My significant health issue was breast cancer with brachytherapy for radiation. I walked around for seven days with tubes sticking out of my breast, so they could put radiation in a specific spot two times a day. This experience was more significant due to my fears of the unknown than it was to the actual radiation. My mental questions were, "How bad is this?" "Is the cancer everywhere?" I was scared shitless. "I'm not ready to be dead" was my continual thought.

Sabra: My restless legs have driven me crazy—sleepless nights, uncomfortable plane rides, plays and symphonies where my legs danced the whole evening. I've always believed in "leaving no stone unturned," so recently I had a neurologist look at my problem with new eyes. Now, after many, many years, I have a medical solution that works, and my restless leg disruption is down to zero.

What part of your body is most important to your health, and why?

Lou: My mind. It drives reactions to what can be construed as negative health issues. My joints ache, but that doesn't mean I'm going to sit down all day.

Sabra: My first year out of graduate school, I worked in a hospital in Flint, Michigan. I was the social worker who went in and talked with a patient before a scheduled surgery. I was often the last person they spoke to in a normal voice before having a laryngectomy. Ever since then, I have valued having a voice, knowing that these patients would never speak normally again.

How has money been a motivating factor in your life?

Sabra and Lou: We are women and, therefore, very security oriented. We are not motivated by money, but we seek the security that money brings. That means that I sometimes give free sessions, or we pay for a painting class and end up providing comfort and support to the instructor. We are selective in how we spend our money. I buy wines I like, and Lou recently bought a convertible six-speed roadster. We travel a lot and love the experiences and adventure that travel brings.

How have you dealt with the physical changes of aging?

Sabra and Lou: What physical changes? Not well; not happy about them! I still think I'm 35 but my body doesn't match my head. Slowing down doesn't come easily or gracefully. Some things are harder to lift. I find myself saying, "This is too heavy." Energy flags somewhat sooner than expected. But, all in all, we are still kicking and still doing. I find myself saying, "Oh, my God, my mother would never be doing this at my age!"

How does your current physical environment bring you joy?

Sabra and Lou: We love our home. It's peaceful and reflects who we are. It is a little funky, a bit eclectic, modest, and much loved. One of the best things about this house is that we will not have to downsize. Unlike many of our friends, we can stay here as long as we can take care of ourselves. The house was perfect for us fifteen years ago and continues to be the perfect dwelling place going forward. We like to share our physical environment and have had a meditation group that has met here monthly for the last eleven years. We hope that people "come as guests and leave as friends."

Mental Clarity

Tell us about a time when you trusted your intuition to make an important decision?

Sabra and Lou: Lou asked me to marry her and changed her will nine days after we met. We both sold our homes and bought one together shortly thereafter. We both knew (intuited) that this relationship was the right thing for us. We had a commitment ceremony in our new home one hundred and eight days later.

What mental skills have you developed over the years to help you navigate the difficult times?

Sabra and Lou: One of the mental skills that come with age is "perspective," being able to see the bigger picture, being able to predict how other people are going to react, knowing what is probably going to happen next. We both follow our intuition wherever we go, in a hospital waiting room, in a Reiki session, on a hiking path, or with our meditation group.

At what point did you recognize that you had stepped into your own voice?

Lou: I found my voice on a professional level when I became a manager and had the autonomy to run a team with a 2 1/2 million dollar budget. On a personal level, I found my voice when Sabra and I became a couple. There I could be authentic to the world.

Sabra: I stepped into my voice when I became a therapist. I finally found my niche—where I fit, where I could provide guidance and support to others, where I could shine. Personally, I don't speak up much out of my office. Instead, my voice comes out in my cooking, my nurturing, my hostessing.

Did you have a definitive life plan? If so, how did you stay focused on that plan?

Sabra and Lou: No, of course not. Neither one of us had a definite life plan. Early decisions were family scripted; later decisions were on our own. Now that we see where we are in our lives, we feel so blessed and so guided. Lou said that after a major life change she looked up at a ceiling fan and said, "God, put me where you want me to be." And she did!

Who in your family inspired you to be courageous?

Lou: While we are all generally timid in some situations, as I reflect, there are so many instances of bravery I can name in my biological and extended families. My mother, knowing she had breast cancer, courageously kept that undisclosed as she cared for my father through his declining years riddled with the effects of Parkinson's disease. My father, imagine, at the Battle of the Bulge, at twenty-something, almost certainly knowing he was going into the ultimate sacrifice of his life. My grandmother, Concetta, who journeyed from Italy on a boat to the U.S. at 16 years old seeking a better life, knowing it was likely she would never see her family again. My own sister, Anne, faced heart bypass surgery while nearly scared to death. My brother-in-law, Jay, who earned two Purple Hearts as a Marine in Vietnam. My dear friend, Cindy, facing a stem cell transplant and uncertain of the future of her multiple myeloma diagnosis. My brother, as he painfully guided our father's transition; he was his best friend. My stepson and stepdaughter and their spouses as they took all the necessary steps to adopt our beautiful Asian grandchildren. Brave is my "God's daughter" as she follows her heart with her gender fluidity. Brave is my brother and sister-in-law as they together heal from his leg amputation. Brave is inherent in my family.

Sabra: After my mother's death, I heard stories about her attending a retreat and speaking in tongues. I also found an Edgar Cayce book on her dresser. While she had a motherly influence on me during her life, the book she left behind had a more powerful influence and shaped my spiritual journey. The book, *Edgar Cayce on Reincarnation* by Noel Langley, opened my eyes to a new world of possibilities. From there I explored other authors: Louise Hay, Sonia Coquette, Carolyn Myss, Judith Orloff and Gary Zukoff.

Spiritual Courage

What safety nets have you relied on over the years, and how have they served you?

Sabra and Lou: Our modest financial safety net has been very important to us, allowing us the freedom to breathe, to enjoy life, and to know we are safe. Our relationship with each other is also a huge safety net, providing emotional security and support. We both know that "Doing" is one of the things that ground each of us.

What have you loved deeply in your life?

Lou: I have loved my pets and my mother. I love and adore my wife, Sabra. And both of our families. I love each of my wonderfully diverse friends deeply. But the "things" I love deeply are kayaking on peaceful waters, starting a new book, getting my passport stamped and all the adventure that entails, a rainy day in Arizona, classical music (particularly Vivaldi), the sounds and smells of Africa, the gentleness of Australia, snuggling with "feathers, feathers fur, and flesh" in the morning, sitting by a fire, having the freedom to choose, coming home to Sabra's car in the driveway, my relationship with the Universe (by whom I am richly blessed), helping, giving, soothing, and being brave!

Sabra: I only learned to love deeply when Lou and I came together.

What advice would you give younger people to help them develop a vision of hope for their later years?

Sabra and Lou: Do the things you love and love the things you do. Understand that our 60s and 70s are not the same as our parents' or grandparents' 60s and 70s. Right now 73 doesn't seem old and so "old" has moved up a bit. "Old" doesn't kayak or hike, doesn't rent cabins with fireplaces for their romantic atmosphere, "old" doesn't buy a six-speed roadster, "old" doesn't take up painting and look into more classes. "Old" doesn't leave the country for trips abroad.

Can you describe a time in your life when you moved from surviving to thriving?

Lou: I was just growing old, much older than my chronological age. When Sabra and I came together I started living. My standard comment is and has been, "If you were any younger, I would be too old for you!"

Sabra: I moved from surviving to thriving when I left an abusive relationship. I used Deepak Chopra's suggestion to hold a word in my mind. For me, the word was "freedom." Six months later I was free, without guilt, without the responsibility or blame for the ending of the relationship. As far as I was concerned, it was a miracle and a direct result of Deepak Chopra's suggestion.

It is said that bravery comes through taking action. How will you continue to live a braver life?

Sabra and Lou: We will continue to live brave lives by "doing"—driving a convertible sports car, taking painting classes, signing up to perform Reiki at the cancer center, trying new recipes, telling ourselves to "be brave" when our courage flags. We will continue to live a brave life by traveling, finding adventures, and believing that everyone has a positive intention.

Sabra has a motto: "When death finds me, let it find me living."

Lou's translation of this motto is: "When death finds me, let it find me alive."

During our interview with Sabra and Lou, they mentioned the expression, "gender fluidity," which I had not heard before in reference to relationships.

I found their clarification fascinating and want to share it.

Lou: I will respond to gender fluidity. Sabra and I have both been married to men—her marriage and my first marriage ended in divorce, and I was widowed at 48 with my second marriage. We have also been in relationships with women. But, by gender fluid, what we mean is that we do not fall in love with a person of a certain gender, but with the person instead. Had Sabra been a Samuel when I met her and had all the lovely characteristics, values, and quirks that she has, I would have been equally attracted to Sam. Gender fluid is to love the light inside, not the "traveling bag of our existence" on the outside. (Author unknown)

Sabra and Lou both inspired Mary Beth and me with the title of our book, *Living Brave*.

DURING OUR INTERVIEW WITH THEM at their home, they took us into their car garage where their convertible sports car sits royally. They couldn't wait to show us the personalized license plate that reads: B3BRAV3. Their pathway together stretches beyond the standard life-style as they move fluidly into being brave!

Live brave.

When our salon client Connie heard about our book regarding women who have lived brave lives and are thriving in their later years, she talked to us about her mother-in-law Raquel.

WE WERE DELIGHTED THAT WE would have the opportunity to interview a 91-year-old woman who was still active, including riding along in her son's truck, and computer savvy, even checking in on Facebook on a regular basis to keep up with her children and grandchildren. We sent her the fifteen *Living Brave* questions and asked if she would answer any of the questions that she found interesting.

A month later we made arrangements to meet with Raquel and Connie for our interview. When they walked into the salon, neither Mary Beth nor I was prepared to meet Raquel. A very young-looking, attractive Hispanic woman—who had just walked up the stairs to our front door and was not the least bit winded—walked in confidently, with a beautiful, full head of silver-white hair and an unforgettably striking face that radiated health. There was nothing old about this woman.

Before we introduce you to Raquel, called Raye by her family, we will introduce Connie, her daughter-in-law.

Connie is currently the president of Adreima. Prior to Adreima, Connie was the vice president of patient care services at Phoenix Children's Hospital. She is the 2009 past chairman of the board for the Greater Phoenix Chamber of Commerce Board of Directors. She served as the 2011-12 president of the Arizona chapter of the Healthcare Financial Management Association and is currently chairing the national Women's Leadership Committee for HFMA. She also served as the 2011-12 chairman of the board for Ryan House, where children with life-threatening conditions and their families may come for respite and, as needed, end-of-life care.

Connie is a registered nurse who graduated with a Bachelor of Science in nursing from Loyola University in 1978. Before joining Adreima, she spent most of her career in children's hospitals where she worked in a variety of clinical, management, and consulting roles in nursing and quality improvement. She earned a master's in management (MBA) from the executive management program at the Kellogg Business School of Northwestern University in 1997.

Connie introducing Raye:

"It is not every day you meet someone truly selfless who doesn't have a victim mentality or a martyr's bone in their body. The day I met my mother-in-law, Raquel, was one of those days. Raye grew up in a poor area of San Antonio where they were often hungry, and their great source of entertainment was a Sunday paper that she and her six siblings shared for a week. Her mother died when she was eight and her grandmother when she was fourteen. Her dad traveled as a barber and generally didn't live with the family. She stopped going to school at 15 and made bombs in WWII. After following her migrant-worker sisters to Chicago, she worked in a factory until she retired in her early sixties. She has three sons. I am married to the oldest, Danny. By now all of her siblings have passed away.

Affectionately known as Gramma Raye to hundreds of grandchildren, nieces, nephews, and friends, Raye enabled me to have a very successful career by providing care for my three sons and my daughter, our youngest, from the time she was born in 1989. Raye was the one there every day to get them off to school and to be there when they came home again. There were traditions I never knew about until much later...like when the kids were in high school and she would bake a huge bag of chicken legs for an after-school snack for the kids and their many friends. Sometimes she lived with us and sometimes she lived nearby. Today, at 91, she lives right next door in a patio home adjoining ours. She still remains vibrant, happy, and engaged and is as active today as she was 20 years ago, climbing, without assistance, into my husband's truck to go shopping. She reads and speaks both Spanish and English and beats us all at crossword puzzles and mind games. Everyone she encounters is better because of her. It has been my honor and my blessing to have her in my life for the last forty years."

RAQUEL, 91

"Just one thing bothers me and that is that, according to what has always been said, wisdom comes with age. Well, age came, and I'm still waiting for "wisdom" to get here, but it's not happening! It's all right; I don't really need it now!"

I WAS BORN ON NOVEMBER 16, 1924, in San Antonio, Texas. I was number six of seven children born to Carlota and Miguel.

When I was eight years old, my mother died, but by then, she and my father had already been divorced for a few years, so father was not around, except for now and then when he would bring money to help with our upkeep. After Mother died, most of the responsibility for the family fell on my oldest sister, Sue, who was around eighteen years old at the time.

I quit school after I finished ninth grade and did nothing to speak of, except to care for three children, until I was nineteen years old when I tried to find a job. Without a good education, I qualified for nothing, but this was during WWII, so I was able to get hired in a factory during the night shift that ran from 8pm until 5am. The first night I was placed on a line packing metal parts into a large crate. I soon learned that these were bomb parts going to the soldiers who were fighting the war. After that first night, I was given the job of spray painting all bomb parts before getting packed, and I did this until the end of the war.

When the war ended, the factory closed down for a month in order to convert their machines back to manufacture their original product, which was commercial refrigerators. Most workers were called back to work, including me, and I continued my paint spraying job, but now I was not spraying the enamel used on the bomb parts. I was now working with commercial refrigerator parts which took a different kind of paint, a powdery one that required baking after application and which resulted in a nice, shiny finish called "porcelain." Well, I never knew this before!

I learned a lot of skills in this factory: to be punctual, to respect and get along with others, to do the best on my job, and so much more. I got to love my job!

In 1949, I asked for a three-month leave from work because I wanted to visit my sisters Lil, Mary, and Esther, who were now married and living in Chicago. I got it, so on Labor Day weekend, I took a train and was on my way. It took close to three days to get there, a real hassle! But I had never been to Chicago and hadn't seen my sisters for quite a while, so I was happy.

When we were nearing Gary, Indiana, the train slowed down and traveled at a very slow pace. Looking out the window, I noticed that it had turned real dark, and there was a very strong smell. It was early afternoon, but I soon learned that this darkness was because of the coal mills running there. Eventually, we reached Chicago, and it was light again. My sister Esther and her husband Horace were there to meet me.

I had a wonderful time visiting and catching up on news with my sisters. I went out with one or the other on their many trips to see their doctors, to go shopping, or to visit with friends, and I began to learn how to get around the city and was starting to love Chicago. My leave from work was coming to an end, so I wrote a letter to my boss back home to thank him for the job but to let him know that I would not be returning to San Antonio, for I was staying in Chicago.

I soon found a factory job in Chicago that turned out to be a much better job, easier and with better wages. Throughout the years, I have worked in many factories, learning different skills for different jobs, and I have enjoyed them all.

In between all that time at the age of 31, I married and had a son in 1956 and another son in 1958. When I was 40 years old, I went to my doctor and told him that I had been feeling strange and thought I was going through some changes, maybe menopause. The doctor proceeded to examine me and, when through, told me that I sure was going through changes, that I was pregnant! Hearing that, I panicked because I had always heard that a woman having a baby at age 40 or older could die while giving birth. The doctor laughed and said that idea is nothing but an old wives' tale. He reassured me, saying that I was healthy and had nothing to worry about.

Sure enough, I was healthy, happy, and worked pregnant at the factory until my eighth month and, in my ninth month, had a third baby boy.

I am very fortunate having always been well, never suffering any major ills or having any surgeries. I used to get the flu or colds, but, knock on wood, I have not had any since I moved to Phoenix, Arizona. I do have allergies, mostly hay fever.

Now at age 91, I still feel fine; of course, my pace is not as steady, my eyes are weaker, my hearing horrible. I have a few aches and pains, but when I have a chance to walk, I can do it at a very good pace. I can take care of myself pretty well. But when I look at myself in the mirror, I still ask, "Who's that old lady?" Then I laugh and say, "You are not going anywhere yet!"

In my life, I don't think that I have ever made any important decisions, I have just let thing happen. I am sort of a passive person. I like to listen to what others have to say and form my own opinions but keep them to myself. I do like to hear others' opinions, but I don't care to give mine. Perhaps it's because a discussion can turn into an argument, and I don't like to argue.

What I love most deeply is my family; each and every one, individually, is important to me. And my happiest moments are when we are all together. At this point, my husband and all my siblings have passed away and relatives are scattered all over the country, so it's impossible for us all to get together like we used to do.

But I live right next door to my oldest son and his family, and we get together all the time, which is wonderful. Also, whenever possible, my second son and his family, who live in Texas, come and spend time with us here in Phoenix, as well as my youngest son who lives in California.

Well, all in all, my life had so many ups and downs, but I think it's the same with everyone in the world. I have made it this far, and here I am! Just one thing bothers me and that is that, according to what has always been said, wisdom comes with age. Well, age came, and I'm still waiting for "wisdom" to get here, but it's not happening! It's all right; I don't really need it now!

I am not good at giving advice; I can only speak of my own experience. When I quit school in the ninth grade, my parents had already passed away, so I had no one to urge, advise, or make me stay in school. I did nothing of importance until I was nineteen years old. That's when I started looking for work and found that since I didn't have a good education, I qualified for nothing! Looking at the want ads in the paper, I saw that there was a factory that needed workers. I went and applied, was asked what experience I had, and replied that I had never worked, so I had none. I asked to be tried, and if I couldn't do the work, they could let me go. I was hired, and soon I learned to do the many chores I was given. I urge all young people, if it is at all possible, to get as much education as they can because the world and its work is very different these days. For a top job, you need preparation. If for some reason that is not possible for you, working in a factory can also be a learning and rewarding experience if you put your heart into it. There are skills to learn, and you will be proud when you learn them. I was always proud of the work I did and applied myself to the fullest, keeping in mind the love I had for my children. They were my strength and the push I needed to keep me going.

After writing her story for us and during the interview with Mary Beth and me at the hair salon, Raquel sat in a chair and Connie sat next to her listening to us going over the paper that she had submitted to us.

WE WERE TAKEN BY HER physical strength, her mental clarity, and her gentle, calm spirit that was humble and yet radiated a deep sense of personal security. We asked her more questions, mostly because we were so impressed by her intelligence and youthful appearance, but Raquel defused any praise that we offered.

As if preparing to give a speech, Connie stood from her chair and said:

"I want to say something. Raye is not going to tell you this, but if it wasn't for her, if she had not moved in with my husband and me when our children were babies so that I could get my education, and if, over the years, she had not been there when our children were going to school, I would not have the career I have today. I could not have done it without her help."

Connie's eyes filled with tears as she stood and paid homage to her precious mother-in-law. Gently, as if not to disturb the moment, Raquel stood, and with two steps toward Connie, she embraced her daughter-in-law and they held each other. (Allow me to emphasize—they did not hug, they held each other) As they so warmly embraced, both Mary Beth and I felt the effect of women supporting women in the most profound way that women do by completely giving of oneself for the benefit of another. Mary Beth and I cried as we experienced the profound affection and love that these two women have for one another.

As both Mary Beth and I are also mothers-in-law, we know that there is a special path that we walk as we deliver our precious children into someone else's lives. If we are fortunate, we are included and our lives expand gloriously. There is a special love that develops within the bond of that marriage and our presence in it. The question becomes how we can be of help.

Live brave.

PART THREE

SPIRITUAL COURAGE

"Life shrinks or expands in proportion to one's courage." ~ Anaïs Nin

CHAPTER ELEVEN

Safety Nets to Rely On

"Being brave requires us to be vulnerable." ~ Brene Brown

KEY QUESTION: WHAT SAFETY NETS HAVE YOU RELIED ON OVER THE YEARS, AND HOW HAVE THEY SERVED YOU?

There are many ways to describe a woman. But never did I think that I would use the word *sensual* to describe an eighty year old woman. Nan is that woman.

SHE IS CONFIDENT, GRACEFUL, ABSOLUTELY a beautiful woman whose stylish attire, inviting smile, and manner of expressing herself are physically attractive. Her appearance is sensual as she radiates an approachable style of self-assurance and care. A client, friend, and my personal home manager, Nan is a woman with a big heart whose word is to be trusted.

NAN, 80

"There is a special bond among women that is unique to our species...that bond is friendship."

I FOUND MYSELF, AFTER FOURTEEN years of marriage, a newly-single mom with two young daughters. My priority became finding a job quickly even though I hadn't been in the workplace for over ten years! Reading want ads, creating a resume, and preparing for interviews...it was all so very daunting. I was fortunate in finding a secretarial position within just one week. I also recognized that this was not a long-term career for me and sought new opportunities as soon as possible.

As the years unfolded, I developed skills that provided opportunities as a project coordinator for a real estate developer, an associate with an interior design studio, an executive in a financial planning firm, and a management position with an international human resource staffing corporation.

When I retired from the corporate world at the age of seventy, I created a home management company providing concierge services for domestic and international clients. A belief in one's ability to meet each new endeavor with confidence and dedication provides tremendous avenues for professional and, most importantly, personal growth.

Physical Strength

What significant health issue have you had to overcome?

Having been diagnosed with breast cancer at the age of 70 (an advanced age, I'm told, for a first diagnosis), it was not unexpected. My mother, father, younger sister, and older sister all died of various types of cancers. Having four of our five family members dealing with and succumbing to the disease was difficult. The first was my father, a strong, loving, larger-than-life figure in my life. He lived a full and accomplished life until age 64. Then my younger sister died at 31: a wife, mother of two young children and a lovely woman with an appreciation and zest for life. My mom and my older sister followed within the next decade or two.

For whatever reason, I was not frightened by my diagnosis. It seemed manageable to me. I felt confident in my surgeon, my radiation, and my chemotherapy doctors. No fear, no panic. A great deal of that attitude came from a strong support system made up of two incredibly positive-minded children, a strong significant other, and many devoted friends.

The process of dealing with breast cancer takes many different paths. First, the biopsy, and then one must experience an MRI that requires you to lie on your stomach and plop your breasts into a trough while the technician (who I swear was 12!) looks at your breasts through some kind of x-ray device. Oh, but first, he places an almond (yes, an almond) at the tumor site. Something to do with identifying the specific area...strange!

Then on to meet with surgeons to get two different opinions, which is always a good idea.

One recommended a full mastectomy, the other a lumpectomy. After a lot of research and discussions with family, the decision for me was a lumpectomy on my right breast. Since my tumor was in the 6 o'clock position, there's quite a sizeable divot under the breast which now causes the nipple to point straight down to the ground. This is NOT attractive. Then one interviews oncologists, makes a selection, and meets with him and his nursing staff. The nurses actually administer the chemicals while you sit in a recliner, wrapped in a blanket, sucking on ice cubes to prevent mouth sores, all the while surreptitiously eyeing other patients to see what they may be experiencing.

Radiation is a many-week process but not uncomfortable, just time consuming. I was working full time so it did require taking time off in the mornings for six weeks while my staff carried the ball at work. The skin at the radiation site became red, then took on a leathery quality, but it was certainly tolerable.

One's strength during a life-altering event comes from deep within and must be recognized as a gift to be appreciated...even treasured. As I said before, each patient has a different path to treatment and recovery. My path was manageable, and the outcome was all one could hope for. I was fortunate to have skilled doctors, caring nurses, supportive friends, and a loving family.

It has been ten years now since my diagnosis, glorious years of living life each day with gratitude and a sense of wonder at my good fortune on so many levels.

Mental Clarity

What mental skills have you developed over the years to help you navigate the difficult times?

It becomes abundantly clear as your husband of 14 years tells you he's leaving you that your life has changed in an instant. A stay-at-home mom, four and nine year old daughters, no job, and a badly shaken sense of self-worth suddenly become your world. Immediate problems loom large: employment, child care, money, self-esteem, embarrassment at one of life's failures; so much to deal with. With great trepidation and almost unbearable insecurity, I began a secretarial job a week later, my kind neighbor watched the children after school, and I started the journey of single motherhood. Forty-five years later, I can say that it worked out just fine. I have two beautiful, self-confident daughters with families of their own, a successful career behind me, and a future filled with love of family, purpose in my life, and great possibilities for the next chapter!

Spiritual Courage

What safety nets have you relied on over the years, and how have they served you?

I believe there is a higher power in the universe. I don't have a name for it. I sometimes wonder why things happen as they do. I question the way in which "it" manifests itself, but I have a deep-seated belief that there is something beyond myself to rely on. My father believed that each person has a soul that travels from one individual to the next until that soul has experienced all of life's happiness, sorrow, heartbreak, and joy, and then can ascend to the heavens. Not a bad approach to the mysteries of life. I can attest to some of his beliefs but must also recognize that I don't have answers; I just wonder at what an amazing experience it has been!

Friendships as safety nets have also been a big part of my life.

When I have an opportunity to tell someone about the two groups of lady friends I have, most people appear to be interested and then, quite frankly, amazed that such connections could be maintained for over thirty years with one of the groups and seventy years with the other. Is it unusual to have this kind of gift? I think so. Am I grateful... undoubtedly! The opportunity to tell you about them is a gift in itself.

There are so many catchphrases today about friendship, support of loved ones, companionship, and what that means to us as we travel life's journey. I have been given, what I believe to be, a unique gift relative to this.

Growing up in Middle America in a comfortable home with caring parents, safe neighborhoods, excellent educational opportunities, and a sense of belonging was a blessing many people never have. And there was a bonus.

Friendships that began in first grade became the basis for friendships that exist today. To still have those same twenty friends seventy years later is indeed remarkable.

In 1999, one of our classmates decided that we needed to see each other on a regular basis to continue to nurture our connection to one another. This became the foundation for a yearly gathering to catch up with one another and to replay our childhood memories: Friday night slumber parties, dressing up for high school dances, pizza parties in someone's rec-room, new boyfriends, the breakups, new crushes, tears, laughter, joy, and sorrow...all emotions experienced by teenagers everywhere.

There are so many memories. It's funny how some people can remember the most precise details about their childhood. My friend Joan, for example, can remember almost every classmate in her homeroom. She recalls her teachers and what made them awful or unique. We often laugh about the "uniform" we wore: a blouse with Peter Pan collar, cashmere (maybe we only had one) sweater, calf-length skirt, bobby socks, and saddle shoes...a vision, to say the least.

When I think of growing up in such an exceptional environment, I realize how fortunate we were. Our high school was rated third in the nation academically. Ninety-seven percent of our graduating class went to college, and our classmates became doctors, physicists, authors, inventors, nurses, lawyers, bankers, investment counselors, artists. Those days were ideal in many ways, but we learned over the years that things aren't always as they seem. The friend we envied because she was so beautiful, smart, and popular faced more tragedy in her life than any of us could have handled. The captain of the swim team never told anyone that his mother was an alcoholic; another girl accidentally killed a small child when he ran out in front of her car chasing a ball. Even as young people growing up, we knew our world was not perfect. We lived with the threat of an atomic bomb attack; our parents had concerns about a foreign nation's impact on our economy; there were many things we were shielded from. Through it all, we held on to each other for comfort, for reassurance, for encouragement, and, as it turned out, for friendships that have lasted a lifetime.

Here is an overview of my second group of friends who have been together for over thirty years.

There are fifteen women in my group. We meet once a month just to be together, to catch up, and to enjoy each other's company. Being involved with these fifteen beautiful, accomplished women since the group's inception over thirty years ago has been one of the true joys of my life. The group is comprised of an attorney, a CPA, real estate professionals, an artist, a therapist, and so on. A diverse and interesting collection of professionals who decided years ago that this would NOT be a networking group, but a gathering of ladies to offer encouragement, support, a bit of wisdom based on life's experience, and, most of all, love and friendship. We were together recently for our Annual Weekend Retreat, and I asked them if they could each describe what the group means to them personally. Their response was immediate and heartwarming. They offered words such as trust, commitment, respect, acceptance, gratitude, sisterhood—all words with deep meaning and all profoundly accurate to describe what we have ... lasting friendships.

It was a chilly February morning, and Lisa was sitting next to me at our monthly breakfast meeting.

Lisa was at the top of the list of these remarkable women, a vibrant, funny, loyal, creative lady who had been the owner of a successful construction company until selling it a few years ago with the desire to spend more time with her husband and 13-year-old daughter. She also wanted to continue to create her exquisite jewelry, which is treasured by all who own it, continue to volunteer at her daughter's school, and give her energy to cultivate a positive outlook to the Girl Scout troop she mentored.

She seemed a bit off that morning, which was very unusual for her. I asked her why. She said and I quote, "Something's going on with my boob." Since I had been through a bout with breast cancer a few years earlier, it was logical that she mention her concerns to me. Her primary physician had prescribed antibiotics three weeks earlier, but there had been no change or improvement in the appearance of her breast or her discomfort. I suggested she see a different doctor as soon as possible. Within the week, she was diagnosed with inflammatory breast cancer, a form of breast cancer that is very difficult to treat and has unfavorable survival rates.

This is where our group of fifteen caring, supportive, loving ladies came in. Through Lisa's three years of treatment—surgery, chemotherapy, radiation, trips to MD Anderson Cancer Center in Houston, more surgeries, more chemo—there was never a moment when she was without the love of each of us.

There is a special bond among women that is unique to our species. That bond is always there, but it's there even more so in a crisis. Perhaps one of us would sit with her on her patio talking about the fun times we had at her cabin in the woods for our annual retreats; maybe it was offering to fly to Houston with her to keep her company during her three or four day stays there; perhaps it was offering to take over her daughter's Girl Scout meetings when she wasn't quite up to it—it didn't matter what she needed or wanted; we had it covered.

Her kind and thoughtful husband brought her to our Christmas meeting in December. She was thinner, her eyes didn't have quite the sparkle they once had, her smile was a bit tentative, but to us ...she was still beautiful. She died just two weeks later.

Lisa brought each of us a piece of her beautiful jewelry that day. Do we treasure these gifts from Lisa? Of course. Do we think of her often and speak of her frequently? Of course.

As adults we recognize that no one gets to the end of this journey unscathed. And, as life would have it, over the years we've lost several of our friends but remember them with clarity and gratitude for the time we had with them.

We have experienced all that life brings: lasting marriages, divorces, successful careers, disappointments in love, death of siblings and parents, the amazing birth of our children and then the devastating loss of a child…and yet we have a common thread that connects us, one to the other. We're not sure what it is exactly, but it's there. Was it the environment our parents provided, was it the era in which we grew up, or was it a desire to remain the girls we once were? Somehow that isn't as important as the fact that we still have today what we have had for so many years…friendship like no other.

The adage that there is strength in numbers is so very true with these women.

HOW FORTUNATE THAT THEIR PATHWAYS of traveling through challenges, joys, loss and re-invention have fortified their paths with care and compassion for each other.

Live brave.

There are statistics confirming that more and more women are choosing to live alone after a divorce or a second divorce, okay, a third.

IT APPEARS THAT NOT ONLY are we doing life solo, but most of us are enjoying our new-found independence. Carefully choosing who we want to share our lives with, we begin the process of meeting and assessing and forming our Best Friends Ever (BFE) groups of women, who, as Nan's story illustrated, stay together to create a family of interconnectedness because, indeed, we need each other. In the book, *Wise Aging*, authors Cowan and Thal describe it this way: *"We live in a web of dynamic relationships and interdependence—we live within the natural world and with each other."*

Here, then, is another group of interconnected women. I happen to know at least half of these women as they are clients at the salon. I must confess a bit of envy as I hear of their travels and Sunday evenings' wine and movie nights. They are having way too much fun, and I'm trying to get myself invited. (Maybe after the book, I'll get "my ask" in gear.)

Immediately upon meeting Kim, I could see that she is punctual, organized, and confident. She is direct in her manner and conversation, and just as you think that the dialogue is going to be straight forward about her hair needs, she says something delightful that makes you both laugh out loud and you discover a light-hearted and very charming woman open for a nice girlfriend chitchat.

It was on the third appointment with me that she shared a bit about the group of women whom she calls her support system. I was intrigued. Being very aware that, as women navigate through the second half of their lives, especially if alone, it is with other women that they find their support, I asked her if she would consider giving us a peak into their brave and incredibly fun group of women.

KIM, 67

> ***"Our group reminded me of the poles for a teepee; they had to lean against each other in order to stand upright and hold up the fabric of the shelter."***

What safety nets have you relied on over the years, and how have they served you?

My answer to this question morphed from safety nets into support systems. I belong to a group of caring, bright, and loving women who have created such a support system.

The nine women sat quietly in the chapel waiting for the Mass to begin. They were an attractive group of 48 to 72 year olds. Some sat with head down, reading the funeral program or just staring at their laps. Some looked up at the crucifix and altar, thinking about their lost friend and her husband, sons, and grandchildren. Some whispered to a neighbor or intermittently rose to hug a fellow mourner. This was the second time that the group had to say a final goodbye to one of their own. Kathy, whom all in this group of women had known for at least 25 years, had passed on at age 72. She had fought a number of health conditions over the past years, many of which came close to killing her. But Kathy, like others in this group, was the epitome of a strong woman. Despite being down to less than 90 pounds, she fought and fought. But once she decided it was time to go (just as she decided on those prior occasions that it was not yet time to go), she calmly and gracefully slipped away. So like Kathy.

Although a few of the women had known each other very early in their careers, most of us met and became friends at a large corporate law firm many years before. During the years we worked together, we mixed socially, grabbing a glass of wine after work or taking in a play or movie on the weekend. Our ages ranged more than twenty years in some cases, but somehow our age differences never entered our minds. Each of us just knew that these particular friends would hold us up when we were down and would applaud us when we were up. Our group reminded me of the poles for a teepee; they had to lean against each other in order to stand upright and hold up the fabric of the shelter.

In 1993 one day over lunch, a number of us began talking about investments and how we wanted to know more about the stock market, bonds, and the like. We decided to form an investment club. The purpose of the club was to learn about investing, make group investments to follow, and meet once a month. Most importantly, we wanted to have fun together. Not surprisingly perhaps, we made a lot more fun memories than we did money!!

Prior to forming the club, many of us had faced challenges, including divorces and deaths, children with learning disabilities and other problems, and either overt or backhanded prejudice based on our position or sex. All had fought to overcome these challenges, and all had succeeded. All were brave individually; as a group, we were nearly unstoppable.

Linda was a young attorney interested in trial work, an area of practice in which some good ol' boys secretly (and sometimes not so secretly) felt women could not be successful as they would not be aggressive enough in a courtroom. Linda was quickly proving that they were wrong. It turned out that being "assertive" is a necessary trait for a trial lawyer, but being "aggressive" is not particularly valuable. We supported Linda through many life experiences and celebrated with a party when she was appointed a superior court judge, adorning her with a black robe and a collar made out of a paper doily, a la Ruth Bader Ginsburg.

The funeral mass we were attending was for Kathy who had been a cardiac nurse for many years before she decided to try nurse consulting, working on medical malpractice and personal injury cases in a law firm. She spent about ten years at a law firm and then returned to her first love, helping people through her nurse practitioner practice.

She received our love and support through her years suffering from rheumatic arthritis and valley fever. We had celebrated the 50th anniversary of the marriage of her and her husband just a few months before with a lovely party.

One morning we all received a very distressing email from Stephanie, the facilities director of the firm and the most dedicated of our group to actually learning something from the investment club. Her email explained that her adult daughter had been involved in a horrendous auto accident in which her lower leg was mangled terribly. She underwent many, many surgeries in attempts to save her leg, but eventually, the doctors told her they had done everything they could and that her leg had to be removed. The group followed the progress of Stephanie's daughter and sent prayers and good wishes. Stephanie's daughter has shown some of the same strength of character as her mother and is doing very well now with her prosthetic leg.

We all received phone calls a number of years ago when Nicole's husband died suddenly at age 51, leaving her with 12-year-old triplets and a 15-year-old daughter. She handled this tragedy magnificently and has raised her houseful of children alone, to the point that all of the kids are now successful and devoted to school and/or their careers. She faced plenty of obstacles, not surprisingly, without a husband and with four teenagers to raise by herself. I actually think Nicole may have supported the group more than we supported her by setting such a wonderful example of dedication to her kids, a "can-do" attitude, and a positive outlook. She has worked very hard her entire life but isn't one to complain or ask why these things happened to her. She just keeps on running like an Energizer Bunny. She is back to her job as a nurse consultant and is justifiably proud of her beautiful children.

Not all of the support offered by the group was of such a serious nature. Janie was one of the first nurse consultants in the state and was so dedicated to the employees of the law firm where she worked that she kept a running log as she measured the blood pressure of the employees who suffered from hypertension. She went through a divorce from her physician husband and a few years later found the love of her life. Love at age 60 is such a sweet thing. We had to really celebrate her upcoming marriage, so we took Janie to LaJolla, California, for a bridal shower weekend. Janie is petite, well-preserved, and although she has advanced degrees, she sometimes seems almost innocent. We paraded around town with her in a bridal veil all weekend. We took a limo with champagne from the airport, had a lovely bridal dinner, and gave her sexy little gifts and lingerie. Because she failed to pack some of the various flavored and perfumed "lubricating" lotions she was given in her checked luggage, the TSA agents were mildly amused to find these potions when she went through the security line for our return flight home with a carry-on filled with liquids. Unfortunately, one of them was over three ounces and was actually confiscated—much to Janie's embarrassment and disappointment! But the bridal shower had been a hit, and she simply glowed the entire weekend.

Then we all met Alexis, who was relatively newly divorced and the mother of two teenaged daughters. We were all so taken by her wonderful enthusiasm for what seemed to be all things. She is truly a renaissance woman who is interested in everything from the Middle East to gardening and who gushes about it all. But not in a way that seems forced or insincere...she just loves everything. Alexis had dated informally over the years but was never serious about anyone until she met Bill.

When they decided to marry, we gave Alexis quite a bridal shower as well, including a gift of a unique book which had daily suggestions for sexual adventures with your loved one. We thought it was so funny...even more so when Alexis would report that she and Bill had enjoyed suggestion number 72 or 36 the night before…with hilarious explanations of what went on. We were all sworn to secrecy, of course, as Bill would have been mortified to think that these women had indulged in this candid conversation about their sex life. Tragically, Bill was diagnosed with ALS only six years after their wedding and rather rapidly became weak and then disabled. Within two years, he was under hospice care. We all came to her aid, providing support through his illness and his last days. Kathy sat with Alexis and Bill all night on the night he died. I was out of town at the time of Bill's death but rushed back the following day and spent the night on Bill's side of their bed with Alexis in case she woke up in distress. But Alexis is very strong and classy, only seldom showing the anguish which Bill's death caused. Alexis had previously survived breast cancer (with the medical members of our group following her care and accompanying her to chemotherapy treatments and doctors' visits), sustained a hip fracture, and a Parkinson's diagnosis, so she continues to receive help and support from the group.

The group's resident Good Samaritan is Samantha, who was also a nurse consultant. She is so knowledgeable about medicine that, to this day, I would trust her diagnosis before most any doctors. She had been married to her pediatrician husband for only a few years when he received a diagnosis of Parkinson's disease. She eventually became his caregiver, taking care of both him and their two boys until his death twenty years later. Samantha probably has more friends than the rest of us combined, and the outpouring of grief and concern after her husband's death was amazing. There is, no doubt, that she has so many friends because she is so extremely caring about everyone else. She is our group's muse.

One of the most traumatic losses the group suffered was the death of our friend and fellow club member, Patti, in an automobile accident. This was so sudden and unexpected. Patti was a vibrant 48-year-old newly-appointed vice president of her company. She loved her husband, her hyper-liberal daughter who was in law school, and her sweet adult son. When we received the phone call with this devastating news, many of us just automatically got in our cars and headed over to Alexis's house to hold each other.

Carol is a 55-year-old single nurse/attorney at a local firm that specializes in defending medical and dental malpractice cases. She was diagnosed with breast cancer, underwent bilateral mastectomies and reconstructions, and then, a few years later, had a cancerous lesion on her face that resulted in the loss of a lot of tissue. She is a beautiful girl, and we worried about the impact this could have on her and, potentially, even her career as a trial attorney. But reconstructive surgery has restored her beautiful face. During the rehab from her multiple surgeries, we brought her dinners and buoyed her spirits.

I am Kim, a 67-year-old law office manager, divorced with three wonderful sons who are the light of my life. Although I feel my life has been relatively free of strife, I did require brain surgery for an aneurysm one summer, followed by spinal surgery the following summer. I started to wonder if I was going to have a "summer surgery" every year, but, thankfully, that didn't happen. As I woke up in the hospital after each surgery, one or more of the girls was there smiling down at me. I received wonderful support (and delicious meals) during rehabilitation. I am also the one who hosts our annual Christmas dinner and gift exchange, which we all consider to be the real start of the Christmas season. We have the best time selecting presents to bring as we get to purchase something that we would like to receive. Then we have a round-robin gift exchange where numbers are drawn and whoever has number one can pick a gift; number two can either take number one's gift or pick an unwrapped gift, etc. until all the numbers have chosen a gift. Some years there is even a lot of snatching of other's gifts. Nevertheless, everyone brings a dish (we are all great cooks if I do say so myself), and it is truly a magical evening.

These women simply will not allow one of their friends to want for anything while facing a challenge. The nurses, of course, follow our various diagnoses as if they were following a patient in the hospital. They are remarkable resources as to which doctors to see, which hospital is best, what to expect in the future, etc. These women are not only delightful, but they are very well-informed caregivers. They don't say "What can we do?" They just figure out what needs to be done and do it without making anyone feel uncomfortable accepting their help.

We have birthday dinners for each other, especially 60, when the birthday girl receives a heart-shaped paperweight with all of our names etched on it. We also love to travel together. At one time or another, we have enjoyed each other during trips to Europe, San Diego, San Francisco, Flagstaff, Tubac, Sedona, Lake Tahoe, Mexico, and on and on. We have discussed that, no matter how much you love your husband, there are no better travel companions than a group of close girlfriends.

Why is it that women can become so close when men do not seem to establish the same type of relationships? Perhaps it is just the role of women because of biology, not only to nurture but to be able to accept nurturing from others. Perhaps it is women's deep-seated understanding of the challenges that they know will be faced and the knowledge that they can better deal with those challenges if they have a support system in the form of a wonderful group of friends upon whom they can rely in good times and in bad. The old saying that "you don't get to pick your family, but you get to pick your friends" is very true. In our case, our friends have become our family and have added such richness to our lives that they are truly precious to us. We are all successful and accomplished women about whom some might ask, "How does she do it?" We always say, "What would we do without each other?"

The nine of us in the chapel prepared ourselves for Kathy's service. Kleenex was pulled from purses and big sighs were heard as we involuntarily braced ourselves. We knew this was going to be a difficult service to get through. A few of us were able to remain stoic and not shed a tear during the eulogy, the homily, and even the beautiful music.

But when the service ended and it was almost time to leave for the reception, we all came together in a group in front of the chapel, held each other, and bawled like babies. But we were still standing tall...just like that teepee.

Somehow, the majority of these women have now become clients of our salon.

WELL! ONE GOOD HAIRCUT LEADS to another and another and another. I'm hoping that I can continue to keep my hands moving and my mind sharp enough to remember if I have cut both sides. Their path to friendship and compassion for each other has solidified their sisterhood and given them the courage to live braver lives.

Live brave.

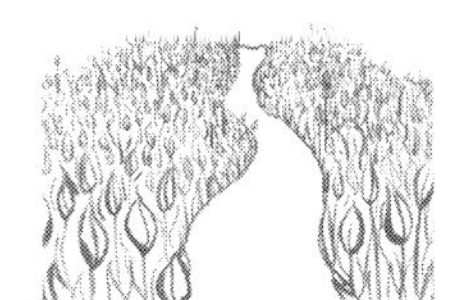

CHAPTER TWELVE

Loving Deeply

"The late, great philosopher Ronald Dworkin recognized that there is a second, more compelling sense of autonomy: Whatever the limits and travails we face, we want to retain the autonomy—the freedom—to be the authors of our lives."
~ Atul Gawande, Being Moral

KEY QUESTION: WHAT HAVE YOU LOVED DEEPLY IN YOUR LIFE?

During the past seven months, four of our clients have lost their children.

Gloria, a client for over ten years, is eighty-eight years young. In November her sixty-year-old son, the youngest of three sons, passed away suddenly on a Monday morning of a heart attack. A few months later in March while attending a class in California, I received a call from a client's husband informing me that their son, an eleven-year-old, bright and beautiful, thoughtful and handsome child had passed away in a tragic accident. His wife, Jennifer, was due in for her hair the following Saturday, and he thought that we should know so that we could be prepared.

In March again, Valerie, an attractive and bright business woman in her fifties, a client for several years, lost her twenty-one-year-old son to an unintended drug overdose. A month later in June, another client in her early eighties, our sweet Gandolfa, lost her 56-year-old daughter from prolonged use of morphine.

The question, What have you loved deeply in your life, has stirred up a variety of answers from women who say they love God, reading, their cats and dogs, their homes and some, simply, the adventure of life. But there is no question that women love their children…deeply. The thought of a child dying before the mother makes her transition is a universal fear for all women from the day the child is born. A natural protective course of action develops within the woman's consciousness, and the radar screen for the child's safety and well-being is created. Losing a child off the screen of her life is inconceivable to a mother. But it does occur, and the process of healing such immense pain takes time.

I asked Jennifer, the mother of the eleven-year-old son who passed, if she would share her story. It had been less than six months since his passing when I approached her and asked if she would open herself and her family to give others a glance into her thoughts and grieving and to share the questions that were filling her mind at this time. Jennifer is an intelligent woman with a soft and welcoming nature. She is a thoughtful and private person, and I wasn't sure if she would consent to sharing while still in the beginning stages of their grieving. But without much hesitation, she agreed, and here is her story.

JENNIFER F, 47

"Every day I privately battle with that voice inside my head and the pain in my heart. Give up; no, keep moving. Finding a purpose, preserving a memory, and trying to make this world a little better is about all I can do."

I AM FORTY SEVEN YEARS old and was born in upstate New York. I have lived in numerous states, including Ohio, Wisconsin, Minnesota, and Montana and currently live in Arizona. I graduated from high school in New York and attended Hamilton College in Clinton where I secured my bachelor's degree. Later at the University of Montana, I prepared for my career as a clinical laboratory scientist. After working in a hospital for several years, I secured additional training and earned a specialty in blood banking. Earning a master's degree in immunohematology from George Washington University, I currently work for a blood donor center.

At the age of twenty-six, I married my high school sweetheart, and we had three children. After fourteen years of marriage, we divorced. Shortly after the divorce, I moved to Arizona with my children where I met and married Thomas, a widower who had lost his wife and ten-year-old daughter to a drunk driver. Thomas had suffered massive injuries, while his eight-year-old son was uninjured. He had been raising his son alone for eight years when we met; we married and blended our families two years later. Our children stood up for us in our ceremony. It was a glorious day for everyone.

The past few months have been hell and a journey on a road I would not wish on anyone. Last March, March 10, Ryan, my 11-year-old boy hanged himself. No indication why, no note, no answers. Just a big empty hole in my heart.

It wasn't too long ago I would have said that we are just a normal family. I still think we are a normal family, but our perspective has changed, and we have a few more battle wounds. When I was asked to share my story, my mind wandered. There were so many layers. Where do I start? Is there really a linear story that is easy to tell? Maybe, maybe not. When I have tried to tell it, I have gotten lost. And I still feel lost.

So let me start with my daughter. She has all the gifts. Brilliant, thoughtful, beautiful inside and out. But somehow, as so many of us know, the teenage years have a way of distorting the brains of the young. She turned to drugs. Truthfully, we have been fighting this fight since she was 13, and I am not going to stand up here and make excuses although there are situations in her past that may have led her down this road. She was a cutter and was dealing with something dark inside. Honestly, I believe the media and pop culture wants us to believe that drugs are cool, so it's no wonder our kids gravitate towards them. She ran away in eighth grade for three days and slept on the street. She was not being abused or neglected. Her home was safe, but this girl wanted to define her life a certain way. When she hit high school, we continued to notice a change. Her grades never slipped, but we noticed the signs. She was pretty bad at hiding them from us. Wanting to cut up cactus to make a mixture that would help her meditate was not exactly hiding it from me. I told her it was a felony, but it didn't seem to matter to her. Every summer was a refreshing break for me because she would spend her summers in upstate New York on her grandfather's farm. It was a time for us to regroup. In the fall she would return and be excited about school and the new possibilities. She turned 16 and got her license. She had a new school to go to and a new group of friends. But then, just like that, she would slip again. She would start using the drugs. I asked her to have her friends at our house so they could hang out there. I could monitor them—no alcohol or drug use. No, Sarah would tell me. Her friends thought I was too aggressive, and other parents were cooler. I even called these other parents and stated that under no circumstances did I want my daughter drinking or smoking. They said they agreed, and they would monitor the activity. Never happened. Sarah drove from a party. Drunk. Smashed into a parked trailer and totaled her car. Drove home and tried to put herself into bed. I heard her come home, and I smelled the alcohol. I was upset, but I figured I would deal with it in the morning because you can't talk reason to someone who is drunk. In the morning, we found the car. Great, she drove and hit something. Now I have a hit and run. I immediately called the police. That's when we found out it was a parked trailer and not a person she hit. We set more restrictions. She got a job. But she also started selling drugs to make money so she could buy a new car. She was driving me crazy, and I really did not even like her anymore. No, I could probably say I hated her, but I was her mother, and I wouldn't give up.

March came. It was a normal evening. My son Ryan was hanging out at the ball park, watching his friends play. I called him to come home for dinner, and he asked to stay. We negotiated and finally agreed on a time but not a minute longer. He came home ten minutes late. I got upset. I grounded him and reminded him that he had given me a time. He never argued. He took his punishment. He ate dinner and went to his room to do homework and talk to his friends on FaceTime. I called him out so he could watch a little TV with us. He came out. I remember he wanted me to dish him some ice cream. I didn't do it. I kept hearing his brother and sister in my head, "He's old enough to do things. Don't do it for him, Mom." After about thirty minutes, he went back to his room. We didn't think anything of that because that's what he did all the time. Twenty minutes later, I got a phone call from his friend asking if Ryan was okay. I said, "Yeah, he was just with us," but I walked down the hall to find his door locked. I pounded, but he didn't answer. I kept beating and kicking the wall. My husband came around the corner. We finally got the door open. Sarah had gone outside to go through the window. I remember seeing her face when we got the door open. She was screaming. We untied Ryan from the ceiling fan and starting CPR. It seemed like forever for the ambulance to arrive. We tried and tried. They took him to Phoenix Children's Hospital to work on him more. I sat in the ER and watched them work on him. I felt numb and empty. And then they pronounced him dead.

I had to call my older son. I asked him to come to the ER. I could not tell him over the phone, but watching him collapse against the wall when his legs buckled after being told that Ryan was gone was just as hard. I had to call his father and my parents. How do you do that? I don't even remember the conversations. I just don't. I remember going home from the ER. My husband, my daughter, my son, my stepson and me...we all sat on our couch together. We all lay on top of one another. We were exhausted, awake, and silent. All night just like that. But one thought kept creeping in my mind, "Why didn't you just get him the ice cream? It all would be different."

We watched my daughter unravel. Less than a week later, we admitted my daughter into an inpatient treatment center. When she was discharged, she attended an intensive outpatient program. I found a trauma counselor for her so she had additional counseling above the rehab. She also had to see a psychiatrist for her medication. That was a trip. She would argue her prescription with the doctor. Really, it was that she wanted to continue to take drugs but was worried about the cross-reactivity with her prescription.

She could not stay sober. She ran away. Her friends hid her from me. She would return and throw fits of rage, and every time she did, I called the police. She would run away again. It was obvious to us that she was taking meth now. She started to pick at her skin. She had sores all over her body. So through my frustration and hatred, I found a promise, and I found hope. I found a program called Teen Challenge. This was a fifteen-month residential program. Believe me, I had done lots of homework. Three month or even six month programs were not going to work. It would take a full nine months off of drugs for her brain to recover. This program indicated the additional six months were because that would be the time needed to work on her. We waited for school to end, drove her there, and left her on June 1. This was less than three months after her brother's suicide. That night was the first night I had slept in ages.

I started to grieve. I started to allow myself to feel a little bit. However, everything was so tight inside, and it was hard. I would get questions like, "How's your daughter?" I would answer politely, but inside I would be screaming, "What about my son?" Most people would not acknowledge or mention his name. Had they forgotten? Work became a chore for me. It gave me no satisfaction, and it felt like a burden to be there. I started to question myself as a mother. How did these things happen to my kids? What did I do wrong? This stuff isn't supposed to happen. I started to think more about Ryan. I tried to push the images of that day out of my mind, and I asked God to replace them with good memories. Day by day, my heart started to beat again.

One morning I woke up from a dream, and it became clear to me. I was going to do something for Ryan. I wanted to do something that would honor Ryan's memory because the world was not going to forget my son. To me and to so many of his family members, a store that honored Ryan and his love for the rhinoceros seemed to make perfect sense. I started to design the graphics using Ryan's rhinos. I snapped pictures and photoshopped them in different ways, creating fun and colorful designs. I talked and networked my idea. I learned a lot along the way and figured I would just jump off the cliff and do this thing. I launched my site, *In Danger*, in December, less than nine months after Ryan's suicide. It gave me such a passion and a purpose for life. I am still learning so much, and the women at Mother's Grace have been amazing. I am so excited to see where this will take me.

So let me end on this final story. It's the story of exactly one year after Ryan's death. I took the day off. I wanted to go to the zoo in Camp Verde. It was the one zoo where I had not taken Ryan, and I knew there was a rhino there. My husband and I got there about 10am. There is a bus you can take that will drive you through some of the enclosures, but I was anxious to see the rhino. I didn't want to stand in a line for a bus that wasn't going to take me to the rhino. So we set off on a walk. Down the road a bit, Lisa, a staff member in a truck, stopped us. She had noticed my Rhino shirt and volunteered, "I love your shirt. I love rhinos, too!" Thomas gave her a flyer that talked about *In Danger*. She loved the idea and said, "Meet me at the rhino exhibit in five minutes."

We walked on and soon were standing in front of Jericho. He had just eaten and was looking a little sleepy. Another woman was standing there, so we introduced ourselves. She said she lived in Flagstaff but often came down to work in front of Jericho. She was in love with this animal. At this point, Thomas was thinking, "Oh, great...now there are two crazy rhino ladies here." The staff member came as she had promised. She wanted us to meet Jericho, but he was not cooperating. So we spent some time talking to them about our son and his love of rhinos. We said that was why we were starting our new business. They loved the idea and wanted to support us. Isa invited us back later at 4pm when they were going to feed the rhino. We were not planning to spend the day there but decided it might be worth it. Finally, at 3:30pm we wandered back to the exhibit where three different staff were waiting. They had heard of our mission and wanted to bring us closer. They unlocked the gate and took us to the back where Jericho was waiting. We spent fifteen minutes scratching his belly and his ears. We took pictures, and I just wanted to hug this giant beast. I fell in love with this animal all over again. I realized I was smiling. Smiling! On a day that should be one of the saddest of my life. Suddenly, all of this made sense. I felt Ryan smiling down on me. It was one of the most amazing blessings I have experienced. The pain of the day was replaced with this most astonishing feeling.

Every day I privately battle with that voice inside my head and the pain in my heart. Give up; no, keep moving. Finding a purpose, preserving a memory, and trying to make this world a little better is about all I can do.

I am happy to report today (at the time of this writing) on my daughter's progress. She is filled with God's grace and is learning healthy coping skills. She is learning that life is not fair but that doesn't mean you cannot prevail. She has centered God and her family in her life. There is a rebuilding of three relationships. It is not perfect and, certainly, not easy. I am tremendously proud of her transformation and cautiously optimistic about her future. Teen Challenge has saved her life. Every time I say that I break down because I know the truth in that. I also understand how many kids are walking around in that same fog, and it breaks my heart.

I still have two questions to ask from those who share this pain of loss with me:

1. *When people ask me how many children do I have—how do I answer?*
2. *I believe in the afterlife. I believe I will see Ryan again, but then there's that ever-so-brief moment that I doubt, and I ask myself, "What if I don't? What if it's all a lie?" I can't stand that thought. When will that thought go away? When will that doubt go away?*

My dear friend and client Mary Lee is intellectually and emotionally smart.

WHEN I ASKED IF SHE would share her story of the loss of her daughter and answer these two questions for Jennifer who had just lost her son, she immediately responded with yes. As you will see by her abbreviated bio, she is a very busy and dynamic woman and her heart is bigger than her busy life.

If public speaking is still ranked as one of the top five fears of a human being, then my friend Mary Lee is definitely living brave. No matter how many times I have had the pleasure of watching her deliver a public presentation, her cool command of the subject, delivery, and self-confidence assures her audience that she is in complete control of the subject matter and that her wisdom runs deep.

Mary Lee has more than forty-five years in healthcare reimbursement management experience. Currently providing consulting support for healthcare clients, she was the Vice President of Revenue Cycle for Maricopa Integrated Health System from 2004-2014. In prior roles, Mary Lee has led teams in organizations on both the provider and vendor sides of healthcare in Oregon, Washington, California, Nebraska, and Arizona.

She is the immediate past chair of the Arizona Hospital Healthcare Association Managed Care Committee, past chair of the National HFMA Revenue Cycle KPI Task Force, and is a member of both the National HFMA Medical Debt Task Force and the National HFMA Pricing Transparency Task Force.

As a single parent, Mary Lee raised three children in Seattle, relocating with Molly, Mike, and Mark to Tucson in 1993. In 1999 at age 23, Molly died of complications fifteen months after a heart transplant for viral cardiomyopathy.

In memory of Molly, Mary Lee became active with the American Heart Association's annual Heart Walk, where she has served as a company leader for the past sixteen years, raising an average of $40,000 yearly in donations by the 350-400 walkers. The AHA awarded her with a Lifetime Achievement Award in 2015 in recognition of her service.

MARY LEE, 68

"How to answer the question: How many children do you have?"

IMMEDIATELY FOLLOWING MOLLY'S DEATH, I was confronted with the mundane demands of daily living that required me to reorganize my thoughts about my family and how I represented us. It astonished me that the world kept revolving and going on about its busyness while I was forever changed. For eighteen years I had been a single mother with three children, one daughter and two sons. Now, I was a single mother with... three? two? Children? No daughter? Just two sons? How should I answer that question? How should I fill in the blank field on a form? How could I possibly explain the fifteen month journey I had been on with Molly's sudden illness, heart transplant, and then her death in one sentence, in two or three words, or with an X in a box on a form?

Initially, I would pause, stammer, and let the tears well up in my eyes. It took me a couple of months, but I did resolve, and then practiced saying, "I have three children.

My daughter died in February 1999; Mark is a student at NAU; and Mike is at the U of A." I made the decision to include Molly in my response and learned to say, "I am the mother of three children." It took repetition until I was confident enough to respond to the question without breaking down. Often, I will ease the impact of my response by adding, "I can talk about it now without bursting into tears, but for the first three years, it was very hard. Thank you for asking." Most adults, particularly adults who are parents, are uncomfortable upon hearing my response. It is frightening. What if this awful thing, the death of a child, happened to them? It's every parent's worst fear. And so, I want to reassure them, help them to feel safe.

I will always be Molly's mom. Her life and presence among us was a gift to me and our family. I want to include her when I am asked, "How many children do you have?"

How do I manage the doubt I feel regarding my belief in eternal life and whether I will see my child again?

The death of a child is the most painful loss of human life that we can ever experience. The instinctive nature of parenting forces us to love, protect, nurture, and care for our child, but somehow, something went wrong, and we lost our child in spite of everything we did. Doubts flood in. Could I have done something differently to prevent this? I don't trust the beliefs I once had because, in spite of everything I did, I lost my child.

The phases of grief are well-documented, but the most important concept to remember is the healing quality of the passage of time. It is slow, but sure. Give yourself permission to doubt, and then move on with your day. The doubt may come again tomorrow and the next day. In time, you will heal, and in healing, the doubts will shrink and disappear. When you have doubt, pause and reflect on your beliefs; give respect to their origins. A personal habit I used was to put my doubts in front of the Lord in prayer. I begin every prayer with gratitude and the one thing I am most grateful for—the gift of my daughter Molly in my life. Too grief stricken to pray? Read the 23rd Psalm out loud. Give your doubts to God and ask him to reassure you.

When I found myself consoling a dear friend on the sudden death of her 22-year-old son fifteen years after Molly's death, I realized my doubts were no more. I had regained my faith and trust in eternal life and was once again confident in the knowledge that I will be reunited with my daughter, my mother, my grandparents, all who have passed into eternal life.

Time, and the love of your family and friends, will bring you through and will heal your pain.

Mary Lee, Molly's mom

Maureen Patricia "Molly" Major 9/11/75—2/11/99

She is almost six feet tall and that, in itself, brings us to attention as she enters our small salon and greets us with, "Hello, my children!"

Her comment immediately announces that she is in control of our space, and she is received with smiles. We love her and appreciate her directness, big heart, and affectionate manner. Florence is young looking and wears a striking short cut on a thick head of silver hair. Her posture is that of a healthy younger woman; she is stylish in her dress and confident in her manner; she is used to being noticed when she walks in a room. She connects with the clients in the salon and always has something pleasant to say.

Retired as a business owner all of her life, she currently volunteers her time at a hospital and is very involved with her sons and her grandchildren.

I asked Florence to share her story of the loss of her son because I had never forgotten her answer when we first met and I asked her if she had children and how many.

FLORENCE, 75

"When people ask me how many children I have, I pause and say—I have three sons: my oldest son Charles is in heaven, my son Bob lives in Phoenix, and my youngest son Jim is in California."

Charles was killed thirty-two years ago. Our last conversation was in February of 1984. He called to tell me that he already had my birthday present picked out. My birthday being in October, I was somewhat surprised! Then he told me that our daughter-in-law Mary was pregnant and due in October!

I wasn't happy with that news. I felt that she was too young at twenty-three, and they had been married less than a year.

Two weeks later, he was killed. Will I ever forget that conversation? It still haunts me. I won't make excuses, but it did teach me to never end a conversation being negative and not letting the other person feel special.

Seven months later my grandson was born and our daughter-in-law named him after his father—Charles. Wow!

The happy ending is that my daughter-in-law and I are very close and grandson Charles just passed the bar exam (first try) and is a very special young man.

To answer the second question: When will my faith become concrete? Faith is looking back on how I handled the devastating news of my son's death and the subsequent life of my grandson. He didn't take my son's place but he did fill a little hole in my heart. God saw to that.

Karen has been a client at our salon for over ten years.

SHE IS DEEPLY ROOTED IN her spirituality and volunteers her time teaching a class, "A Course in Miracles," at a local church. During the years, I have come to respect her curious mind, her efforts toward continual personal development, her ability to move forward fearlessly (at least, it appears fearlessly to me), and her easygoing manner with a propensity for laughter. A gentle spirit and a calm nature endear her to us, and when asked if she would share her story of losing her daughter, she agreed graciously.

Karen considers herself to be analytical and logical. After receiving her BS in Liberal Arts from Arizona State University, she had a fifteen-year career in retailing. She then returned to school and graduated from the University of Dallas with an MBA and an interest in financial planning. She joined American Express Financial Advisors and spent the next seven years working in this field and loving every minute of it.

After the death of her daughter in 2001, it was clear to her that her analytical mind and logical skills did little to prepare her for the emotional roller coaster ride of grief. Leaving the corporate world behind her, she embarked on a new path. Her life is now about finding meaning in whatever she is doing. She wants to find a way to help people deal with change. She facilitates a study group based on the teachings of *A Course in Miracles* and is a long-time volunteer for the New Song Center for Grieving Children, a program of Hospice of the Valley.

KAREN, 67

"My daughter, Janette, pursued her dream as if her life depended on it."

Little did I know that it would be the price she had to pay to reach her goal. Her dream was not unusual or difficult for the majority of women. All she ever wanted was a baby and to be a mother.

There were countless challenges for her to face that began with a partial hysterectomy at age 19. She was left with 2/3 of one ovary that was connected to a blocked tube. The good news is that her uterus was perfect. Doctors gave her a 10% chance of ever conceiving a child. Surgery was done to clear the blocked tube, but it was unsuccessful. The only answer appeared to be in vitro fertilization. This is an emotional and financial draining process, and I watched as Janette continued to take the next step without looking back or giving up. She was ecstatic when the second attempt at in vitro was successful.

It was not smooth sailing after the pregnancy was confirmed. The hormones that surrounded the egg did not reach the appropriate levels, and the doctor did not want to aspirate the three eggs that were the strongest. The doctor also suggested genetic testing based on the date of her ovulation. Next, Janette began to experience symptoms of a hypertensive heart and was sent to a high-risk clinic.

She never questioned her decision to have a child and never became a victim of her circumstances. All I could do as her mother was to love her and support her in her pursuit. My conversation revolved around letting go of fear. I felt as if she could not accept the reality of the pregnancy after her relentless pursuit.

Janette did deliver her beautiful baby girl, Angel Grace, but Angel's first breath was to become Janette's last.

My daughter's story ended at age 32. Her baby girl is now a beautiful and intelligent teenager. I am reminded of her mother when I look at her. One of my goals is to help her understand who her birth mother was and to know how much she loved her even if she was not here to raise her. I am creating a photo journal for Angel that is filled with stories and pictures about her mother. This project has been a healing experience for everyone.

I used to think that a mother was here to teach her children about life and love, but for me, it has been the opposite experience. After my daughter passed away, I learned how to live and the importance of keeping my heart open.

Answering Question 1: When people ask me how many children do I have—how do I answer?

My response to this question has changed in the fourteen years since Janette passed away. I try to avoid this conversation with anyone because, however I answer, it is difficult to respond. I feel as if someone kicks me in the gut before the question is even asked. I sense that it is coming. I never initiate this question because I don't want to be asked in return.

For the first few years after Janette's passing, I told my story to anyone who was willing to listen. It was my identity. I was a member of a club that nobody wants to join. If I answered the question and said that I have a son who is 37 and a daughter who died at 32, questions would immediately follow:

"How did it happen?"

"Did the baby live?"

"Where is the child?"

My story is then the focus of the conversation, and this is not my intent.

I finally reached the stage of acceptance in my grief journey and did not want to repeat my story to random strangers. It no longer defined me, but it did change me in profound ways after going through this experience. My current response is, "I raised two children, a son and a daughter, but now I am into grandkids."

I meet incredible women who have also lost a child, or in some cases, multiple children. Each finds her own way to respond. One of my favorite answers is, "My child is forever 32."

What I have learned is that there is no right or wrong response. Follow your heart and be authentic.

In response to question two, the doubt ended for me when I began to receive signs and messages from two of the people that I lost before I was ready to let them go. My messages come in dreams, songs on the radio, and random events that grab my attention. It became clear to me after receiving many messages that there is more to life than just what I can see and touch. The love that I had for another person is still in my heart and that love never ends.

I received a sign several years after my daughter's death. Here is the story:

I like to sponsor flowers at the church service on the Sunday before the anniversary of my daughter's death. This is a small gesture that allows me to honor her memory, and I am touched when I read the dedication in the church bulletin. I signed the form to secure the desired date and wrote a note in the margin of the paper: Please order an arrangement of pink and purple flowers. Pink was my daughter's favorite color and purple is the color of healing.

There was a little snag in my plan because, after I signed up for the flowers, I had an opportunity to be out of town over July 4th weekend. I chose to modify the original sign-up sheet for flower dedications. I drew an arrow to indicate that I would sponsor the flowers on July 9th instead of July 2nd. The community administrator of my church called me to confirm the change in date, and everything was set.

My trip out of town was cancelled, but I decided to leave the date of the flower dedication as July 9th. I arrived at church on July 2nd and saw a beautiful arrangement of pink and purple flowers. However, the dedication was not what I had written. The flowers were to honor someone else. I felt confused, irritated, and a bit frustrated. All I wanted to do was honor my child on the anniversary of her passing, and it was all wrong. She might be honored the next Sunday,

July 9, with the dedication that I wrote, but the pink and purple arrangement would not be there.

On Sunday, July 9, the dedication was in the church bulletin, and the flowers were lovely. The only thing I could see from where I sat in the back of the sanctuary was that they were not pink and purple.

It is customary for the person who sponsors the flowers to take them home after the service. I went to pick up the arrangement and discovered something that sent a chill down my spine.

It was one of those moments when I knew that I was receiving a message. The bouquet contained three yellow roses, which happen to be my favorite flower. The number three was also significant because it let me know that the two people I had loved and lost within three years of each other were still with me.

Any feelings of irritation about not having pink and purple flowers quickly dissipated. I realize that everything worked out perfectly.

CHAPTER THIRTEEN

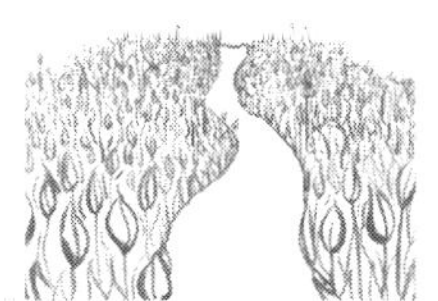

A Vision of Hope

"This is not the moment to wilt into the underbrush of your insecurities. You've earned the right to grow."
~ Cheryl Strayed, Brave Enough

KEY QUESTION: WHAT ADVICE WOULD YOU GIVE YOUNGER PEOPLE TO HELP THEM DEVELOP A VISION OF HOPE FOR THEIR LATER YEARS?

I have had the advantage of knowing LaRae for over forty years.

As a client of the salon, we, the salon team, have had the opportunity to have her as our mentor, advisor, and coach in all areas of our professional and personal lives. She is strong, intelligent, and always informed about the current world, the social and political climate. She reads everything and is one of the most interesting and interested women that I have ever had the pleasure of knowing.

Currently, at age 85, she is taking classes through Encore University's "Adventures in Lifelong Learning" on Southwest historians, the Italian Renaissance, American literature, brain exploration, world religions, the US Constitution, and French impressionism. I know that she will continue her learning as long as she is alive. It is her nature to be curious and to keep her mind sharp and receptive to information.

LaRae travels extensively throughout the year. When asked how she developed her love and inspiration for trekking the world, she answered, "As we age our passions change. Some stay with us, such as family, reading, and the wonders of traveling. My father fostered the passion of travel. His inquiring and adventurous mind took us on many wonderful Sunday driving trips, exploring the country. For twenty years, I have traveled with a group of professional women. We have explored and absorbed the cultures of third world countries like Mexico, Central and South America, Morocco, and Turkey. We even camped in the Sahara Desert for several days where we experienced one of the dust storms that we read about in books. My husband and I also experienced many interesting adventures traveling to Mexico, China, Europe, the UK, Asia, Cook Islands, Turkey, Greece, Canada, and the islands in the Caribbean. Some of these destinations warranted visiting twice."

They say there is a slight distinction between fearing and respecting someone that you hold in high regard. While fearing her disappointment and, simultaneously, respecting her high standards and common sense approach to living, I have asked for her advice and, at the same time, dreaded her counsel. Although I have always known that her vast knowledge and sensible thinking will give me the best results, I've not always followed her guidance. I will always be twenty years younger than she is, so I am still learning from her and from my own mistakes. But I have recently noticed that I am experiencing fewer mistakes and surrendering to her opinions much easier. Gratefully, LaRae has yet to give up on me and still offers her love and friendship...and lots of guidance.

In his book *Aging as a Spiritual Practice*, Lewis Richmond writes about people who have beaten the odds of aging. They build teams around them of people who support their lives—strong friendships, trusted doctors, financial advisors, family ties—and, through curiosity and openness, they live a higher quality of life. He calls these people Extraordinary Elders. LaRae is an Extraordinary Elder.

Born in Tacoma, Washington, and raised in a surrounding rural area by pragmatic parents with common sense, high moral values, an honest work ethic, and good healthy genes, she recalls being a tomboy working the fields and climbing trees. She remembers her childhood as happy and healthy and that she was always curious.

LaRae attended The University of Arizona in Tucson where she acquired a teaching degree. Her teaching career spanned 30 years in the primary grades, mostly teaching reading, until she retired to spend time with family and to travel the world...which she does often.

LARAE, 85

"When you get older, you begin to realize that everything has its rewards."

Physical Strength

What significant health issue have you had to overcome?

Born with shallow hip sockets, I started at the age of 41 with my first hip replacement and have had three replacement surgeries since. Currently, I have been diagnosed with adult scoliosis, but it doesn't stop me from doing anything that I want to do.

How have you dealt with the physical changes of aging?

I'm able to participate in most everything. I travel and do crazy things with the boys (son and grandsons) like getting into high trucks and boats and going out at night to hunt for scorpions.

How does your current physical environment bring you joy?

The artwork in my home, the paintings, tapestries, sculptures, reminds me of the colors of the cultures I have visited and loved. The expansive windows of the living room display the earthiness of my native desert landscaping. I feel a strong connection with all of it.

Mental Clarity

What mental skills have you developed over the years to help you navigate the difficult times?

I have developed the ability to make good decisions and to think of the consequences first before making the decisions.

When you get older, you begin to realize that everything has its rewards. Sometimes an old friend has to be out of your life. Negative people are not good as we age. Instead, it is important to have a sense of humor and not live in the past!

Who in your family inspired you to be courageous?

My father inspired me. He never used swear words; he was intelligent, educated, loved to travel, and was a business owner. I was fortunate to have wonderful parents.

Spiritual Courage

What have you loved deeply?

I have loved reading and I love my family.

What advice would you give younger people to help them develop a vision of hope for their later years?

Make decisions by first thinking ahead of the consequences.

Take classes and develop hobbies if you don't already have them. My favorites are reading and helping people in many ways. Be a good listener and not a gossip. Keep your promises to others and spend time with your family.

Make friends with younger people; they bring so much to the table.

Try new ideas and expand your mind. Develop a good work ethic and read everything!

Save money and have a nest egg for your older years because being comfortable when you are older makes life more enjoyable.

It is said that bravery comes through taking action. How will you continue to live a brave life?

By being proactive with my health, accepting diversity, loving my family and spending time with them, and continuing to read everything—from novels to store signs! And to continue planning for the next travel adventure, for as I always say, the best trip I ever took is the Next One! I am really pleased with my age as I continue to see life more clearly. I remain curious and open to what life will bring me next.

As you have surmised by her short answers, LaRae is a woman of few words, even when asked for her counsel.

BUT IN THOSE FEW WORDS, she captures the essence of who you are, and because of her solid and enlightened state of mind, not many words are needed to get her point across.

Similar to the feelings I hold for my own mother, I feel a deep sense of love and reverence for LaRae. The thought of losing her leaves me afraid that I will miss the stability that I have felt for over forty years knowing that she would always be accessible.

If you are reading this book and are in your twenties, thirties, forties, or even your fifties, I wish for you that you will come across a curious and interesting woman who will lend herself unselfishly to your personal development. Treasure your relationship with her and let yourself grow in her shadow. Then someday you will be a shadow for another.

Live brave.

One way to develop a vision of hope for the later years is to ask questions.

OR AS MY FRIEND AND fellow *Living Brave* woman Connie Kadansky says: "Get your ask in gear!"

I started thinking of the women who walk into the salon who have *that* way about them who *always* ask us how we are. They take an interest in us, not just because we are about to work on their most precious image (hair is everything to us in the industry) but because they genuinely care about others. Let's face it, when you make someone feel special, they, in turn, want to make you feel special. Or at least that is how it feels to us in our salon. Pay attention, ladies; this is significant information.

I first met Lisa several years ago through her mother, my next door neighbor, who suggested that Lisa come to me for her hair. Her mother quickly let me know that she herself would not be coming to me. She said she knew that she was a very difficult and demanding client, and that as neighbors, she could not afford to have her hair come between us having a good, neighborly relationship. As it has turned out, I like Lisa's mother very much, and we are good neighbors. With that said about her mother, Lisa is one of our favorite clients. Not only does she have a great head of healthy, thick hair and body enough to experiment with a variety of styles and lengths, but she is also one of the most easygoing, punctual, flexible, bright, and fun clients on our schedule. She is a very attractive woman and has an amazing figure to boot. Her overall look is stylish and smart, and her sense of herself appears to be comfortable and relaxed. Always with a ready smile on her lips, she is indeed a treasured client.

When I shared with her that I was writing a book about aging gracefully with the help of other women who were trailblazing ahead of us, she had a few questions to ask of the women.

LISA, 49

I EARNED A BBA IN finance from Hofstra University and graduated in 1988. I have worked in the healthcare insurance industry for twenty-seven years, and for the last eleven years, I have worked for a major national insurance company. I've worked with C-suite individuals at multiple employer groups to help them provide cost effective and quality healthcare programs for their employees to improve their health and to become better healthcare consumers. Currently, I am the senior director of the third-party private exchange department. I grew up in Long Island, New York, until the age of twenty five. I then moved to California where I lived for three years and for the past twenty one years have lived in Arizona.

I have three fabulous boys in my life: my sons are 21 and 18, and my 51-year-old best friend and husband of twenty-two years.

I enjoy reading books and love to stay active, running and working out with friends. I enjoy going out to dinner and a glass of wine with good friends and am looking forward to living out the next few decades with my husband and getting in some international travel.

Here are a few questions that Lisa asked of our trailblazing, *Living Brave* women:

How should I live my life entering my 50s so that I will have no regrets?

Sabra, LCSW Therapist

In answer to the question, "How to live life so that you have no regrets," Lou has a quote:

"Do not let work define you. You are here to have a life, not just to make a living."

And I have a quote to follow that one: "When you are what you do, when you don't, you're not."

So, since we don't want to hang our personal well-being on our professional identity, what can we do?

First and foremost, we have to understand that, as women, we will do things for our children, for our spouse, for our extended family, for our church, for our profession, but when we start to do things for ourselves, we feel guilty and selfish. Somehow, in our wiring, doing for ourselves is wrong and bad, so we have to know that we are important and push through those feelings of selfishness and guilt.

How? Find at least one personal interest and pursue it.

One woman, who was turning fifty, did fifty arts and crafts projects, which she abandoned during the weeks prior to her birthday. Apparently, there is an Abandoned Art movement and lots of other people are doing it too. (Abandonedart.org)

Another woman was given horseback riding lessons at the age of fifty, and she hadn't ridden in thirty years! The instructor said that she hadn't lost her seat in all that time.

Then there is an organization called November is National Writing Month. If you sign up and write 50,000 words in the thirty days of November, Amazon will publish it in hardback for you. I learned of this from a woman who told me that she had written two novels. Of course, she said that they weren't very good, but they were in print, and she was proud of her efforts. (NaNoWriMo.org)

My partner gave me piano lessons forty years after my last lesson as a teenager. She planned to rent a piano for me to practice on, but the piano store was closing its doors, so instead of renting a piano, we bought one! I took lessons for the next four years and still enjoy playing the piano in my spare time.

I know we come home from work exhausted and ready to collapse. We say that we have no time or energy for something new. But I discovered last spring that this is not true.

My Cairn terrier, Oz, was invited to be Toto in a live theater production of *The Wizard of Oz*. I was so excited to be invited and get to be a stage mom. What I didn't realize was that Oz and I would have to be at every rehearsal

Monday through Thursday and Saturday mornings for six weeks!

Through this theater experience, I discovered that I had more time than I realized. I learned that my battery of energy recharged when I changed from the working woman to the stage mom. I actually had more time and energy to expend on something else. I had been selling myself short.

Here are some other ideas for enriching your life:

Painting classes, drawing classes, or a photography workshop (you don't have to be good at something to enjoy it...and you don't have to make money from the resulting product)

Yoga, hot yoga, aerobics, kickboxing, weight lifting and bodybuilding (have you thought about bodybuilding competition?)

Piano or violin lessons, guitar lessons

Dog obedience training, dog agility competition, or pet therapy (assuming you have a dog)

Knitting, quilting, crocheting, glass blowing, jewelry making, stained glass work or any other craft work that you can think of

Kayaking, canoeing, hang gliding, horseback riding

Study to become a master gardener or a sommelier or a certified jeweler

Get certified as a scuba diver

The ideas are endless and fun and recreational...and there are other people already doing them!

Don't wait until you retire to do these things; start doing them now, and you will be amazed at how your world expands.

Remember—Life before 50 is just a warm up! So get going!

HOW SHOULD I, AT THIS AGE, BEGIN TO LOOK AT MY LIFE AND CAREER AND BE REALISTIC AS TO WHAT IS MOST IMPORTANT AT THIS NEXT STAGE?

Linda, Personal and Professional Life Coach

REFLECT FOR A MOMENT ON how fast the last fifteen years of your life have flown by. Now double the speed of that time because, before you know it, you will be almost 65! Every year goes by faster; you may have noticed that!

So this is a good question to ask now, and one that must be taken seriously. The next fifteen years have the possibility of being some of your very best. The good news is that you are now mature enough to let go of many of the insecurities that may have been drivers to your younger self. Many worries, concerns, and insecurities have indubitably fallen by the wayside. However, you know the ones that still dog you. Now is the time to really look at yourself with rigorous honesty and take steps to reduce or illuminate the critical and/or negative internal voices that may still have power in your life. Nearly fifty years is long enough to have listened to those negative thoughts. If someone had been following you around being critical to you non-stop, you would have walked away or ended that relationship by now. However, if you had a critical parent when you were a child, this may seem normal to you! It isn't normal or healthy! Being self-critical to the point that it makes you anxious is a bad habit that can be broken and the sooner, the better.

It is also the time to determine if you have been too driven or not driven enough and to make some corrections about that aspect of your behavior. If you have been too driven, you risk missing out on the sweet time in your 50s of the pure enjoyment and satisfaction of what you have created, and you also set up the possibility of injury or disease as you grow older. Now is the time to work smarter, not harder. Make a serious assessment of your talents, ability, and capacity, and apply them efficiently. Working with a personal or professional coach at this time in your life can be of real benefit. We are often blind to our worst failings, and it is important to work with someone you trust who will also tell you the truth.

If you determine that you have not been driven enough, there is time to get serious about what you want and apply yourself in a more serious and/or consistent manner. Sometimes it is easier to determine what you don't want and motivate yourself to avoid that outcome. For instance, maybe you don't want to have to live with your grown children when you are older. If that is a sincere desire, it might be enough to motivate you to save money you have been unconsciously spending or to take a second job to accrue more savings. Don't be seduced by the thought that there is plenty of time left. Remember how fast time flies by?

It is also valuable to decide that you don't want to be more driven. In that case you can arrange your life to accommodate that decision. Here is the key to that stance: It is only really valuable and authentic if you do that without guilt. If that is a heartfelt and sincere choice, you must give up other people's opinions and your internal critic. The vast majority of Americans are not overly wealthy and uber ambitious. That's the caricature of Americans, but that is not the largest majority! If you don't want to be more driven and you feel guilty for not being more ambitious, it is like a haunting. Something has to give in that case! Making peace with yourself and your values with no regrets is important.

Sometimes you are not working at your capacity because you are burned out or trying to fit in a career or marriage that no longer has passion or meaning for you. That is a hard realization to let in but one that is vital for you to acknowledge. No job or marriage is perfect. Are you expecting too much? Are you carrying resentments from the past? Have you put the effort in to change the dominate patterns in yourself, or are you waiting for your career or marriage partner to change? Have you just given up and begun to feel like a victim? Those are good questions to ask yourself and really listen to your own answers.

If you determine that you are stuck in one or more of those beliefs and patterns, try a new tactic. Pick someone you trust, share how you feel, and ask for feedback. Don't ask someone who thinks you are so great or loves you so much that you won't be told the truth. Pick someone you respect who tells it like it is. That might be a co-worker, minister, counselor, therapist, or life coach. There are many different solutions to your dilemma that you haven't thought about or considered. Trying to figure this out by yourself is like trying to do surgery on yourself! The world is filled with people who can open you up to new ways of thinking, believing, and behaving. Never before in history has it been so easy to get suggestions. However, you have to ask to start the process. If you have already done so, find someone new to talk to about your situation. Some people are best when you are asking in the beginning while others are better as you get closer to making decisions. No matter who you talk to, you will still be the only one who can make decisions for yourself.

The type of career any one person has throughout life has really changed in the last forty years. It used to be that your grandparents had one career all of their lives. Now adults have many different careers, called the second or third act! Try not to get stuck in a belief that what you are doing is all you can do. As long as you are computer literate or willing to learn, you would be surprised at the skills that transfer from one career to another!

If you love your life as it is, there is no need to change anything as long as you are not exhausting yourself, are not under a lot of constant pressure, and have a good financial plan for your future. You might begin to notice what could be intriguing and satisfying either as part-time work or as a volunteer, so you will have some ideas to consider when you choose to reduce the amount of time you work.

It is best to set achievable goals along the way and measure your results. That is also why being accountable to someone else is a good idea. Otherwise, goals and good intentions can end up like New Year's Resolutions that quickly fade after a few weeks.

WILL YOU SHARE SOME WISDOM ON THE PHYSICAL, MENTAL, AND EMOTIONAL CHANGES THAT ARE COMING MY WAY, AND HOW TO EMBRACE THEM?

Becky, PhD. Therapist

LISA, THIS TIME IN YOUR life is significant in so many ways. It represents a portal into a whole new chapter where you can begin to shed some of the roles that have absorbed you. But let's start with the physical. The 50s usually involve menopause, which for some women can be hormonally difficult to endure. You will also start noticing signs of aging. In my field one definition of good mental health is "the ability to adapt to an ever-changing environment." This time in your life provides a physical landscape that is constantly evolving. Your challenge is to find the adaptation that works for you. Some women choose the route of Botox and facelifts. While this is certainly an option, I believe it only delays the real challenge of the 50s: How do we slowly embrace and gracefully accept our body's many changes? I found this challenge easier to face when we added dimmer switches in the bathroom.

Mentally you will remain strong, especially if you are challenged in your profession. The possible downfall in the 50s is succumbing to the many internal messages that arise from a culture that continues to over-value youthful beauty. Thus, the 50s and beyond can invite all the negative thoughts that we tell ourselves about our changing physical appearance. But what a great opportunity to habituate new positive thoughts about ourselves as strong, independent women with more freedom than any generation before us. It can be quite liberating to stand up to those distorted and limiting cultural messages.

This newfound freedom can only evolve when we first allow ourselves time and space to grieve the loss of what no longer is. There is often a necessary sadness in letting go of the important role of parenting a child or the energy of our youth or the passion of an early relationship. But it is the grieving that creates the space for something new to generate. So I would encourage you to be kind to yourself in ways that you perhaps haven't been kind for all the years of caretaking others. This is your time to caretake yourself, and it can be amazing!

I WOULD LOVE TO KNOW HOW THE RELATIONSHIP IN MY MARRIAGE WILL CHANGE GIVEN THE "EMPTY NEST" AND HOW

TO LIVE LIFE TO THE FULLEST WITH MY PARTNER AND ENJOY EVERY DAY.

Becky, Ph.D. Therapist

MOST MARRIAGES GO THROUGH A profound evolution with the "empty nest" years. Without the focus of parenting, the relationship with your husband has the opportunity to develop new intimacies as a couple. Many marriages go through a growth process at this time...where each of you reclaims the other in new ways. If there has been too much focus on raising the children and little feeding of the marriage, it can be a difficult transition. This is a time when many couples seek couple's counseling to help them transition out of a parenting relationship and back into a marriage.

In my role as a marriage therapist, I often suggest that couples think back to the activities they enjoyed during their dating years and before children. These activities can be a comfortable avenue for reconnection. This time in life can also create space and energy for discovering new ways of being in a relationship. It can be helpful to reinstate date night where each week you trade off choosing an activity to share. Similar to when we were young, it can be fun to push the edges and find new areas of interest.

For women, the need for conversation and emotional intimacy continues throughout our lifetimes. Given the hormonal changes in both men and women, these years can often bring a new emotional closeness to a marriage. Many men in their 50s are feeling a drop in testosterone that generates a greater percentage of estrogen, which means more capacity for emotion and emotional expression, which, in turn, most women crave. So, you see, the best is yet to come!

How can I be more confident in myself and who I will become over the next few decades and embrace being me?

Arlene, Life Coach

How to be confident in yourself?

Over time, I have found that being confident in yourself is an ongoing project. It requires the courage to dig deep and know yourself. It means peeling off the layers of not me, and letting the true self shine through. Most of us grew up in a society where your ranking matters. Because of this, we jump through a lot of hoops to become someone who can rank high enough to be respected and accepted. True self-confidence comes when we dare to take off the mask and gain respect for being authentic. When that occurs, our confidence is infectious and not contrived for recognition.

How to embrace yourself and who you will become over the next decade.

In order to fully embrace ourselves, we need to take the time to know ourselves. Self-awareness is the greatest gift we can give ourselves and is the gateway to true self-confidence. Making time to explore your passions, interests, and unfinished business is a top priority. Who you will become over the next decade will not be determined by some grand plan but rather a day-by-day and moment-by-moment commitment to be true to your own path. There is really no way to predict what can happen to a person over a decade. What we think today will change over time as we meet the challenges and opportunities that life offers us. After all, that is what living brave is all about. The wisdom we need will always appear at just the right time. Our quest is to seek, savor, and share.

We enjoyed receiving the wisdom from these trailblazing writers and are grateful for Lisa's questions.

IF THERE IS BUT ONE morsel of insight that you can gather from our contributors, allow it to be a pathway to your thinking and direct your actions in moving gracefully into aging wisely, all the way to the finish.

Live brave.

CHAPTER FOURTEEN

Surviving to Thriving

"It's not that the things and opportunities that we want in life don't exist yet... It's that we're not yet aware of their existence or the fact that we can really have them."
~ Jen Sincero, You are a Badass

KEY QUESTION: CAN YOU DESCRIBE A TIME IN YOUR LIFE WHEN YOU MOVED FROM SURVIVING TO THRIVING?

On Tuesday, March 6, 2001, I presented my first keynote speech to an audience of one thousand Native American women from the United States and Canada.

THE CONFERENCE IS HELD YEARLY in San Diego, California, and is sponsored by the University of Oklahoma through their American Indian Institute Outreach division. I can assure you that I was scared out of my wits.

Two years before this event, I had applied to the university outreach division and had been accepted to teach at their yearly conference and at some other smaller tribal women's conferences held throughout the year in other Western states, including Nevada, New Mexico, and Washington. These classes held forty to fifty participants and were approximately one to three hours in length, depending on the subject matter. My expertise is in the field of anxiety disorder and storytelling, and my workshops utilized my book *Living on the Other Side of Fear*, as well as other books, research material, and articles that I continually updated.

My father was one hundred percent Indian born in Mexico, but I had not been raised with any traditional Indian culture. My parents immigrated to the United States, and our family followed instead the Mexican culture and incorporated the American way of life. My siblings and I were born and raised in the United States. Nevertheless, in the two years of working with the Native American population, I had become familiar with various cultural rituals and traditional beliefs and had developed a genuine fondness for the people.

Although every tribe is distinctly diverse in their individual beliefs and customs, I found similarities that I could incorporate in my classes. I taught classes to the Yaqui, Navaho, Tohono Odom, Hopi, and Puyallup tribes, just to mention a few. Most of the tribes allowed the ceremonial "smudging" to prepare the space where the teaching would be occurring. Using dried sage and cedar (sage, the female plant, represents the female energy; cedar, the male plant, the masculine energy), I invited and integrated both the energies into the room. I burned the dried leaves of sage and cedar in an abalone shell and used the smoke and my sincere spiritual intention to clear the area of any unwanted spirits. I learned a good deal traveling, working with the different tribes, and incorporating a variety of rituals, and I treated them reverently. I also learned that most of the women were shy, respectful, and reserved, especially those who still lived on their reservations. Eye contact was minimal, and interruptions were few. But they did love humor and laughing. Oh, my goodness, did they love to laugh. The time spent with this community of people was deeply rewarding.

Monday, the day before I was to present my keynote speech for a full ninety minutes, (yes, ninety minutes in front of a large group can seem like a lifetime of anxiety), I decided to attend and listen to the Native woman who would be presenting her ninety minutes that morning. My intention was to gather as much information as possible so that I could be better prepared for my own presentation the next day. After all, I wanted to make sure that I was following the itinerary of the Native American Wellness Conference for Women.

Walking into the ballroom where the event was to be held, I couldn't help but notice how large and brightly lighted the room appeared. It was a bit overwhelming. Women were still entering, and a few men who had joined the women were coming in with them and taking their places in the chairs. The stage was set with a hotel-style lectern centered near the front of the stage and a large screen set behind and above the speaker for a PowerPoint presentation. The time arrived, and a Native woman board member of the wellness conference introduced the key note speaker. The speaker was a stunning, large and tall, dark-skinned woman with jet black hair pulled away from her face and set in a coiled braid at the base of her nape. It was difficult to guess her age, but I thought that she might have been in her mid-fifties. She wore a dark blue flowered muumuu from her native state of Hawaii. She was introduced as a distant relative of one of the early, most notable, native rulers, King Kamehameha. She was indeed impressive.

As she took her place behind the lectern, I became aware that her voice was especially strong and steady as she began to welcome the audience of a thousand women and men to the Native American Wellness Conference. And then she began her presentation.

Because this book is about uplifting women, I will only share a small part of the story that she told. She spoke from her wounded heart that continued to ache for her people and for the loss of the freedom that the Hawaiians gave up when they were taken over. On her PowerPoint, there were artist renderings of James Cook, the famous British explorer, the first white man to visit the islands in 1778–79, looking aggressive and dangerous. There were depictions of Protestant and Catholic missionaries who became influential in the political and business decisions and allowed outside (U.S.) interests to gain power in the islands. Remarking that eventually political unrest developed in

1893 and ultimately led to the takeover of the islands, her presentation was harsh toward the "White" aggressors. And, within minutes of starting her talk, the women began to leave the room. But her presentation continued, and her wounded heart was now showing the negative effects of long-term disappointment through her voice inflections and body language. As I sat and watched the PowerPoint, I understood how she could be so frustrated and wanted to share her story and wanted to reach consensus with the room of Natives. Just as her people had been wounded and betrayed, she knew that the people who now sat in front of her had felt the same pain.

Before the entire ninety minute presentation was over, more than half the room had emptied out. I sat and felt the sadness overtake my body, not only for the women in the audience but for the speaker. I could certainly empathize with the Natives and with the speaker, but wondered what good this had brought about for them. After all, this was a wellness conference. What change could be brought about by hearing and reliving this story?

Coincidentally, the title of my keynote presentation the next morning was "Moving beyond Surviving to Thriving."

I arrived an hour early with my assistant, and we quickly placed our handouts on each chair. The handouts were six pages of quotes, reflection questions, short articles, writing exercises, and amusing cartoons all tied together on the upper left-hand corner with raffia ribbon, a beautifully colored bead, and a feather, a spiritual symbol for most Natives. I had refused a lectern or even a stage to stand on. I had no PowerPoint to demonstrate, and I would be standing and presenting from the same level as their chairs.

As the women and fewer men started coming into the room, I stood at the doors and greeted as many as I could personally, making eye contact and shaking their hands as they walked in. Some were hesitant, but most would take my hand, look me in the eyes, and smile warmly.

To my surprise, my son, who was twenty-nine years old at the time, drove down from Los Angeles to hear me speak. He had never been to any of my presentations before, and I was delighted to have him there. He sat in the front row. Okay, so now I was even more nervous. What, I thought to myself, if they get up and leave the room as they had the morning before?

When the time came and the conference board member introduced me to the audience, I took a deep breath and asked the questions: How many have fought a good fight and lost and still feel the pain of the loss? How many have won and have forgotten to stop and celebrate that win? I asked a couple more encouraging questions, and then, slowly but surely, I invited each one of them to join me as we all looked at our stories of surviving and considered the possibilities of thriving. What would that look like to them?

With humor, stories, and attention to their wellness, I worked hard to bring them into each other's lives and to share with each other victories of the good that surrounded them currently. Some women stood and shared their stories of survival and recovery, while others talked about their faith and the desire to deepen their trust in the Creator.

They answered questions from the handouts and laughed at the cartoons. At one point as I looked at my son's face, I recalled and shared how my son and I had struggled through my raising him as a single mother and how much I had learned about myself and my strengths because of it. They too had memories of their children and pride for those who had left to attend college and would be coming home soon. I started a wave on one side of the room, and we stood and sat with arms above our heads. They were active and interactive with each other, and they stayed in the room...for ninety minutes.

I share this story because it reminds me that painful events happen to everyone, and we must deal with them when they are happening to us. Sometimes there is nothing that we can do about something that occurred long ago. But carrying the pain in our bodies will weaken our resistance and render us not well. If we transport it in our minds, it muddles our thinking and the ability to make good and sound choices. And if we wrap our spiritual essence in our pain, the essence will fade, and we will not become the "real deal" of who we were born to be. We will continue only to survive.

We all have options in our everyday lives. As the Buddha teaches, pain is inevitable, and suffering is an option. On that morning, I once again learned that all of us have pain in common, and we can endure much in our lives. But we must come to the understanding that each one of us has the ability to decide what we want to experience in our lives.

Shall we simply survive, or shall we decide to thrive? The choice will be ours.

Live brave.

Mary Beth and I attended a lecture at a friend's home titled: "Chronic Diseases and Their Symptoms Have Everything to do with Digestion!"

If you are not digesting properly, you are causing a catastrophic body deficit that can lead to low energy, premature again, illness, disease, and most cancers." There we met Karen, a passionate and knowledgeable specialist in nutrition and poop! Yes…Poop! As she recounted her life story of illness after being diagnosed at nineteen with Crohn's disease and her subsequent, extensive hospital stays struggling with the illness, she made a compelling argument to her audience of the importance of good nutrition and having good poops.

Obviously, Karen used humor to transform a much-talked-about subject, food and well-being, and made it entertaining and jammed-packed, filled with excellent information. (No pun intended.) But her point was clear and unforgettable. Healthy, natural, and enzyme-rich foods will, in return, deliver great results. Her high energy and fervor for sharing her knowledge to make a difference in other's lives is contagious, as she "PowerPoints" her way through her presentation. Half of her visual aids (quotes, photos, statistics, and illustrations), I would position on my refrigerator door as a reminder of conscious eating, healthy eating, happy life.

In her book *Rising Strong*, Brene Brown writes that we need each other to rise strong in our lives and that we truly cannot make it on our own. She urges us to ask for help and not be afraid to let others help us. It is the balance of giving and receiving that we all crave and must embrace to thrive in our lives. Because both authors of this book are committed to conscious eating, healthy eating, happy life, we encourage our readers to make the time to understand the importance of good nutrition, as it relates to their own bodies, and to ask an expert for help in developing a stronger relationship with the proper balance of nutrition toward a life of well-being...all along the way.

Here, then, is our next passionate *Living Brave* woman:

KAREN, 46

"As I look back on my life, I realize that I have been guided my whole life."

I AM A WIFE TO an awesome husband and a mum, guide, and coach to three awesome children and two rather furry rambunctious cats.

My mission in life is to pay it forward by sharing my knowledge and my story with health advocates to health professionals so that they too can pay it forward by helping their clients to live happier, healthier lives.

I have the honor and opportunity to work and live in three countries. I am also a speaker, a trainer, and an internationally-recognized holistic nutritionist, an orthomolecular health practitioner, a therapeutic lifestyle educator and functional medicine consultant, a somatic intuitive training practitioner, a live cell microscopist, and an early childhood educator.

When not working with others, you can find me either barefoot on the beach or wandering the grocery aisles and farmer's markets in the pursuit of real food.

Physical Strength

What significant health issue have you had to overcome?

I was diagnosed at the age of nineteen with Crohn's disease. An awkward time to receive this type of disease (however, when is a good a time right?) as I was in college, working three jobs, and trying to figure out who I was while dealing with the pain and discomfort of the disease, as well as being in and out of hospitals. I overcame this disease six years ago with my last diagnosis of "no evidence of Crohn's disease."

What part of your body is most important to your health, and why?

That's a tough question because every part of my body is important to me, as well as my spirit is connected to my body and my mind. In fact, after having a temporary colostomy, I had to learn how to accept and love my body as it was, and in that moment, I developed a ritual that I would do every day. I start at my feet and work up to my head, identifying and acknowledging each part of my body, saying how grateful I am for this part and why, and ending with "I am grateful…I love you." So, every part is important to me, even if it is missing (because the energy is still there), and I thank and love each part because we are energy, chemical reactions, and one big energy machine that all parts create to make a whole.

How has money been a motivating factor in your life?

My idea of money has changed throughout my life. We did not talk about money growing up, so I did not understand that it takes money to have the essentials. When I moved out on my own, I had a poor concept of money and always felt that if someone wanted to buy something from me I was afraid to ask for what it was worth for fear of hurting their feelings. I had no concept of money. And, interesting enough, I have come to learn even with my own business that my ability to accept money was a direct reflection of my own self-worth, so I always charged too little. I had to learn this along the way. It was tough. Money is a motivating factor so that I can make sure my needs and my family's needs are taken care. I can then move forward to do the things I love.

How have you dealt with the physical changes of aging?

What a great question! Have I dealt with the physical changes? I think a lot about it. I look at women who are ten years older than I am and I think, "I am going to be there soon. I wonder how they deal with it, and how has it impacted them? How will I deal with it?" I have always looked extremely young for my age, so that is not the issue. It is like there is something that changes within you without your knowledge and you see things differently; it is like a vibrational frequency change, and I no longer vibrate in this case with 30 year olds or with 20 year olds.

I know that with each passing decade I will look different, and that is okay. I have come to accept that I will change. I am changing on the outside, and as each wrinkle creeps on my skin, it reminds me of my wisdom and my vibrational energy. Each wrinkle allows me to vibrate even higher, attracting those with the same vibrational energy, and a new chapter will begin. So, yes, I am good with the physical changes and will stay young at heart on the inside.

How does your current physical environment bring you joy?

When I purchase a house, it is just a shell. I add the things to it that make me feel good inside, that make me feel comfortable and happy inside. I also fill my house with plants because they are living energy. I don't have designer or fancy things because I don't need those things. The paintings on the wall, which I get many compliments on, were done by my children, and we have tons of plants and two cats. Anyone who comes to my house always says that my home feels so comfortable. And those who do not like cats usually end up saying, "I don't like cats, but your cats are different." I love that! The comfort that I create others can feel, and then it is my home. Comfortable to me means a feeling of warmth and comfort that makes me feel safe. And, that is exactly how I like to feel and that makes me feel joy.

Mental Clarity

Tell us about a time when you trusted your intuition to make an important decision?

As I look back on my life, I realize that I have been guided my whole life. I wish I could explain this better; it is like I have a presence, a grandmother presence that is always there, especially in my time of need. And, oddly enough, decisions are, at times, told to me in advance, and although my heart is not in agreement, I have this knowledge that it will happen. I feel like I have an undeveloped sixth sense, and this alone is tough for me to speak about because I have been unable to find someone who is willing to help me with this, to help me understand it.

What mental skills have you developed over the years to help you navigate the difficult times?

I would have to say it is really believing and trusting in the universe. I have been in situations where I did not have money coming in, or in a position of illness where I never believed I would be well again, but through it all, I have somehow allowed myself to just trust, and I am not one to trust easily. When my husband's job was eliminated in the economic downturn of 2008, we both went through stages of panic that were so severe for me that I was experiencing anxiety attacks and I thought I had to do something. So, I turned to the universe and had a dialogue. I let the universe know what was going on and what I needed, and it ended with giving my trust to the universe to bring what I or my family needs. And, it always does.

At what point did you recognize that you had stepped into your own voice?

I think I am still doing so. I think the older I get the less I worry about how people see me and what they think, and this has allowed me to come into my own voice. Along the way, letting go of my past traumas has also opened me up to coming to a place of truth. My whole life I came from the voice of a deeply traumatized child.

Then when I became a nutritionist and began public speaking, I froze. Suddenly people were listening to me for what I had to say, and I did not know what to do. I did not think I had anything intelligent to say so I shut down; I got severely sick. I had to learn how to incorporate the entertainer in me with the intelligent side of me. Once I did this, I was able to speak publicly, but I lacked confidence and was once again "hiding" behind the microphone to hide my intelligence. I still had a ton of work to do. It was not until I truly let go of most of my childhood and young adulthood traumas that I could truly step into my own voice.

Did you have a definitive life plan? If so, how did you stay focused on that plan?

I was not raised to have a plan. And because of the abuse I suffered as a child, I did not start thinking for myself until

I was in my late 30s when I was on my own and had no influence from others. So, I call myself a late bloomer.

WHO IN YOUR FAMILY INSPIRED YOU TO BE COURAGEOUS?

Wow, if this question had come along even five years ago, I would not have been able to answer this. Once I was able to clear all of my hurt and anger and be at peace with myself I can now answer questions like this. It would be my mother. My mum had me very young and did not have the skill set to raise me or my other siblings. However, she did the best she could with the resources she had. She was a single mother working 12 and 15 hours a day to keep a roof over our heads and food on the table, a person who did not rely on social assistance and had no family support—she was it! I am inspired by her courage to raise us and to provide what we needed. She always stood up for herself and did not allow anyone to stand in her way.

SPIRITUAL COURAGE

WHAT SAFETY NETS HAVE YOU RELIED ON OVER THE YEARS, AND HOW HAVE THEY SERVED YOU?

Before I learned to trust myself and believe in trust, intuition, and the greater connection to the universe, I turned to books. I did not come from a family where I could have discussions about how I was feeling. If I found myself in a situation where I was not sure if I was doing the right thing, I would find books so that it could affirm I was doing the right thing. My psychologists, if you will, were books!

What have you loved deeply in your life?

I would say the first thing I ever loved deeply in my life was my daughter, and it grows each day because I look at how different her upbringing is in comparison to my own.

She taught me to learn to adapt to situations. She taught me to experience the world as if it was the first time I was experiencing it. She taught me to be patient and to laugh and to be proud. She taught me to be honest with myself and with others. She taught me to trust in her and myself.

What advice would you give a younger person to help them develop a vision of hope for their later years?

Whatever your upbringing, know that it may shape you. However, you have the power to allow for the final mold. If you did not like what your mother, father, aunt, sister, brother, uncle, or whoever did to you, let it go. Remember that they too have their own stuff they are going through, and that is not your fault. Take whatever has happened to you, look at it from a different perspective, analyze it without emotion, learn the lessons you need to, and let the rest go. If you cannot do these on your own, find someone who can help. You are not a victim of your circumstances because you create the victim, no one else—break free and soar!

Can you describe a time in your life when you moved from surviving to thriving?

I did not know that there was a difference, and I think I still struggle with the difference. Perhaps I could say that when I was dealing with my illness, I was surviving. I had to pause to look up the terminology for the two. To thrive (of a child, animal, or plant) is to grow or develop well or vigorously: prosper; flourish. To survive is to continue to live or exist, especially in spite of danger or hardship.

So, perhaps my surviving was during my illness. However, I believe I was thriving because I was growing and developing. I truly believe that being diagnosed with an illness is a gift. And, my gift was my Crohn's disease because it was my body's way of trying to put me first so that I could put myself back in balance and harmony. Perhaps for a time I was merely surviving when I was in the depths of pain and misery. Then my daughter came along and forced me even more to put my health first and fix my imbalance. And, maybe this is when my growth and expansion began. But, eventually, I had to come out for air and nourishment and right back into thriving.

It is said that bravery comes through taking action. How will you continue to live a brave life?

Am I brave? I have never thought of myself as brave. I believe that every single one of us does something brave every day. So, if I am considered brave, then I will continue to be brave by stepping outside of my circle to embrace new ventures and ideas. I will continue to be true to myself and my purpose on this earth. I will continue to smile at others, maintain eye contact, hold their hands, and show others I care. I will continue to hand out my knowledge. I will continue to do things my way and not what others think I should do. That is the most important thing I can do as I continue my journey by being brave.

As a nutritionist, what information on aging healthy and thriving would you recommend women develop at any age?

When it comes to aging and being healthy and thriving, it really comes down to what you are doing now. Beauty is from the inside out. We hear this all the time that we are beautiful from the inside, and I think that it is so true. The inside is our mind, spirit, essence, and physiology, and the way we respond to our beauty is what we reflect on the outside; beauty truly is more than skin deep. Our cells are constantly communicating with every other cell in the body. How the body and all its cells react is based on what we are bringing into our body.

If we are bringing in toxic food, breathing toxins and pollution, soaking our face and body in toxic personal-care products, cleaning our home and washing our clothes with toxic endocrine and hormone-disrupting cleaners that overload our detoxification system and store toxins in our fat cells, it will age us and keep us in an unhealthy state. Our cells will go into protection mode where there is no expansion or growth; then we are merely surviving. If we do not feed our internal systems with the right nutrients, over time they cannot perform their proper functions; we lack energy, we become run down, we live with vague symptoms that become a part of our normal every day being and later may lead to diagnoses of conditions, syndromes, disease, and cancer.

Get rid of the plastics—the bottles, bowls, drinking water bottles (and stop microwaving them too) full of xenoestrogens, including BPAs, that affect our ability to reproduce, that are robbing women and girls of the right to develop beautifully developed babies in the future. These same harmful chemicals are also in our cleaners and personal-care products, toxins that are being stored in our fat tissues. Fill your home with non-toxic substances, and soon your energy will change. There is a new cellular communication taking place: expansion and growth. Soon you are full of energy, life, vigor…your inner child is even more joyous—you love easily, you glow, you live to love, and you take on a youthful appearance.

If our outlook on life is more on the negative side, we spend our time gossiping, thinking negatively, watching the news, hanging around toxic people, looking for the negative in every situation; this communicates to our cells to go into protective mode where there is no expansion or growth. Over time our body responds to the cellular communication; we don't stand tall, we don't give eye contact, our hair lacks luster, our skin is scaly and rough as if to ward off anyone touching us; it is like we become a rough fortress, impenetrable. Our thoughts become darker; we vibrate at a lower energy, attracting others of the same thoughts, beliefs, and attitudes. We begin to feel hopeless; we internalize everything. Our body responds with dark circles under our eyes, pale skin tone; we get sick easily; we have low energy; we feel hopeless, hopeless for others, hopeless for our future.

We MUST fuel our body with foods that come out of the ground. They are full of the nutrients of the earth's energy and microbiome that interact with our own microbiome and provide us the nourishment for our cells to be able to function properly, as well as to repair and revitalize. Mother Nature's blessings give us everything that we need to run our hormones, to allow us to detoxify harmful toxins so that they cannot negatively impact our health. When we eat quality organic foods that grow out of the ground, filled with luscious humus of microorganisms, we take on the live energy, and it fills us with live energy. We want more; our cells want more; our consciousness grows, and from this comes a place of joy and happiness. Our inner child is at play once more; we are full of youthful vigor and look young; we glow.

We need to drink quality water, full of minerals, so that it too can fuel our body and our mind, hydrate our organs, help expel wastes and toxins, plump our skin, and keep us looking youthful and full of energy.

In order to feel young and full of life at any age, we have to look at our body as a whole: mind, body, spirit, essence, and being. We need to let our inner child play all the time while our watchful inner voice guides and coaches us to the better qualities of life: food, products, choices, vibration. We must pay attention to what we digest, what we put on our skin, what we breathe in, what we eat. These are simple changes you can make that have a greater impact than any surgery, nip, tuck, or cream can ever do for you. Beauty is truly from the inside out. Our skin, our stature, our eyes, all are a reflection of our internal dialogue. To feel young at any age and to gracefully transition through the decades starts with what and how you are living and where you are thriving.

I have known our next brave woman for several years but have only been around her a handful of times.

EACH TIME THAT I HAVE been with her, I am filled with a feeling of peace and a gentle reminder to relax and breathe deeper. I'm not sure if it is because she is such a calm presence, or if it is her soft, long hair that is naturally turning silver that she wears in soft waves on her shoulders, or if it is her soothing voice, welcoming smile, and tender eyes. Or the fact that I know she teaches yoga and her entire being represents the Yoga principles. She is a beautiful presence of a delightful woman.

She attended a holiday party at our salon during the writing of this book, and I felt compelled to ask her if she would consider answering our *Living Brave* questions. After reading her answers, once again I was reminded that everyone comes to their life's calling through a variety of ways. It is not always smooth sailing on the journey to get there, but those storms that disturb the voyage can fuel the desire for change and will eventually become the anchors for a committed life purpose.

I did not know her life story until I read her answers. No matter how often I hear a woman's journey to self-reliance, I think of the courage that it takes to say no and at times even more bravery to say yes, I can!

ABAGAIL, 56

"I have loved the continuity of how everything has happened to me and how I became the person I have become."

I was born in Jerusalem, Israel, and moved to Amman, Jordan, within months of my birth. In the early seventies at the age of twelve, we moved to the United States. My parents had divorced, and my father brought us (his new wife, his father, my half-sister, my brother, and me) to live in Kansas where we moved into a one bedroom house.

My life journey has been a magical flow. Early in my childhood, I lived in fear of so much. In my late twenties, I began to wake up to an inner power and strength and healing through the divine presence in my world.

I experienced yoga in the seventies, which saved my life, and in the late nineties, I experienced the power of the breath during the home birth of my first child. The spirit within filled my heart and mind to be present to the breath and God within, and the babies' births took care of the rest. I have two children, a daughter, 21, and a son, 16.

The thread of yoga continued to wind through my life, filling me with awe as I began teaching and witnessing my students shift and transform through yoga. Expanding my teaching to working with seniors, military veterans, children of all ages, and those with special needs, I continue to encourage students and clients to "Tune into the Breath and uplift your Being!"

I have participated in many community services and have created media presentations. I have the following certifications and education:

- International Teacher Certification in Kundalini Yoga, Kundalini Research Institute
- Muscular Strength and Range of Movement Certification, Silver Sneakers
- Trauma Release, Recovery Assessment and Prevention, Facilitator
- Mastery of the Adolescent Brain Certificate, University of Arizona
- Group Exercise Certification and Healthy Lifestyle Principles
- Rewind Senior Yoga Therapist Certification, Ymedica Foundation
- Sedona Yoga Festival Mindful Yoga Therapeutic Yoga

Physical Strength

What significant health issue have you had to overcome?

Some significant health issues I had to overcome included frequent migraine headaches, an abnormal fear of water, and the fact that I lived constantly in fear. I was literally afraid of my own shadow.

What part of your body is most important to your health, and why?

My heart and my mind are the most important to my health; as I lead with my heart, my mind follows.

How has money been a motivating factor in your life?

Money has not been such a large motivating factor in my life. I am grateful to have it as I share and serve from my heart; money shows up grander than I envision, at times beyond my expectations.

Once I asked God for some financial help, and within a short time, someone broke into my home and took my jewelry box, which I had organized to let go of gold jewelry that I was no longer using. I received a nice amount of money from the insurance company.

A year later, I asked again for financial help to show up. Someone hit me and damaged my car, but not me, and again I received a nice sum of money. You have to be clear about what you ask for, and at the end of every request, add "with ease and grace." It doesn't always come that way, but you can at least ask for it to come that way.

How have you dealt with the physical changes of aging?

I have dealt with the physical changes of aging in my life by staying active, focusing on strength and gratitude, slowing down a bit, resting and taking care of myself, and honoring myself.

How does your current physical environment bring you joy?

My current physical environment brings me joy because my home is my sacred sanctuary. I am surrounded with joyful spiritual and inspiring images, art, stones, and pictures of nature and gardens and words that fill my heart with gratitude and bliss. I have also built a labyrinth in my back yard. I have created a sacred sanctuary for myself.

Mental Clarity

Tell us about a time when you trusted your intuition to make an important decision?

I was married for sixteen years to a man who came into my life and was the calmest person that I had ever met. He was the opposite of my father. He was a huge support, and he would let me go through my stuff and heal my fears. He helped anchor my support within myself and claim the strength within me. It was years later, in my fifties, that I came to see this as the gift he had given me.

During the time that we were married, as the years went by and I grew stronger and wanted to expand myself to keep growing and to go higher and to live a fuller life of giving to others, he was incapable of giving me the intense emotional support that I needed, and he was not interested in growing and expanding with me.

When I was at home with him, I felt as if I were dying inside. I was emotionally starving. I felt I was dying, and my children would not know who I really was. My connection with him had disintegrated, and we no longer had a bond. I began to struggle and think of how I could leave, but I equated divorce as abandonment of my children because that is what I had experienced as a child with my mother. Once, toward the end of our marriage, we went on a big vacation, but instead of enjoying it, I found myself constantly crying. My daughter asked me, "Why are you crying, Mommy?" I responded, "I am healing my heart, honey." I had no idea that I was grieving and preparing myself to leave. I thought of leaving for years until one January morning, I woke up and said, "This is it. I am leaving. It's time."

After I left the marriage, I cried myself to sleep many nights, and it was a painful experience for all of us. I thought to myself, "What have I done?" I moved out without my children initially until the divorce was final, and then we settled on joint custody and a new rhythm of life was created for us.

What mental skills have you developed over the years to help you navigate the difficult times?

Some mental skills include focusing on what I want and not what is in front of me at the time. I also use chanting, walking, education, playing, and having fun. Trusting and knowing the Divine Presence is always there to guide me, breathing deeper, and being still.

At what point did you recognize that you had stepped into your own voice?

When I decided to give birth to my children at home, my husband was hesitant, but I stood strong in my decision. Both children were born in our home, and their father helped in the birthing process. I had found my voice.

Did you have a definitive life plan?

Nope! I did not have a definitive life plan specifically. I stayed focused by connecting deeper with the spirit within and asking for support from my spiritual community to remind me to go to a higher place and connect with God.

Who in your family inspired you to be courageous?

The family member was my adopted "mom" and friend Patty who showed up in my world in my early twenties. She worked at the nursing home where my grandfather was living, and she was the kindest person that I had ever known. She could give me a penny and make me feel like I had a million dollars. She was very kind, generous, loving, and an amazing being. She gave me confidence in myself by unconditionally loving me and being present to me, and she reminded me how much God is with me and loves me and protects me all the time. She was there for me, and I could talk to her about anything; she became my good friend and "mom." Patty had five boys and said God had sent me to be her daughter.

Spiritual Courage

What safety nets have you relied on over the years, and how have they served you?

Earlier in my biography, I said that yoga saved my life. At the time I was in my early twenties, living with my father, attending college during the day, and working the night shift at a computer shop from 11pm to 6am. This went on for two years, so my life was stressful. I had no support from my father, either financially or emotionally. I supported myself completely, including paying him rent and paying for all of my expenses, as well as my own food. One day a friend took me to a yoga class at the college we were attending, and it was the first time I felt calm, strong, and relaxed. I tried other things like running, aerobics, and other healthy modalities of exercise during the years, but I always came back to yoga. Eventually, in the nineties, I came back to stay.

What have you loved deeply in your life?

I have loved the continuity of how everything has happened to me and how I became the person I have become. My father, in taking me away from my mother, taught me and gave me the strength to know how to be on my own and to come to trust in myself. I have also loved deeply the practice of yoga, my spirit, my children, my community, and the amazing unfolding of my precious life.

What advice would you give younger people to help them develop a vision of hope for their later years?

The advice I would give is to always take care of yourself and don't abuse or take for granted your body, your health, your life.

Can you describe a time in your life when you moved from surviving to thriving?

I had dreams and messages of needing to leave my marriage, and people showed up on my path to remind me that is was time. Once I decided to act on it, I went through the darkest night of my soul, but by allowing myself to dive into that place, I received the gifts of clarity and knowing my heart. Once I understood how everything that had happened in my life had served a purpose, I moved from victim to victor.

It is said that bravery comes through taking action. How will you continue to live a brave life?

I will continue to live a brave life by living through faith instead of fear. I trust that I am always loved, protected, and supported, and that I just have to ask! And I will live outside the box, as that is where my heart soars. Also, I will give because in giving I am most fulfilled.

A couple of weeks after completing the questions for us, Abagail called and asked if she could share our *Living Brave* questions with the women's group that she was currently facilitating.

"Of course," I answered. "Let's all walk this path together."

Live brave.

CHAPTER FIFTEEN

Living Bravely

"Sometimes you have to have a good flood to wash away the debris…the bad habits, bad behaviors for things to get better."
~ Donna, a Salon client

KEY QUESTION: IT IS SAID BRAVERY COMES THROUGH TAKING ACTION. HOW WILL YOU CONTINUE TO LIVE A BRAVE LIFE?

I feel fortunate to have a loving, protective, and brave mother for me to love.

THE THOUGHT OF LOSING HER reminds me that my own inner self yearns for consistency and stability and that includes the presence of my mother in my life. As the winter of her life enfolds her and envelops me and my siblings, we are reminded that the end of her existence is close, and I am acutely aware of how strong she has had to be all of her life. Finally, by escaping the selfish thoughts of my own existence, I am able to see that those times when I saw her as weak and stubborn, she was being strong and holding on to what little self of her was left. She was protecting her children by compromising herself in an abusive marriage, working at home and away from home, and all the while, keeping us in the country that gave her hope, Los Estados Unidos. And she worked and pushed herself endlessly and tirelessly until her body gave out, time and time again.

Indeed, my mother kept us where she felt that we would have the opportunities that she had not been born into. She fought every step of the way for us to have the best education that was affordable at the time; of course, the Catholic school in a small mining town was considered the best. She made our clothes, stretched out meals, protected us from harm, and kept us clean and healthy. I cannot imagine what she did without so that our lives would prepare us for a future beyond which her own imagination could conceive. And now, all four of her children, all in our sixties, don't even want to imagine what life would have been like without her determination and courage.

Thirty years after their divorce with both my father and mother widowed from their second marriages, my father was rushed to Mayo's hospital in Phoenix. As he lay in the emergency room waiting to be transferred to a different hospital, my mother, who was visiting our sister, came into his room. While interviewing her for this book, I asked her what they had said to each other on his death bed. This is what she said: "I thanked him for giving me my four children. And I thanked him for having brought me to this country so that my children could have been born here."

I am proud to present my mother to you...one of the bravest women that I will ever know and love deeply.

Maria was born October 13, 1926, in Sonora, Mexico. Her mother died while giving birth to a baby when Maria was only three years old. She attended school until the third grade in Mexico and lived with her father and one older brother in their one-room home built of adobe walls and a dirt floor. By the time she was eight, she was pulled out of school to stay home where she cooked, cleaned, washed and ironed their clothes, and knitted blankets to sell. The home did not have running water or electricity. Her father, Jose, was a blacksmith, and Maria recalls turning a heavy crank that stoked the fire to heat the irons for making horseshoes. At the age of twelve, she was sent to live with a relative in Ajo, Arizona, where she attended three more years of school. Unfortunately, her father pulled her back to Mexico, and she did not return to school again.

At age twenty, Maria married her next-door neighbor, and together they moved back to Ajo, Arizona, where her husband, my father, worked as a laborer in the copper mine for over forty years. Their four children, Carlos, Maggie, Hilda, and Connie, were born in the first seven years of their marriage. Apart from raising a family, Maria worked many jobs to help support the family. She became a seamstress to many in the small town where her dressmaking skills included wedding dresses, a variety of clothing alterations, and the customary slacks, dresses, blouses, and embroidered dish towels and pillow cases that she sold. In addition, she worked outside of the house in a laundromat, a tamale factory, and a drive-through liquor store. With much pride, she became an American citizen in her late thirties. She divorced the father of her children after thirty-two years of marriage and two years later married a family friend; that marriage lasted twenty-three years until she was widowed in her seventies.

MARIA, 89

"Don't tear your life apart for someone not worth losing yourself over."

PHYSICAL STRENGTH

WHAT SIGNIFICANT HEALTH ISSUES HAVE YOU HAD TO OVERCOME?

Three hip replacements on one hip and one on the other hip, deviated septum nasal surgery, three bouts with Bell's Palsy, and a variety of surgeries, including a hysterectomy and surgery to repair an arm broken in a fall.

WHAT PART OF YOUR BODY IS MOST IMPORTANT TO YOUR HEALTH, AND WHY?

My heart. It keeps me alive.

How has money been a motivating factor in your life?

I never had much money, but there was always enough to live on. In my second marriage, my husband had a little more money, enough that I finally felt financially safe.

How have you dealt with the physical changes of aging?

Up until now, I had never felt the changes of aging. Now, I feel as if it is time for me to feel the years upon me. I don't remember ever in my life saying, "Oh, I'm getting old." I really never thought of it...aging. Now I have surrendered... and that is how I feel. A time ago, I had good times, and now what is happening is the same as always. I have good times, and I still have my four children. And that is what keeps me happy.

How does your current physical environment bring your joy?

In this moment, right now, I am very happy. I have joy because I am spending this day with my beautiful daughter Hilda in her home. I want to be happy where I am, and now that I do not live in my home where I lived with my husband and then alone, I miss being there. But I can't go home anymore. I have to be happy right here.

Mental Clarity

Tell us about a time when you trusted your intuition to make an important decision?

When I left my husband after being married for thirty-two years, I felt sure of myself and of my decision. I had been working hard and making my own money. Not a lot, but I thought I could make it on my own. My children were grown and gone from home for a long time by then, and they were all married with children of their own. I took a chance and left, and it was good.

What mental skills have you developed over the years to help you navigate the difficult times?

When something bad happens, I think to myself that I am going to get out of this, too. I pray, I think about it, and I worry, and then I get out of it. And that is happening right now!

At what point did you recognize that you had stepped into your own voice?

Again, I think that I stepped into my voice on the day that I said to my husband, "Here! I am done!" I was fifty years old; he got mad at me for not doing something and hit me across the face. And that day I walked out on him, left years of abuse, and filed for divorce.

Did you have a definitive life plan? If so, how did you stay focused on that plan?

I never had a plan for my life. I waited to see what would happen and then I would do what I had to do next. I never had the mind to be able to make plans for myself. In those days, women didn't know about making plans for their own life—not in Mexico.

Who in your family inspired you to be courageous?

My father taught me to be strong. He encouraged me and protected me when I still lived at home. He was smart and a hard worker, and he was an honest man. I respected him immensely. At one point when I was young, he was appointed to the position of judge in a small town in Sonora, Mexico. People liked him and trusted him. He was a good man.

He never knew about my hard life with my husband. I didn't want him to know because he would have done something, and I was too afraid that he would take me back to Mexico.

Spiritual Courage

What safety nets have you relied on over the years, and how have they served you?

Well, what has held me up is my God! What else can hold us up?

There was also my neighbor Rosenda who became my best friend and who was with me when I needed to be held up. We were young mothers, both raising our children, both husbands working the copper mine, and she would encourage me to leave to save my life and my children, but I never did. Not while they were young. But she was always there until she and her husband moved to California to raise their family. I missed her so much. But I did visit with her later in California, and our friendship was good. She died a long time ago. I miss her.

My safety net now is still my God and my children who have always been there for me.

I pray and ask Him to be with me as I get through this also.

What have you loved deeply?

I love being peaceful. But that did not come soon to me.

I struggled so much in my life with my body, and I still struggle but not all the time anymore. I have some peace now.

I also love my children and God...deeply.

What advice would you give younger people to help them develop a vision of hope for their later years?

Don't tear your life apart for someone not worth losing yourself over.

Watch how the world is now and get a good education for yourself and respect yourself enough to not do anything that is not good for you. Make something of yourself. This is your life!

Can you describe a time in your life when you moved from surviving to thriving?

In my fifties when I finally spoke the words and said, "Enough." I could do what I wanted to do. I could walk out that door of our house and not come back. Maybe I couldn't do everything that I wanted to do, but it was much better than nothing at all. I was free.

It is said that bravery comes through taking action. How will you continue to live a brave life?

I live brave every day when I get up in the morning. If I am alive, I give thanks to God for another day of peace and life.

During the writing of this book, my siblings and I decided to move our mother out of her home where she had lived for over thirty years, the last twenty alone as a widow. We moved her to Mesa where she would live with our sister Maggie and her husband who were home during the day. With the diagnosis of congestive heart failure and Alzheimer's, she could no longer be left alone to care for herself in the small town of Ajo. As many Sundays as possible, she spends the day with me at my home where we watch Mexican movies, sing her favorite Spanish songs, work on jigsaw puzzles, walk the distance of the house from one end to the other for her exercise, eat healthy meals, and laugh at jokes while she also tells her stories of growing up. I love hearing her stories.

Growing up in a small mining town without any distractions of city life, my siblings and I grew up with a hearty dose of supernatural beliefs through the stories of our mother, our father's mother, a Yaqui Indian from Hermosillo, Mexico, and the neighborhood women. Storytelling was a big part of our lives. We did not grow up with television or any other electronic devices, including telephones until high school, that would disconnect us from each other and from hearing these life experiences that had been handed down through generations of storytelling.

And indeed, in the evening after the dinner hour, it was the women who told the stories as they gathered us outside in the backyards to lie on cots and old spring beds covered with weathered tarps and handmade flour-sack quilted blankets. There were no street lights to fade the immense view of a star-filled sky, nor any sounds of traffic nor hums of electric wires traversing our silent, stark dark nights. Most of the men would be out in the bars, and it would be hours before they made their way home, walking and stumbling into each other on dirt roads, stinking of alcohol, cigarettes, and other women. The nights belonged to the women and the children, huddled under the covers with just our heads poking out to look at the women sitting in their old, creaky wooden chairs, tired from their days packed with housework and cooking, still wearing their aprons as we begged to hear the tales of the Mexican legends.

Like American and European fairy tales, Mexican folklore always has its scary demons, monsters, witches, and wild creatures that endanger the souls of misbehaving children by taking them away, flying them high in the sinister sky, never to be seen again if those bad children don't listen to their parents. We spent hours listening to these stories, and our minds became fertile to the supernatural way of life that filled us with strong beliefs in spirits, ghosts and spells, and things that get loud in the dark. When we were in our preteen years and misbehaving and our mother was worn down from the daily grind of children, cooking, working, and not enough sleep (I never saw our mother in bed sleeping unless she was ill), I recall her saying that she wished that her mother had not died so young and left her at three without teaching her how to be a good mother to us. At this point, she would begin to cry a bit. Feeling terrible that we had misbehaved, partly because we were afraid of those witches that would come and take us away, but also because we could see that she was sincerely hurt, we would settle down and show our love for her. Many times during these moments, she would tell us that, as a child lying in her bed at night, she would awaken to see her mother standing at the foot of her bed watching over her. It would comfort her to know that she was there. Without any question of her sincerity, we believed that our grandmother did indeed stand at the foot of our mother's bed when she was a child.

It had been years since Mom had shared of her stories with me, but on this particular Sunday as she spent the day at my home, she surprised me. We had just eaten and were about to pounce on a 1000-piece jigsaw puzzle of a blue butterfly in flight when she said, "Mija," a Mexican term of endearment that an older person calls a younger loved one, "I want to share a story with you today while I am with you." I instantly thought of the nights of the backyard storytelling and the star-filled sky we experienced as children with our mother and the neighbor women.

At the beginning of Mom's stay at my sister's home, she was moved into a group home. Within those two short weeks of her stay, she had an experience in her room that brought back a childhood memory of one of her earlier supernatural encounters.

At the group home, she was given a private room with a big window that looked out onto the front yard. Besides a healthy green grassy area, there were beautifully maintained flowerbeds, well-manicured shrubs, and a couple of older trees that shaded the house. She was glad to have a room with a view.

The room was small with a comfortable hospital bed supplied by hospice, a nightstand and chest of drawers, and a nice blue fabric armchair so that she could sit and watch her own television set. The door that opened to the hallway, which led to the great room and a large kitchen, was left open most of the time so that the caregivers could occasionally look in and keep an eye on her if she chose to be in her room.

On her first evening sleeping in her room, she noticed a light above the frame of the door that led to the hallway. The light, about the size of a nightlight, slowly dimmed and brightened and then dimmed and brightened again and again at a steady pace as she watched it from her bed. She remembers thinking that the rhythm of the light dimming and brightening reminded her of her own heartbeat. She tried to see if she could make sense of where the light would be coming from but could not remember seeing anything during the day that would lead her to believe that a light would be coming from atop the door. Finally, after an hour or so of not sleeping, she gave in, and sleep came over her.

In the morning, as much as she could, she investigated the area above the doorway to see if there were any signs of an electrical outlet. She checked the position of the window but, by looking out to the front yard, could not see a street light that would be reflecting into the room. There were no other lights in the yard that could possibly reflect to such a high area of the room. She thought that she would make sure to close her curtains tightly so that no outside light could enter her room in the evening.

This went on every night, until at the end of two weeks, she was moved back to live with Maggie and her husband. She did not tell anyone of this incident until this day at my home when she decided to share the childhood story that it brought to her mind.

When she was eight and living in a small town in Mexico, her father decided to send her to live with her older sister, Angelita, her husband, and their two children: Ruben, six, and Carolina, five. She was to help her sister with the children and with chores because Angelita was pregnant again.

The family moved into a one-room house on the outskirts of town that had been abandoned for quite some time. Similar to the home in which she had lived with her father and brother, this home was also only one room with adobe walls and a firmly packed dirt floor. A small window was beside the front door made of wooden slats with a separate makeshift screen door stretched on a thin wood frame. There was no running water or electricity, but there was a shabby wooden structure that might have been used for a closet with a few shelves that had been built against one of the walls. There was no stove or any other household items that she could remember.

On their first night sleeping in the home, she could recall the sleeping arrangements. Ruben and Carolina slept together on a small bed with a thin mattress and a blanket against the opposite wall of the "closet shelves," and she slept next to them on a small cot. Angelita and her husband slept a few feet away, just to the side of the door to the outside.

Sometime during the night, she was awakened to a small light coming from the "closet shelves" that dimmed and brightened, dimmed and brightened. From the middle of the shelves, this light hung there with nothing around it and went on and off. At first she felt uncomfortable because the only lights she knew were candles and kerosene lamps, and in her mind, she could not imagine how this light could be there. The light went on and off, and it continued for some time until she finally fell asleep.

In the morning she talked to her sister about it, but her sister dismissed the story and only gave her the chores of the day to accomplish. She decided to forget the incident and did not think about it again that day.

On the second night, along with the light, came the sounds of crying and moaning and other indistinguishable noises. At first the sounds were a whisper that seemed to go with the rhythm of the light and, strangely enough, the rhythm of her own heart, and again the next day she talked to her sister about it. But to no avail.

The third night came, and the light presented itself again, and the sounds were louder. This time she crawled from her cot to her sister and husband, who slept on the floor on a heavy blanket. They were sound asleep, and she lay next to them until the morning came. When she talked to her sister about it, the sister promised to wake up with her and that together they would investigate this light and the sounds.

A week passed, and nothing appeared again until the third week when Angelita's husband was away working in another town. Suddenly, Angelita was awakened to the light and the sounds of crying, moaning, and unusual noises. Years later, my mother would describe the noises as something that was scraping and dragging on a wooden floor. Both awake now, they could not deny that there was a presence in the room that was not of this world. Angelita was convinced that they had to leave.

The family moved from the home as soon as Angelita's husband returned, and it was then that the neighbors confessed that they knew the home was indeed haunted and had been unlivable for years. Even at the tender age of seven, my mother had been privy to a world that exists that not many have the opportunity to experience.

Her short time in the group home had brought back memories of an entire lifetime of fears, of being alive and yet dead to the real her, but not completely dead, just as the ghost in the one room home was dead but not gone, or the memories of her deceased mother standing at the foot of her bed watching over her, dead but not gone. Asking herself, when do we die for sure?

As my mother shifts from her physical limitations to a lifetime of memories of giant choices that she made and small pleasures that she still enjoys, she readies herself for the journey on the other side of the veil. And she is not afraid.

I share this story because I have come to believe that our lives on this earth are much bigger, richer, inclusive, and expansive than what our senses can conceive. Although our physical body seems to be the indicator of our limitations, especially as we age, how much more is available to us when we increase our belief beyond that of what we can taste, hear, see, smell, or touch.

A full and expanded life can only be experienced when one chooses to allow a consciousness beyond limitations. Consider that there is much more to life to investigate. I am not suggesting joining a ghost buster's group or organizing a séance in your home.

I am recommending openness to living that includes some mystery and magic, perhaps shifting the focus from our younger lives of doing, accomplishing, and acquiring to the time of simply being open to the world of possibilities. There is magic in the universe.

Live brave.

PART FOUR

NURTURING THE INNER GARDEN OF WELL-BEING

"I like living. I have sometimes been wildly despairing, acutely miserable, racked with sorrow, but through it all I still know quite certainly that just to be alive is a grand thing."
~ Agatha Christie

CHAPTER SIXTEEN

Nurturing the Inner Garden of Well-Being

Although I am not a hands-on gardener, spending time planting, pruning, spraying, watering, and inspecting for anything that might come along to bother the natural flow of a growing and thriving garden, I do enjoy the visual impact that my backyard has on my well-being and on my contentment. The garden I nurture and enjoy most in my current life is the one that is flourishing within me.

THROUGHOUT THIS BOOK WE HAVE shared mini-life stories of women who have not always cared for or nurtured themselves in their younger years, but who, with a full measure of past experiences to draw upon, eventually arrive to an awakening and a desire for being well, and they stay the course of caring for themselves physically, mentally, and spiritually. After reviewing our interviews with the women and with our own observations and external research, we have identified twelve healthy areas of significance for nurturing the inner garden of well-being that is of the utmost importance for becoming the best we can be in our lives.

Once again, we have requested from a group of *Living Brave* women their wise counsel and asked them to share their stories as mentors for those who are waking up to the task of being in charge of their own inner garden. Although I don't consider any of our contributors in the elder's category, yet they are wise and are masters of their words.

I found this piece in the book *From Age-Ing to Sage-Ing*, by Shalomi and Miller on mentoring that I must share with you before you read the twelve healthy areas of significance for well-being. *"What do elders have to teach? Over and beyond an exchange of verbal information and technical skills, they transmit what can't be acquired from books. ......When an elder fertilizes a young person's aspiring mind with his knowledge and seasoned judgment, the student receives a living spark, a transmission that may one day blossom into wisdom."*

The statement reminds me that we are all tellers of the stories and every day is a new story. Like water and fertilizer of thoughts and emotions that move through our families, friends, co-workers, clients, audiences, and fellow travelers, we all have the ability to transmit a living spark, the sunshine on our gardens, and to mentor others in caring for themselves until one day when they blossom into their own wisdom.

No amount of medicine or surgery will replace nurturing oneself from the beginning of our time in our human body.

Physical self-care and emotional attentiveness, along with the understanding that our lives are sacred, are significant pathways to thriving. In his book *Being Mortal: Medicine and What Matters in the End*, Atul Gawande writes that the role of medicine and doctors *"is to enable well-being. And well-being is about the reasons one wishes to be alive. Those reasons matter, not just at the end of life, or when debility comes, but all along the way."*

Reading his book, I appreciated the responsibility that he personally felt in caring for his patients, but I also thought of our own personal accountability to our well-being "all along the way."

As keepers of our own bodies, minds, and spiritual health, what is it that we could nurture within ourselves to give us the best chance of living fully all the way through? For myself, I wish I had had this list of areas to nurture within my inner body and that I could have grasped the implications of following a plan. But since I didn't have a plan, I can only say to the reader—do as I say and not as I did. Because... I don't think that it's ever too late to start a well-being course of action.

After the list of the twelve areas we have identified as important for you to consider, you will discover an article for each subject written by a woman who said "yes" to sharing her story. Once again, we suggest that you not rush through this in one sitting but savor each one separately and enjoy the offerings...preferably while sitting in a beautiful garden.

- **Engage Your Body**
- **Be Curious**

- **Invite Adventure**
- **Stay Flexible**
- **Refresh**
- **Dream**
- **Be Attractive**
- **Discover Passion**
- **Hold Close Relationships**
- **Forgive**
- **Give**
- **Believe**

And here each of these subjects is addressed by our panel of *Living Brave* women.

ENGAGE YOUR BODY

JUDI, 68

WHAT DOES ENGAGE REALLY MEAN? Why is it important to engage your body? As a physician focusing on health and wellness, I hope to impart some words of wisdom taken from forty years of experience. What I have learned, in essence, is that your body is worth the effort you put into it.

Engage is a verb that has many meanings, but the one I like the most is "to bind, as by pledge, promise, contract, or oath." It sounds stiff and a little scary, but living in a body requires us to pledge a commitment to it. We all want our relationships to work. It is the same with the body. It wants you on board making sure all systems are working like a fine instrument. Tuning, repairing, lubricating, and nourishing the body are all part of our commitment to it. A healthy start would be to state that you love your body. Most people don't love their bodies. So, every day look in the mirror and say, "I love my body." Love it as it is right now, and vow to make the changes that will make it more functional and healthy.

The changes you will need to make include mindfulness, good nutrition, and exercise. Incorporating all three will release you to a state of wellness. Remember, you are not necessarily looking to achieve your *own* perception of a perfect body. You are looking to do the best you can for the physical body you have. Learning mindfulness is important to be able to engage with the body. Mindfulness is a technique in which one focuses one's full attention on the present to experience thoughts, feelings, and sensations, but not judging them. Yoga and meditation are two techniques that will bring you to a more mindful state. In this state, you will be more able to work on your physical body. Yoga breathing alone can balance your brain neurotransmitters. These brain molecules regulate mood states such as anxiety and depression that can sabotage your commitment to care for your body. The mind becomes too fretful, unfocused, and self-centered to be of much use. It is thought that a person living in the past can suffer from depression. A person living in the future is more apt to be anxious, but a person living in the present experiences more peace. Peace… a lovely thought and a good feeling!

As far as exercise, just become someone who moves. Count your steps. Ten thousand steps daily is a good goal. Add a stretching routine. Lift light weights a few times a week. Get your heart rate to 120-130 for ten minutes every day or a half hour every other day. Check with your doctor to determine the safest exercise for you. Walk, walk, walk… move, move, move. Sitters get sick. Movers get healthy.

Everyone knows that good nutrition is important for health, but do you know why?

Nutrients "turn on" genes. This may not be a sexual relationship, but it is certainly an intimate one. Food manages our genes. Foods laced with pesticides and trans fats that are dense with calories *turn* on genes that express illness (physical and mental illness). Foods that are fresh, organic, and full of nutrients turn on genes of health (physical and mental health). This concept is simplistic but true. Adelle Davis told us, "We are what we eat." So eat a diet that is rich in fresh vegetables and fruits. It will reduce your risk of cancer and heart disease. Also, make sure you are eating those foods that provide oils and protein, such as nuts, seeds, meats, and fish. Eating organic food is the key to avoiding pesticides. An easy way to get the 5-10 servings of vegetables per day is to juice organic vegetables and fruits. Add coconut oil to enhance absorption of the nutrients in the blend. Become familiar with the "Super Foods" and include them in your diet. Drink eight glasses of water between meals. Water is the great detoxifier and can help prevent stroke and dementia. Engage your body with the earth by growing some of your own food. Talk with a specialist to see if you need high quality supplements. There are tests available that check your nutrient needs.

Mindfulness, good eating, and exercise will indeed engage you with your body. Tonight, sit in a tub of warm water with salts and lavender oil. Relax into a mindful state and make plans for truly honoring your body. You can do it! Get engaged; it feels good. As Wayne Dyer said, "You don't need another diet, workout manual, or personal trainer. Go within, listen to your body, and treat it with all the dignity and love that your self-respect demands."

Dr. Judith Ingalls *has been a primary care physician for 25 years and is presently specializing in the health care of women. She is former medical director of the Telluride Medical Center, former director of an emergency department in Oregon, and presently presides over her longevity and hormone consulting practices in Carefree, Arizona, and Telluride, Colorado.*

BE CURIOUS

GAYLE, 60

THERE IS AN OLD PROVERB that warns, "Curiosity killed the cat." One might suppose from that advice that being inquisitive could get you into trouble. A bit of digging shows the original form of the proverb was "care kills the cat," where "care" meant "worry" or "sorrow." And it turns out there is even more to this proverb. What is often left out is the rest of that adage, "satisfaction brings it back," suggesting resurrection or return. So maybe being curious isn't all bad?

As a psychotherapist specializing in psychological trauma, I have worked with many people weighed down by painful life experiences, by worry, by sorrow. Studies show that unresolved traumatic stress impacts our physical, as well as mental health, not only complicating chronic medical conditions such as hypertension but, in many cases, causing them. The famous Adverse Childhood Experiences (ACE) Study is one of the best examples of this research.

No one goes through life without bad things happening—natural disasters, accidents, illness, death of a loved one, divorce, job loss, bullying, and the list goes on. We all experience such things. It turns out that with psychological trauma, it's not so much the terrible thing that happened but what comes after. Did we hide away from the world in fear? Or did we reach out for help to recover? Did we tell our story? Did we heal and make meaning from the experience?

The field of neurobiology is a fascinating new area of scientific study. What these experts tell us is that being curious is wired into us as part of the life-enhancing circuitry of our brain; in this case, what's called the "seeking" circuit. Interestingly, this circuit sits across from the life-protecting circuit of fear. So what if we fire up the seeking circuit instead of letting fear take over? What if we approach the world with interest and curiosity, rather than avoiding risk and hiding out in fear? Seems easier said than done sometimes, I know.

Years back, after my second divorce, I was weighed down with "care,"—worry, sorrow, and, yes, with some fear. Yet I did something some people thought was crazy; I went back to school. Again. After two master's degrees, I set out to complete my doctorate. I fired up my curious-seeking circuitry and plowed onward. It turned out to be the right divorce recovery strategy for me. I see the same good outcomes for my patients time and time again. Being curious is not only a characteristic of well-being, but it can contribute greatly to our return to health.

Perhaps then, there is something to that old proverb after all if we consider it in its original form, as reflected in Shakespeare's 1599 play, *Much Ado About Nothing*: "What courage, man! What, though care killed a cat, thou hast mettle enough in thee to kill care."

It seems whether we draw upon the findings of 21st century neuroscientists or the wisdom of the ancients, the examined life is the way to go (indulge me here, Socrates).

So, be curious!

***Gayle Cordes** is an Arizona state-licensed psycho-therapist, providing counseling and psychotherapy services focused on issues related to relationships, divorce, sexuality, and addictions. She assists adult and adolescent clients with recovery from trauma, abuse, depression, chemical and behavioral dependencies, stress and anxiety, self-esteem issues, troubled relationships, infidelity, and divorce.*

Gayle has experience across the continuum of care, including inpatient treatment in independent private practice and integrative primary care.

She holds a doctorate and two master's degrees and has completed post-master's training in the treatment of trauma and abuse. She is also an EMDRIA Approved Consultant, as well as an IITAP Certified Sex Addiction Therapist.

Prior to her career in psychotherapy, she spent twenty years in the corporate sector, serving in several executive level positions in Fortune 500 companies in the business of staffing and human capital management. She holds a master of business degree.

INVITE ADVENTURE

SABRA, 73

ADVENTURE DOES NOT COME INTO your life uninvited. You have to put yourself in a place for adventure to happen. When rafting the Colorado River many years ago, an old river man said that stories about the river always begin with "and there I was." And there we were getting ready for the helicopter to fly us out of the canyon and back to civilization. Me, with my leg wrapped in an ace bandage from a torn hamstring, and my partner, white knuckled from the rapids we'd just gone through. As she said, "It was the best of times and the worst of times." But it was definitely an adventure!

So you have to be someplace for things to happen, and it usually is not at home. Stories worth sharing rarely begin with "So...today we decided to stay in."

For me adventure is all about exploring the outdoors. My partner and I took up kayaking about five years ago. We have tried to explore as many different kayaking venues as possible...lakes and rivers in Arizona, the coast of California, the bay of Cabo San Lucas, the San Juan Islands with Orca whales, and the Coral Sea surrounded by dolphins. We expanded our kayaking to kayak camping. And while I never loved camping, somehow kayak camping is different. One of the biggest challenges for me is driving the kayak trailer and backing it down the ramp. I have anxiety every time about backing the trailer in a straight line like the fishermen do with their fishing boats. But somehow I manage, and the kayaks get put in the water, whether the trailer is straight or not. And once on the water, all the anxiety goes away...until the next time.

Adventure for me is about doing new things, going new places, trying something different. There is always a risk in going to a new restaurant. What if I don't like the food? What if the service is lousy? What if the people I invite don't like it? Recently, I was going to meet friends before a play, and they asked me to find a restaurant for the occasion. I researched the area and located a restaurant where we all planned to meet. When I walked in, I discovered that it was small, had plastic chairs, and bare cement floors. My heart dropped, and inside I was quietly saying, "Oh, no." However, when the food came, all kinds of empanadas and plantains, it was delicious and loved by all! It was so good that we have been back there several times. I've seen this same restaurant recommended on *Check Please Arizona*, a PBS original television presentation.

There is excitement and anticipation that comes with inviting adventure into your lives. But there are other emotions that keep many people from venturing out of their comfort zones. These emotions have to do with anxiety and fears: fears of not being good enough, fears of being laughed at, fears of failing. Because people don't want to feel uncomfortable or fearful or anxious, they stay in their comfort zone. As a result, anything outside of your comfort zone qualifies as an adventure. And know that you will feel very proud of yourself for taking the risks, for trying something new, for being brave. These feelings are excitement, pride, exuberance, and confidence.

A friend of mine hiked Mount Kilimanjaro after months of strenuous training. Now, that is an adventure! But your adventures don't need to be that monumental. Anything out of your comfort zone constitutes an adventure, whether it be a painting class or signing up for a 5 K run or going somewhere you've never been. They all count as an adventure because they are new to you and you invited them into your life.

I have a patient who went out and bought a gun, a Glock, and took a gun safety class. Both these actions, buying the gun and taking the safety class, were definitely out of her comfort zone. But she reported feeling excited and empowered and plans to take more classes in the future. She has started on an adventurous path, and who knows where it will lead her next?

My partner and I are not spring chickens. She is in her 60s and I'm in my 70s. In the past five years, we've added a number of new things to our lives: kayaking, kayak camping, painting lessons in acrylics, decorating bird houses with rocks, attending plays and musicals we've never seen before. We worked with a youth theater group to put on *The Wizard of Oz*. Of course, the fact that our dog was playing the part of Toto is what got us involved in the first place, but we loved being theater moms and now are interested in working behind the scenes on future productions. We've traveled to many different places: Australia, Aruba, Botswana and Kenya, Alaska, and Mexico. Our future travels are going to take in Kauai, Italy, Croatia, and then Namibia. We tried a vacation on a clipper ship and loved it. We've snorkeled with nurse sharks and manta rays off the coast of Belize. I've been to my first polo match and stomped on the sod pieces just like they did in the movie *Pretty Woman*. As I write this, my partner is off to her second glass blowing class.

We purchased a Miata this past summer. It has a six speed transmission, and I haven't driven a stick shift in over forty years. Also, as I recall, I was never very good at shifting back then. So now we have this car, and I have been afraid to drive it. I avoided driving it; I would tell Lou to drive it instead. But yesterday I drove, and the fear is gone. Well, almost gone. And today I drove the Miata to work. I'm actually shifting better. I'm proud of myself. I'm excited about the prospect of driving again. So we invited adventure into our lives by way of a car, and I'm finally enjoying the ride!

Please be aware that the degree of difficulty in adventures will decrease as you get older. Your adventures won't be as extensive or as physically demanding. But do what you can while you can. Age and physical limitations will influence the rest.

So, invite adventure into your lives, do something different, something you've never done before, something you might not be good at, and enjoy the rewards of taking a risk. Enjoy the feelings of pride, exuberance, accomplishment, confidence, and bravery that come with taking a risk.

***Sabra House** is a licensed, certified social worker in the state of Arizona. She has been a psychotherapist for over thirty-five years. She first practiced in Flint, Michigan, and then moved to Scottsdale, Arizona, in 1990 where she opened her own private practice, The Lighthouse Center. Sabra has authored a self-help book entitled* Who's Walking Around in Your Head With Muddy Boots?

STAY FLEXIBLE
BRONWYN, 52

THINGS DON'T ALWAYS GO THE way I plan.

It felt like someone had just punched me in the stomach. I was lying in a heap on my kitchen floor more than six years ago. I heard a woman's voice wailing off in the distance, only to realize it was mine. I screamed until there was nothing left. Then the tears were streaming down my face as the pain, the heartache, and the anger replaced the piercing shrieks. Numb and in shock, my eighteen-year marriage was crashing down around me.

As I sifted through the rubble that represented my broken dreams, I could feel God holding my hand, wiping my tears, and letting me know that everything was going to be okay.

On that significant and fateful day when I thought the world went wrong, I learned that it was the day the universe was making everything right. God had a whole new life waiting for me, something much better than I could have ever imagined.

Before I could step into a new day or start fresh, I had to learn how to be flexible and adapt to change. There were many firsts that I had to face after the divorce: living alone, being a single mom, making new friends, going out on a date, and even filling out an application for a corporate job. I was scared and unsure of myself. Had I not learned how to stay flexible and present in each moment, I would have missed the gift of discovering my true strength.

I now choose to make flexibility part of my spiritual practice on a daily basis. It gives me a platform to grow better instead of bitter. I learned how to look at things differently, switch gears, and find new opportunities, not only to survive the circumstances of life but to walk through them with God. I not only walked through them, but I found a way to thrive. I am happier now than I've ever been.

I still have a lot to learn about staying flexible. It requires me to "unlearn" old patterns and ways of thinking, doing, and being. No more autopilot and taking things for granted. I gently question my thoughts and actions every step of the way. I am curious and ask myself questions, "Does this hold truth for me today?" "Does this serve me and help me become the highest and best person that I can be?" If it does, then I keep it. But if it doesn't, I let it go without regret. When I release it, I start to dream and imagine what a bigger, brighter version of me could look like. That new vision encourages innovation and transformation. I try on different scenarios and keep going until I find one that fits me just right for where I am on that day.

Staying flexible is good for my emotional well-being, but it has also had a positive effect on my physical health and vibrancy. Being flexible has taught me to honor and celebrate my body through the process of aging. I used to feel upset when I saw a wrinkle, a laugh line, or noticed some gravity pull. But now I know that these changes represent a life well-lived and that I have known love.

I began to practice yoga regularly about five years ago. It is a physical example of flexibility, and I loved the way it made me feel to stretch and move my body in new ways. Unfortunately, I sustained a wrist injury that took me off the mat for over a year. I used my spiritual practice to look at what I really wanted. I could remain physically active by brisk walking, hiking, and biking. Physical therapy and rehabilitation have helped to heal my wrist, and I look forward to getting back to my yoga practice.

Staying flexible becomes the norm for women who choose to live bravely. It's no longer just an option because we never know what life has in store for us. We can learn how far we can bend without breaking. We learn that adapting to change is an essential part of life. It helps us find hope, joy, and love when we feel like our world is falling apart.

***Bronwyn Marmo** is the award-winning and best-selling author of **The Food Is A Lie: The Truth Is Within**. She is the associate producer and one of the featured experts in the documentary film **The Inner Weigh**. Bronwyn spent more than ten years in the broadcasting industry as a television news anchor and reporter. In Phoenix, AZ, she was a popular guest on Channel 3's **Your Life A to Z** with her regular segment entitled, "Spotlite on Success."*

REFRESH

MARY LEE, 68

Throughout our lives we are given repeated opportunities to pause and refresh ourselves.

Sometimes we recognize the opportunities and embrace them with gusto, donating maternity clothes after the baby is born, changing our names following divorce, purging closets when moving from one home to the next. These are the obvious opportunities, and they arrive with a predictable checklist of things we must do in order to leave the old behind and move forward into the future.

It is more challenging to identify the opportunity to refresh ourselves when we lack a significant event or change that motivates us to stop and take inventory.

How will I recognize the slow decay of a stale career that saps my creativity and shrinks the future, limiting the time I have left to make a meaningful contribution?

A poor relationship with my supervisor may motivate me to make a change, but if the relationship is strong while the job is on autopilot, it is more difficult to recognize.

Will it be my primary care physician who gives the direction to start moving in a regular exercise program? Yes, a few pounds have crept on over the past few years in combination with increased hours of keyboard/monitor time; I had no idea I now fit the definition of obese! Denial precedes action.

How will I know when it's time to purge the closet of items I no longer wear? Is it when the rack pulls away from the wall brackets and crashes to the floor? (Yes, this has happened to me, as well as to friends of mine.) Is it when I have begun arranging my clothes by size versus color and item type? How many pairs of black slacks are too many?

Am I satisfied with who I am and where I am personally, spiritually, professionally, and financially? What are the flags waving to get my attention? How do I know when and where I have opportunities to pause and refresh? And, in the process, to let go of the old and embrace the new place, the new way of being, with my eyes focused on the future.

We all have those inner voices (which we must stop ignoring). I encourage you to take the time to pause and listen to the messages:

"You've stayed too long in this position. It's time to put your plan together and move to the next opportunity." *Scary!*

"This relationship is sucking you dry. Stop worrying about the impact on your partner and take care of yourself." *Really Scary!*

"You are spinning your wheels and avoiding the reality of your destiny. Set the daily routines aside and now reach for your stars." *Terrifying!*

The annual ritual of creating New Year's resolutions has never appealed to me. It seemed so pointless to have resolutions which you knew would be abandoned within the month. Lofty goals, something to talk about in the break room, but I just didn't relate to the process. A few years ago, I had the opportunity to hear a motivational speaker, professional football player, Joe Theisman, share his life experiences and how, throughout his career, he achieved his many goals, rewards, and recognition. He was compelling as he described his approach, how he writes out his goals every year. As I listened, I became engaged, "Why not try it?" It worked for Joe, and clearly, he has had great success in his career. So I tried it two years ago; I wrote my goals on my PC, printed them, and put them in a cellophane sleeve placed on the side of my desk. Every day I saw them. I didn't intentionally plan actions, but I was reminded daily, "These are my goals."

At the end of the year, the most amazing outcome was when I realized that I had achieved eight out of ten goals. I had had success without having to try very hard. I used a process of aligning two specific goals within each of the following areas where I was striving for growth.

Personal (save for the dream vacation, spend more time with family, write)

Professional (update the resume, ask for the promotion, apply for a new position)

Spiritual (meditate daily, create a quiet place for my inner thoughts and dreams)

Financial (eliminate debt, save for a vacation, meet with financial advisor)

Health (schedule that colonoscopy, lose weight, move all of my joints and limbs every hour)

I'm continuing to focus on my health; however, I am encouraged by the success I have enjoyed the past two years.

Years ago when I was a suddenly single parent of three children under the age of five, working through a child custody battle, and hanging on to my home and sanity by my fingernails, I had a first-ever experience where I divorced a girlfriend. I didn't plan to do this; it came about gradually. I had known this woman through grade school and high school, and we had maintained the friendship although it stretched thin as the years went by.

She invited herself and her children to come spend a weekend visit with us. She announced to her children (and to mine) that they were here to "help" this poor family going through this hard time. Throughout her stay, it seemed to me, she continued to flaunt her success—photos of her doting and romantic husband, their financial trophies (Mercedes, boat, beachfront vacation home), trips to Hawaii, and upcoming plans they were making to cruise the Mediterranean. This went on all through the weekend. At that time, I was barely able to put macaroni and cheese on the table, certainly not able to plan extended vacations in exotic locales. It became unbearable to me. Relief folded in as they departed on Sunday evening. Going forward, I stopped taking her phone calls, did not answer her letters, and pretty much, "cut the cord." It was too painful to feel the constant comparison of her success with my dire straits.

I chose to leave the friendship and move forward without her. I felt relief. I did not have to prove myself or try to show a happy face when happy faces were in short supply. I did not feel guilty; I felt free. I learned a very important lesson: not every friend is a good friend.

What prevents us from moving forward? Even the most mundane opportunities like purging the bulging closet seem daunting. Fear holds us back. Ask yourself the question: What is the worst thing that can happen if I do this? For me, when I write it down, I realize I have the solutions within myself. This is my release. I have the knowledge within me; I've learned to trust myself; this means…I can do it.

In each phase of our lives, our priorities and our goals will change. Leaving babies and diapers behind in Phase 1, we will move into the next phase, which will be different for each one of us. For some, it will be a focus on family; for others, a focus on the career; and, for a few, basic survival (food, shelter, safety). Be aware of the phase you are in today, right now. What do you want? What do you need to let go of in order to achieve your life goals? What is the contribution you wish to leave for others to learn?

Each day, consider what is your opportunity for that day. Embrace it, own it, and celebrate it when you complete it. And then Refresh!

***Mary Lee DeCoster** has more than 45 years in healthcare reimbursement management experience. Currently providing consulting support for healthcare clients, she was the Vice President of Revenue Cycle for Maricopa Integrated Health System from 2004-2014. In prior roles, Mary Lee has led teams in organizations on both the provider and vendor sides of healthcare in Oregon, Washington, California, Nebraska, and Arizona.*

Mary Lee is the immediate past chair of the Arizona Hospital Healthcare Association Managed Care Committee, past chair of the National HFMA Revenue Cycle KPI Task Force, and is a member of both the National HFMA Medical Debt Task Force, and the National HFMA Pricing Transparency Task Force. As a past president of Arizona HFMA, she earned the chapter's first Lifetime & Leadership Achievement Award in 2010. In April, 2014, Mary Lee was selected by Arizona Business Magazine as a finalist for the annual Arizona Healthcare Leader Award in the executive category.

DREAM

JENNIFER, 50

"To Sleep, Perchance to Dream"... William Shakespeare (excerpt from Hamlet).

AHHH...TO DREAM...WE ALL LOVE TO dream. We speak of dreams, we sing of dreams, we write of dreams, and we dream of dreams. Just the word drips from our lips like honey.

From Shakespeare's *Midsummer Night's Dream* to Martin Luther King's *I Have a Dream*. From the Aboriginal "Dreamtime" to Aerosmith's "Dream On." From Einstein's sleep time discovery, the speed of light, to Ramanujan's, the theory of pi. From Mary Shelley's dream-inspired *Frankenstein* to Paul McCartney's "Yesterday." Dreams inspire our prose, initiate our discoveries, and inject our creativity.

But what is a dream? Why do we dream? Can we control our dreams or, better yet, harness our dreams?

The subject of dreams dates back 5000 years to the earliest recorded civilizations, the Sumerians of Mesopotamia. Dreams were recorded on clay tablets, and the Sumerians believed that, in the dream, your soul left your body and actually visited the people and places in the dream. In these earliest recordings, we see the interpretation of "good dreams" from the gods and "bad dreams" from demons. Prophecies and omens lived in dreams. Throughout history, such themes have been woven into spirituality, religion, and theory. In 2000 BC, ancient Greeks wrote their dreams on papyrus, incubated dreams, and slept on special dream beds to seek advice, comfort, and healing. The Bible documents God speaking to and through angels in dreams, including the angel who appears to Joseph in a dream instructing him to take Mary as his wife and name the baby Jesus. Judaism, Hebrew, Christian, Muslim, Native American and New Age, all have a place of honor for dreams and their interpretation.

But what is a dream?

Dreams are most often referring to a series of thoughts, emotions, or feelings occurring during sleep. The neurobiology of dreams is now well-documented and scientifically proven. Dreams occur during REM sleep or the state of rapid eye movement, the stage of sleep in which the brain activity is most like wakefulness. We dream about every 60 to 90 minutes of sleep, and our period of dreaming extends with each occurrence. Thus, if you want to dream more, sleep longer. We do not recall 95% of our dreams, but those most vivid or experienced just before awakening become the source of our interpretations and manifestations. The prefrontal cortex, responsible for logic and planning, exhibits decreased activity in REM sleep; thus, we fly, we create, we…well…we dream the impossible dream.

Back to the important unanswered question, why do we dream? Science does not know as biology and physiology have not revealed why we dream. It is unknown if there is a single origin of dreams or multiple portions of the brain or even if the purpose of dreaming is for mind or body. Dreams remain a mystery to the scientific mind. Yet for 5000 years, we have documented, investigated, interpreted, incubated, and celebrated dreams, regardless of the physiological how and why. And still we crave harnessing and controlling our dreams to unlock the potential into our waking state.

In our quest for control we have focused on "lucid dreams" as a potential pathway into the sleeping state of dreams. Lucid dreams, or the conscious awareness of dreaming while dreaming, only recently have been sanctioned by scientific evidence showing individuals who not only know they are dreaming while dreaming but who can communicate such to an outside observer. This may be an entry way to control the outcome of dreams, have intentional dreams, and play in the fertile ground of the mind, unhitched to outer reality. Tibetan Buddhists have practiced Dream Yoga for 1000 years in which daily practice heightens the mind's awareness of dream versus wakefulness to increase the frequency and control in lucid dreams. Maybe someday we will unlock a key to controlling our dreams during sleep state.

For those of us non-Tibetan Buddhists, there are tools you can use to increase your use of dreams in the daytime, such as a dream journal in which the moment you awake, you write the vivid memories of your dreams. Others claim that if, just prior to sleep, you set an intention to remember your dreams, you are more likely to recall a dream upon waking. Simply placing a pencil and paper next to the bed and writing any memories of the dream state upon awakening has led to such discovers as Einstein's and Ramanujan's. Vivid dreams with music and character have been captured immediately by those such as Shelley and McCartney, propelling their nighttime creativity into fame or fortune. Thus, you can clearly understand why many seek the key to nighttime dreaming and long to capture and control this creativity.

But before we accomplish our quest for control of the night, do we fully control our daydreams?

Merriam-Webster defines dreams as "something you very much wished to do, to be or have for a long time." Aristotle proclaimed, "Hope is a waking dream," and Walt Disney built an empire upon, "If you can dream it, you can do it." But how do we get from "dream it" to "do it"? If you believe Walt, wishing upon a star will make your dreams come true. I enjoyed this as a child but would not base my next paycheck on the North Star, probably to find out it was just a slow-moving satellite. So how do we harness our daydreams?

Lao Tzu states, "A journey of 1000 miles begins with a single step." So what is that first step? To do the undoable, to think the unthinkable, you must dream the undreamable. So let's dream, then think, and then do. That is how you get from "Dream it" to "Do it."

Start now. Close your eyes (after you are done reading, of course) and let's dream together. Dream big, but dream. Dream the ridiculous, but dream. Dream of who you dream of being, just dream.

Now let's think. Think of your dream, not from another time in your life, but right now. Not from the future or the past, but think in the present tense. Think in detail. Think in full living color. Think sound, smell, and taste. Think the dream is your life now, happening live. Think I am, I have,

I do. What does it look like? What does it feel like? What are you doing? Wearing? Living? What is out your bedroom window? What is the view from your office or your airline seat? Who is on your arm? What made you laugh today? What made you smile, and what did you do today of which you are the most proud? Get specific. All the way down to the meal you had for lunch, the place you are living, and the car you are driving. Remember, it is happening now; you are already in it, so just look around in your dream.

Next step? Capture this new reality. Record it in a format that you can look at every day. Select one that is your style, visible to you and easy. Google what works for you, take a course, read a book, create a vision board, write in a journal, ask a coach, seek out your tribe, or do what has worked before. But capture your dream in the now.

Step two. Take one action that leads you closer to your dream. There are resources all around you for step two, and I strongly encourage you to select one that fits your style. Take these first two steps, and you will begin to harness the power of your daydreams.

Whether we control our dreams or not, as human beings, we do dream. Dreams are healthy. For me it is no coincidence that nighttime dreams only occur during our healthiest stage of sleep. Adequate REM stage of sleep has been espoused to increase clarity, weight loss, disease prevention, longevity, higher income, and more than a few books, songs, and discoveries. It is no wonder that in the genius of God's universe it is paired with something we humans so long to enjoy—vivid dreams, ensuring we will seek out more of this magical REM sleep.

Waking dreams are, in fact, hope. Hope is the one thing humans cannot live without. We have endured torture, imprisonment, crises, downturns, heartbreak, abuse, divorce, physical hardship, and a loved one's death if there is a ray of hope to light the way. To daydream is to bring the future into the now and remind us that hope exists. It is no wonder why we daydream. Daydreams are hope, and to live we must have hope.

So sleep, per chance to dream, and don't give up your daydreams.

***Jennifer Erickson** is a passionate leader, implementer and self-proclaimed 'executioner,' with a talent of fearlessly executing on powerful ideas, business models, dreams and missions alike. As CEO of Kirk LLC, she manages, incubates and supports wholly-owned start-up companies, inspiring creativity in business models with an emphasis on innovative products and services.*

Jennifer honed her tenacity to overcome obstacles and execute in her roles as CFO, COO and CEO of small to large companies across many industries.

After years focused in healthcare, Jennifer co-founded a motorsports company, becoming one of the largest in the US. She has continued to work with other start-ups and young companies.

Jennifer brings her passion to all she does including her role as a founding member of the HFMA National Women Lead HERe Advisory Board. She also co-chairs the HERe newsletter and often contributes in book reviews and blogs.

BE ATTRACTIVE

SILVER, 56

It was 1983. I was living in Los Angeles and having trouble with yet another boyfriend, so I went to see a therapist a co-worker had recommended. Dr. Shuman, my age and easy on the eyes, wanted to know why I was there, so I told him, "I'm 30 years old, and I've never had a healthy relationship with a man, and it's just now occurred to me that I might have something to do with it!"

I had moved to LA in search of yet another fresh start, but as the saying goes, "Everywhere I went, there I was." I continued my relentless pursuit of men who agreed with my poor opinion of myself. I was drinking too much, and I lived in constant fear, afraid of losing my job, afraid I wasn't pretty or thin enough, afraid that others could sense my desperation.

After a few sessions, Dr. Shuman told me (get this), "You are clinically depressed."

I said, "Doc, are you nuts?" (By the way, they really don't like that term.) "What makes you think I'm depressed?"

He replied, "You come in here week after week and tell me all these sad stories and not just about men. Don't you FEEL depressed?"

I stared at him for a long moment before I responded, "I'm from New England. How would I know?"

Okay, so I use humor to defuse stress.

Depressed!?! Hmmm. Not good. Not good at all. Depression is not for us solid New Englanders. My father once told me that therapists are for people who have no friends. Just going to see one was a huge leap for me, and I wanted to get this over with as quickly as possible. I figured I had better find a way out. I continued to go to therapy once a week, but I also began to look for answers on my own.

I read every self-help book I could get my hands on; *The Power of Positive Thinking* and *As a Man Thinketh* were two favorites. I went to tons of workshops. I did transformational seminars; I quit drinking; I even walked barefoot across hot coals with the famous motivator, Tony Robbins. (I always say WITH Tony, but I've never actually seen him do it! He just stood on the sidelines yelling, "Go, Silver. Go, Silver. Go!")

I tried everything—scream therapy, laughter therapy, retail therapy.

Here's what happened. One night, two years after I started therapy, I had what you might call an epiphany—a big one.

It was winter. I was lying in bed with the lights out, staring at the ceiling, pre-complaining. You know, in case I'm too busy in the morning or I forget—I figured I'd get a head start.

I'm thinking, "Aarrrggggghhhh, I have to go to work in the morning. And those PEOPLE are going to be there. And it's that time of year it's dark when I get up. I HATE that."

And all of a sudden, I started to laugh. Everything I had been talking about in therapy, the information I had studied in all those books, my work on sobriety, and every one of those workshops clicked into place.

I said to myself, "Silver ('cause that's my name), you are lying here in a queen-sized feather bed under a warm, yummy down comforter (because we all know how cold Los Angeles gets in the winter). You have just turned off a ridiculously large TV with a remote control (heaven forbid, I should actually have to get up). There is food in your kitchen, a car in the driveway; you have indoor PLUMBING! In any third world country, Missy, YOU would be the empress!"

Which, to tell you the truth, I really liked the idea of!

In that moment, when I focused on what I had instead of what I didn't, I got my first glimpse into how the Law of Attraction works: you get more of what you focus on. Until that night, I had been focusing on how terrible things were, and guess what? They kept getting worse!

And just like that I started to focus on being grateful instead of resentful.

Here's what happened: I began to "Be Attractive" on purpose.

Where previously I had focused on everything that was wrong in my life, I started to focus on everything that was right: the amazing bed I slept in, the feel of a warm shower in the morning, the delicious food I put into my mouth, and the love of my friends and family.

As I observed the many gifts and happy circumstances I was starting to attract, I dove deeper. What would happen if I focused on the positive attributes of the man I was dating instead of looking for his flaws? What if I gave myself that very same gift?

As I learned to "Be Attractive" on purpose, I went from being a depressed, fearful woman who drank too much and dated men I wouldn't have been friends with if they were women to someone who is so happy today that my siblings think I've been taken over by an alien life force.

I have—it's called joy!

In this third quarter of my life, "Be Attractive" has even more meaning. In a society that can seem to worship only youth, I found myself feeling invisible. Worse than that, I began to resent young women. I caught myself thinking unkind thoughts: "Oh, sure, sweetie. You look good now. You'd better enjoy it; it won't last forever!" Yuck! I knew if I continued to focus on my lost youth, I would begin to attract people around me who agreed with my "has-been" self-assessment and that would not help my cause at all.

Here's what I did instead. I started to look for older women who were rockin' it, still vital and full of energy. The more I focused on them, the more I embraced my own age and vitality and the more I celebrated young women. I realized I'd had my youth and that this time is equally good.

Actually, I think it's even better because I DO know now what I wish I'd known then.

This is the essence of "Be Attractive." You attract more of what you focus on, and it's important to focus on your own beauty in every stage of life—your inner beauty, your energy, and your hard-won wisdom.

I challenge you. What would happen if you were to "Be Attractive" on purpose? What if you were to flip any negative focus you have to a positive one? What would your life be like if, with that simple switch, you could attract what you've always wanted?

Don't take my word for it. Try it yourself! Try attracting happy circumstances when you're in a bad mood. And try attracting negative circumstances (although I don't know why you would) when you're in a GOOD mood. It cannot be done.

"Be Attractive" has nothing to do with your looks. It has everything to do with shaping the life of your dreams on purpose. Join me. It's fun!

Silver Rose, *born in 1953, left a corporate career in 1997 to pursue her entrepreneurial dreams. President of Silver Rose Enterprises, she is a speaker, consultant, and coach who is known for revealing to others how to achieve amazing results by applying the Law of Attraction into their work and personal lives. An Employee Engagement Thought Leader, she infuses* ***ENERGY*** *into organizations and teams with strategies for:*

1. *re-energizing employees*
2. *increasing profitability*
3. *freeing leadership from the necessity of micro-managing results*

Her proudest accomplishment is having successfully raised her two daughters, at-risk teens she adopted from foster care at the ages of 12 and 15.

DISCOVER PASSION

TERRI, 51

MARK AND I MET WHEN he was seventeen and I was twenty. He worked in our neighborhood grocery store in Marcy, New York, where we both lived and also attended high school. He was a senior, but I had graduated three years prior and was already working as a hairstylist in a salon. He was very tall, more than six feet with a mop of dark, thick, curly hair, beautiful, dreamy blue eyes, and a great, big smile. Every time I went into the store, he asked me out, but I always said no because I knew he was younger than I was. And at that age, three years mattered, or at least they did to me.

After a few months of his asking, I finally said yes to lunch, just to get him to stop asking. Well! He was so much fun and so sweet that we ended up dating for a year. We had our birthdays together, celebrated Christmas, and met each other's parents. I went to his parent's home to hang out with his mom. He was the first boyfriend that I had that my father even gave a nickname. He called him My Sweet Baboo, taken from the Peanuts cartoon because Sally called Linus My Sweet Baboo. Things were going well for us dating. Then he went off to college. His mother and I drove him three-plus hours away and dropped him off. I didn't realize at the time, but that would be the end for us.

Four years later, Mark came back to town and into the hair salon that I owned for a haircut. This was the first time that I had seen him since he had left for college. By then I had married, was twenty-five, and was invested in what I thought was a happy marriage. Once again he said goodbye, and this time he was headed to Florida where he had a job waiting for him.

As life progressed, when I was twenty-nine, my husband and I decided to move from New York to South Carolina. My brother had moved there earlier, and when we visited him, we loved the sunshine, the outdoor life, and the weather, all of which attracted us to what we thought would be a better life for us both. So together we just went about living our lives again, what I thought was "living life." It would take me until I was in my mid-forties to realize that, in fact, I wasn't living at all.

At the age of thirty-six, my husband and I built a second home in a small community where all of the houses were built on one street that surrounded a lake. Most of the residents were summer visitors just as we would be, but a few lived there full time. It was very isolated as the nearest town and grocery store was twenty minutes away. Eventually, we moved permanently into the neighborhood, which is when I met the next door neighbor who had just given birth to a terminally ill baby boy who needed 24/7 care.

She was married and a school teacher who taught third grade. She was twenty-nine, and this was their first child. The baby was born with an underdeveloped brain and spinal cord. He was incapable of movement, could not lift his head, could not hear or see or cry. He was on a feeding tube and on oxygen full time. She was housebound and only left her home if either her husband or a nurse were there to care for the baby. Mostly, she was home with him.

We struck up a friendship that, only later, would I realize we both needed desperately. By this time I had taken up running, and I got her out of the house to run with me. Sometimes I would hang out with her when she just needed some adult conversation while caring for her son. She, unknowingly, opened my eyes to how unhappy I truly was in my marriage.

I watched her with her dying son and realized that she had more passion for life and living it to the fullest and to the best of her ability than I did. They did not know how long he was going to live, but she was determined to make his life the best...every day and to make memories with him... their first child. In the fall when the leaves dropped off the trees, she brought in an array of colorful leaves, surrounded him with them, and took photos of him to remember him during this season. On his six months' birthday she threw a party for him. She was thrilled that he made it that long. Birthday cake, party favors, and people came with gifts that she would eventually donate to the nearby hospital for other children in need. Christmas was yet another amazing celebration with lighted Christmas trees, decorations, music, presents, and even a Santa who was hired to pose for photos with him...and this was in June.

As I witnessed her passion and the joy that it gave her in giving to her child, I started to wonder if I would ever be that happy again in my life, or if this existence with my husband in our isolated marriage was just what my life would be until I died. I didn't lack for anything. I had great parents, a beautiful home, all the things I could want, and a healthy body, and yet I felt as if I didn't know who I was any longer.

The isolated home built on the one street surrounding the lake was like my marriage…alone and lonely, living with a good man that I did not love.

A year after the experience with my neighbor and her baby, I finally left that life, decided to find me again, and filed for divorce. I wanted to live life with enthusiasm, to reconnect with friends, and, most of all, to reconnect with my family. My husband and I did not see my family often because he did not enjoy being with others that much. He liked it when it was just the two of us. I had been secluded for too long, and I also wanted to put more into my career in hairdressing, which was the one area of my life that I still had passion for. I also wanted to do the traveling that I always said I wanted to experience. There was so much that I longed for. I moved away from the home around the lake and into town where I was working as a stylist. A month and a half after I left, I heard that the baby died. He had lived thirteen months surrounded with so much love and care, and his life had planted a seed inside of me…to live.

One day when I was forty-nine and at work, I received a call from Mark, just out of the blue. It was April of 2014, and I had not heard from him in twenty-four years. He had somehow heard about my move to South Carolina, said that he was going to be "in my neck of the woods" golfing with some of his friends, and thought it would be fun to run into me and catch up. By this time he was now living in Arizona.

I said, "Well, you're not just going to run into me in Charleston. We're going to have to make an arrangement to see each other. I'm away on the weekends a lot, so give me a call, and if I happen to be in town, I can meet up with you." Many weekends I spent visiting my parents 300 miles away, but, of course, I wanted to see him, and I was going to be in town, available, and ready to jump into seeing those dreamy blue eyes again. I couldn't wait to see him again.

A week later when he arrived in town and at the airport, I was at work with a client when he called. He said, "Can you meet me and my friends for lunch today?" I said, "Just finishing at work. What perfect timing!" I then looked at the client sitting in my chair with soaking wet hair and said to her, "I'm sorry, but you are going to either blow dry your own hair or leave it wet because I am leaving to go and meet up with my high school sweetheart." I then ran out the door and got to where he was having lunch with his friends as fast as I could. As he saw me coming toward them, he stood up, walked across the restaurant, and hugged me so tight that I thought he was going to break my neck. And at that time everything in my heart came alive!

We saw each other a few more times, and at dinner one night we sat for three hours and talked as if we were the only ones in the entire restaurant. Three days later, he changed his flight for a later time so that we could have more time with just the two of us again.

I took him to the airport to drop him off, and we were both feeling and saying the same words, "I don't want to let go of you. When will I see you again?" We both had the same feeling of not wanting to say goodbye. And then he left!

We started calling each other every day. Even with our three-hour time difference, we scheduled breaks in our workday to talk on the phone. Then he sent me a ticket to come for a visit to Scottsdale, Arizona, then another, and then another, and by the time December rolled around, I was flying out almost every other weekend. This back and forth went on for eight months.

On one of my weekends visiting him in Scottsdale, I said, "I'm tired of saying goodbye and missing you so much." And he said, "So am I. Let's figure out how to move you out here so we can date for real." Three months later, I finally made the move. I knew I had nothing to lose and everything to gain. So I took a passionate leap of faith and courage and, at the age of fifty, moved to Arizona to start my life over with the love of my life.

***Terri Edwards** has been a professional hairstylist for over thirty years. Within her tenure as a stylist, she has excelled with an educational approach to cutting and styling, dimensional coloring and body-waving, and an eye for fashion to ensure her customer's desires are translated into beautiful results.*

Terri has been a salon owner for the majority of her career and understands that quality work and customer satisfaction are what it takes to make a business successful. It is the love and care for people and her passion for hairstyling that set her above and beyond in her industry and an instant success in her field. Other passions include participating in fundraisers in the fight against breast cancer, keeping physically fit through exercise, sustaining an optimistic attitude, and enjoying the sunsets in Arizona. She is a master stylist at Pluma Designs in Scottsdale, Arizona.

In the article by Sabra House, Invite Adventure, she writes; "Adventure does not come into your life uninvited."

As I read Terri's story about passion, I can't help but wonder if passion may also require an invitation for it to burst into our hearts as it did for Terri. I speculate that if we can still recall the feelings of uncontrollable desire to have a major shift in our life at any age, and especially during the second half of our lives, I say go out of your mind and open your heart and burst out with passion!

HOLD CLOSE RELATIONSHIPS

BECKY, 64

I am and always have been fascinated with relationships—both the development of deep connections and the struggles that occur on the way to intimacy. Relationships can take on many forms, but whether interacting with lovers, friends, or family, we seem to progress through a similar pattern.

There is the initial attraction: fueled by hormonal forces and/or genuine interest, we focus on similarities—all the ways in which we are alike. For some, this period lasts for years; for others, mere months. It is easy at this juncture to hold someone close. What follows, however, is the crux of the relationship: we begin to notice the differences between us which can invite either curiosity/interest…or defense.

With enough differences…or enough defenses, we may choose to leave the relationship…or be left. The differences don't have to be great, just significant. Having moved long distances several times during my life, I know that the *difference* in geography alone can sometimes change the course of a friendship. So how do we hold close relationships, given the variables that seem to overwhelm attempts at intimacy?

I believe the core close relationship, the one that remains intact and secures us, no matter the emotional papercuts we may receive out in the world, is the relationship we develop with ourselves. This task is much harder for women than men. Many psychologists believe that, unlike men, women develop a sense of self in relationship to an "other." This essential element calls for us to choose carefully those "others" that will mirror and support our internal development. It also suggests that over time our relationships *will and must* change as we grow.

Thus, in the second half of life after we have raised children, supported partners, cared for aging parents, we often turn more definitively to female friendships for anchoring and support…like a return to ourselves…to those who can best mirror our female experiences in the world. For some women, the friendships that have been there all along will take deeper root in the soil of their hearts. For others, it will be the development of new relationships, more fitting of their current sense of self.

Therefore, every relationship, whether we stay, leave, or are left, is an opportunity for our own personal growth, growth that can lead to an even greater ability to love. I truly believe that our primary task in life is to learn to love deeper, better, more fully. In this regard, we actually *hold all relationships* close. It's just that some change form over time; therefore, sometimes the relationships that have been the hardest, that seem the least successful, in hindsight may have provided the greatest venue for the strengthening of our own heart muscles.

Now in my sixties, I have reached a time when I can finally acknowledge the men and women whom I held close at one time or another, those folks who have been "runners" in my life, running in to shine a mirror on some aspect of myself that was impinging my own growth and capacity to love. Somewhere along the way, I began to realize that love is not a zero-sum game, but rather with each endeavor, our heart holds the capacity to expand a little more...and thus, opens the door to greater opportunities for love and intimacy.

Becky Jandrey, *Ph.D. is a licensed psychologist with private practices in Santa Rosa, California, and Scottsdale, Arizona. She has been interested in gender differences since she was a little girl, curious about her mysterious and quiet father. Her* *practice invites adults and couples who are struggling with all life issues, including the complexities of relationships, managing stress, anxiety, depression, as well as spiritual struggles. She is EMDR trained for the management of trauma.*

As a frequent presenter/educator for Kaiser Health Education in California, she combines psychological insight, humor, and practical solutions for coping with life's obstacles. Her talks have varied widely from topics like "Why Does He Act Like That?" to "Heart to Heart: Caring for your Heart Emotionally and Physically."

FORGIVE

NANCY, 64

One thing that gets revealed with time is that we are arriving at an important choice point. Up until now we felt we had so much time ahead. Now it dawns on us that there is an urgency to make changes if we want to reach for and reap the rewards of a full life. It's time to let go, untie, and unburden ourselves from patterns of thoughts, emotions, and behaviors that have kept us down, held us back, tripped us up, and prevented us from enjoying the best of ourselves and our relationships. If we truly want to make this next period of life a time of release, joy, growth, and fulfillment, then we need to start with learning to forgive. First ourselves. Then others. Then just about everything.

I was stuck feeling victimized and needed to make a decision to release myself from feelings that locked me up. It turns out that, for me, learning to forgive myself and others is "self-centered" in the best possible meaning. When I began forgiving myself, I created a foundational building block that opened up a path to forgiving others. As I'm maturing, I'm dipping into the deep well of human compassion, and it has given me evidence that it is not only possible, but vital, for me to have the next chapter of my life unfold with freedom and without guilt.

What do we need to forgive ourselves and others for, and how do we do it? We need to be forgiving for whatever we have done, neglected to do, failed to achieve, or for whatever has been done to us or we perceive to have been done to us. Like a snake shedding its skin, we can wriggle out of past constraints, beyond past perceptions of ourselves that make us feel unworthy, and let go of feelings that perpetuate sadness, guilt, anger, regret. Shedding the past promotes our well-being and decreases our dis-ease. Once the urgency is felt and the choice is made, each of us can find the tools and pathways to do it, whether it is through deepening our faith, starting a new course of therapy, meditating and visualizing, joining with others to explore "wise" aging and "age-ing to sage-ing," or any practice that will take us toward compassion and forgiveness.

As we age, we can more clearly see the effects of carrying grudges and being harsh and unforgiving. It's sad to encounter overly negative, hard-hearted, joyless people who learned from the past that the future will be bleak and that people will disappoint them. They seem to have an unwavering commitment to one way of seeing events and people with no counter-balancing force to rethink, release, re-imagine either what happened in the past, what the effects have been, or how they can release the jail cell they've put themselves in and walk free.

It's easier to see in others, but not so easy to see pieces of it in ourselves. Take a look in the mirror. Look carefully for places where you hold hurts. Is it around the mouth, pulling the lips down into a frown? I deliberately and slightly pull up the corners of my lips. Is it around the eyes, dulling the reflected light of the world? I try deliberately and slightly smiling with my eyes. See where a lack of forgiveness might be freezing you and picture how being compassionate and forgiving could free you. We all make mistakes. Think of a time when someone forgave you or extended compassion to you. Feel the forgiveness and compassion. Let it seep into you. That's what you can give yourself and others. Ask whether you want to stay glued to past dramas, whether you need to carry what happened, whether it might serve you well to release it. I find peace of mind and relaxation of tension by letting the past go and leaning in to a tranquil present.

We all make mistakes. What is welcoming is an ability to recognize shortcomings and want to change. Whatever we see and feel and think and however it shows up in our bodies, we can be grateful we're allowing it to come up. Put it in the light and examine it. It's probably not as large and important as it seems when hidden.

Eventually, with whatever practice you choose to open up and forgive, you will be free to walk out of your cage and wave goodbye to it. Take this newfound opening and try it on friends and family. What have you not forgiven them for? What's the price? If there's an opening for a choice, grab it! If there's forgiveness to be extended, do it! Don't expect others to be ready exactly at the time you are. That's not important. Just be willing to change the dynamic on your end, and, inevitably, it will change on theirs.

What is the pay off? Your forgiveness muscle is now active, ready to respond to new perceived transgressions and disappointments caused by you and others. Your attitude is a blessing for you and your next chapter, as a continuously learning, evolving, open, and accepting person who meets the challenges of life and aging by gracefully keeping a simple, yet significant, flow of forgiveness for yourself and others.

***Nancy Dallett** practices the art of public history, which requires the skills of a historian combined with the skills to communicate to diverse public audiences. She collaborates with curators, writers, graphic designers, artists, and scholars in a variety of subjects to bring good public history to museums, television, radio, events, publications, trail signage, and public art. She often uses the tool of oral history to get multiple perspectives. Early in her career, she had the privilege of traveling the country and recording personal stories of people who had immigrated through Ellis Island. She is interested in the intersection of memory and history, how collective memory is formed and carried, and how it shapes current understandings and relationships among people and places.*

GIVE

GABRIELLE, 71

We have all heard the expression, "It is better to give than to receive." However, looking at the culture in which we live, we certainly hear more about self-focused taking than other-focused giving. Consumerism tells us to go out and shop and get what we need: "Take care of yourself." It seems that that our cultural motto, "What's in it for me?" more accurately describes our national behavior. Interestingly, in the research on happiness that has compared cultures and countries all over the world, we Americans are the wealthiest population in the world, but we are ranked as one of the least happy countries. Could it be that a self-focused, "What is in it for me?" and "Take care of yourself" approach does not jive with being truly happy, but that a focus on giving to others does.

Elizabeth Dunn, a professor at the University of British Columbia, studies human happiness. She recently told an international conference that charitable giving not only makes people feel better but can lower their blood pressure. In her study, subjects were given money and a choice to spend it on themselves or to give it away. She found that those who gave it away reported feeling happier than those who kept it for themselves and that their blood pressure dropped. She and others have concluded that giving makes you happier and is healthy for your heart. Brain scans of those who give show that giving to charity lights up the pleasure center of the brain and gives that "warm glow" feeling. Studies on altruism indicate that altruistic (other-focused) emotions and behaviors are associated with greater well-being, health, and longevity. In other words, we are happier and healthier when we are thinking of and helping others.

Why is this so? The simple truth is that we are hardwired to give. Our brain got most of its hardwiring about 60,000-100,000 years ago when we lived as small family/tribal groups in very dangerous environments. Helping each other and working together cooperatively ensured group survival. Early *Homo sapiens* needed each other to stay alive. Love, concern, shared group goals, and physical closeness bonded them and created safety. Interdependence was an essential. Taking care of each other was hardwired into the brain then and still is now.

However, today in our high-tech world, we don't live interdependently. We don't hunt and share the kill together. We have Safeway and Fry's where we pass through the aisles trying not to touch the other's cart: God forbid that you should risk a smile, make eye contact, or say, "How are you?" There, we hunt in our modern, shiny, brightly-lit forest filled with abundant pre-fab, pre-killed food. We are surrounded with plenty and more than well-fed. However, all of our plenitude has not made us happy. We are a wealthy nation, but all of our stuff and gadgets have not made us a happy nation.

So giving–what does giving have to do with all of this? The answer is really quite simple. When we focus our thoughts and behaviors altruistically on giving to and helping others, it awakens long ago, unused neural pathways, bred into our DNA many thousands of years ago. It helps us to feel like we belong, are needed, and are loved. It helps us to feel whole again, happy and safe.

So tomorrow or the next day, you will go hunting for what you need, out again into our shiny modern forests. However, try something different. Take time to smile at the clerk who helps you. Ask him about his day. Think of a friend who might need a card or a call from you. Find a favorite charity—donate, volunteer, or get involved by giving of yourself in some way. Whatever you do, no matter how small it might seem, it *will* make a difference. In our modern, high-tech world, we have forgotten who we really are and that we need to give to each other and care for each other in order to be truly happy. So try an experiment. Just for a day or two, focus on others by giving of yourself in some small way. Then, notice what happens to you and to those you reach out to. Notice the smile that lights up in your heart and on others' faces.

They say that wisdom comes with age. For me, although it has taken time and many bumps and detours along the way, a truth has emerged, which is that patience, forgiveness, acceptance of others, and a generous, loving spirit provide the keys to true happiness. Love shows up as gift. And, it is the power of giving that has the power to change everything one smile at a time.

***Gabrielle Lawrence**, Ph.D. is a licensed psychologist in private practice in the state of Arizona. She is a clinical member of the American Association of Marriage and Family Therapist, Registered Play Therapist and Play Therapy Supervisor, and a trauma and loss specialist for children and adults. Additionally, she is certified in EMDR and is completing advanced training in Somatic Experiencing Therapy. She is a recognized clinician working in the area of grief recovery and traumatic loss. Dr. Lawrence received her master's in Early Learning and Development and her doctorate in Counseling Psychology from Columbia University. In 2002 Dr. Lawrence was a recipient of the Hon Kachina Award for outstanding service to the community as a volunteer and founder of New Song Center and, in the same year, also received an award for her work with children from the **Scottsdale Life** magazine Five Who Care award.*

BELIEVE

GLORIA, 77

"What we think, we become." ~ Buddha

BELIEVING IN GOD HAS ALWAYS been with me.

As a child around four or five years old, I remember being in the church, which was an old large cathedral-like structure with marble pillars and a domed ceiling with pictured angels floating in clouds overhead. It was beautiful with holy images of Jesus and various saints everywhere in the statuary, the paintings, and the stained glass windows.

As I gazed at it all, I felt myself being held by all the holy ones, and I felt perfectly safe and "heard" when in that space. I believed in God.

My belief was tested early because at six and half, my father was killed in WWII on the island of Sabu in the Philippines. This was the time when children were "seen and not heard," so no one told me my father had been killed; however, I sat in front of my mother as she opened the telegram with the terrible news. In that moment, I saw, I felt, I knew and perceived the depth of his loss in myself. Everything changed as now I had a problem with God. I had prayed for my daddy daily since he'd left for war. This was the first time in my life I had asked for something and not received it! It took me about two years to accept this loss; my heart ached, and the only one I could talk with was God. The only place I felt seen or heard was sitting in the silent, empty church and sharing my suffering with God and feeling heard and held. Not fixed, but at the same time, not alone. I prayed to the guardian angel pictured above my bed each night.

My personal connection with God has always stayed with me, even when I left the church at 17. It was then that I heard the contradiction between the clergy's words and God's presence as I had experienced it. Even after leaving the church, I still believed in God, in fact, perhaps believed more strongly. By leaving, I put my trust in myself and my connection with God, not in the teachings of the clergy. Through grace, ten years later, I met a system of inner work that addressed the esoteric meaning of life and spirituality.

I learned about myself and the universe, which enabled me to return to church with a much deeper understanding and with the ability to separate in myself the wisdom, the mysteries of Christ's teaching, without expecting the "organization" to mirror that or change its ways. What a gift!

I have always been an avid reader. Books were my friends, and they opened the doors to many worlds, internal and external. Literature, history, and every form of psychological study attracted me. As I discovered deeper, unknown parts of myself, books revealed avenues of inquiry and increased my understanding of myself and the world at large. This adventure has held my attention for more than four decades. The studies have enlivened me and brought me clear realization that I am and have always been in God's hands the entire way. Yes, of course, there have been ups and downs, joy and sorrow, pain and suffering; that is the way of transformation, as I understand it. Yes, life is full.

It is interesting to look back…my health has been normal in that issues have shown up and been overcome, perhaps eventually due to lack of denial on my part. My recognition and acceptance of "what is" has always allowed solutions to emerge that have brought me back to full health. The biggest challenge, almost four years ago and out of nowhere it seemed, was a brain aneurysm that seriously threatened my life. Again, grace entered when I realized that I may die at any moment and… I surrendered to that possibility. I was able to consciously leave it in God's hands, believing that if I die that is the right thing, if I live that is the right thing. I did not have "to do" anything, just accept and let go. The aneurysm was removed safely and is no longer a threat. I am healthy; I am alive.

I believe the most helpful tool so far in my life has been the introduction of meditation, of which I have partaken in many forms. The form is not so important as the practice. One of my greatest weaknesses is and has been the tendency to do too much, meaning I am able to stay in motion most of the time, which then eats up my remembrance of myself. Meditation practices have taught me to embrace stillness: bodily stillness and internal stillness and to allow for a quiet mind when all is working rightly.

I have learned to be still internally and listen to my mind, listen with my heart, feel and sense with my body, all of which gives me the information needed to recognize the truth of a thing. As a blessing, I have found my own voice along the way. To me living bravely means increasing my ability to embrace stillness and my ability to be present to the internal and external worlds.

Gloria Cuevas-Barnett *is Director of the Center for Development of Human Potential. She is a certified Enneagram teacher in the Helen Palmer, David Daniels Narrative tradition. The center has developed a unique, highly intensive format for using Fourth Way Inner Work & The Enneagram of Personality Types for self-understanding, as well as personal and spiritual development. Gloria provides individual coaching and spiritual direction.*

She is a longtime student of esoteric studies, a facilitator of Fourth Way Inner Study groups and workshops for over 45 years, leading spiritual retreats in the United States, Europe, Canada, and Mexico.

AFTERWORD

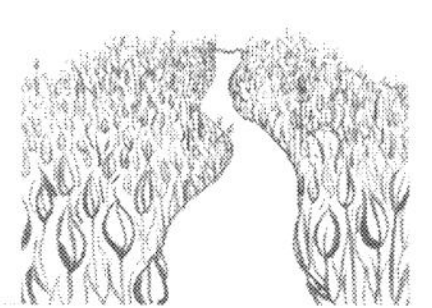

JOY

MARY BETH, 61

We often hear the phrase "surprised by joy," but what exactly does it mean? Should joy be a surprise? When we're young, joy is a natural emotion, a given. It comes organically without much thought. But as the years pass, we're reminded to "look for the joy in life." We question whether we even experience joy; if we do experience joy in our younger years, we wonder whether it will dissipate as we age.

The words *joy* and *rejoice* appear in the Bible over 300 times. Numerous books have been written about joy: *The Joy of Cooking*, *The Joy of Sex*, *Choose Joy*, and many more. Many often say they have been "surprised by joy" over the years: surprised at the joy of a romantic relationship, surprised at the joy of solitude, surprised at the joy of launching a new business, surprised at the joy of grandchildren.

We need not look any farther than into the eyes of a child to see pure joy. It is so pointedly expressed by my 2 ½-year-old granddaughter. Does she bring me joy? Oh, absolutely, but it isn't the joy she imparts that affects me so intensely. It is HER joy, so simple and pure: the joy of picking up a rock, examining it, and putting it in her pocket as if it were a jewel, the joy of completing the same puzzle over and over again, and the joy of swinging higher and higher each time at the park. She, like so many other toddlers, squeals with glee when she splashes in the bathtub and breaks out dancing the minute she hears music. It is clearly pure joy, and it has had a profound effect on me. Her behavior is a reminder to set the worries of life aside and just "be." So then it begs the question: why is joy so elusive for us adults? Is it because we are so busy chasing the right partner, the right career, the right house as a means to finding joy in our lives?

Perhaps joy isn't elusive at all; we simply need to recognize it and embrace it. According to Sandra Brown, author, lecturer, and psychopathologist, "Joy comes when you make peace with who you are, where you are, why you are, and who you are not with." If not a child to remind you to recognize joy, then find your "joy catalyst"—that one person, activity, or possibly moment of solitude that causes you to recognize that you are experiencing joy in its purest form—perhaps even causing you to squeal with glee!

During the process of interviewing the women for *Living Brave*, Hilda and I discovered that most of them are experiencing joy at their various stages of life. In fact, in many cases, their joy felt contagious. We left many interviews feeling exhilarated . . .joyful, in fact! These women find joy in viewing something as seemingly mundane as a rock while hiking or exploring. They find joy in many of the repetitive tasks they perform each day, and they feel unadulterated joy with each accomplishment, however small it may be. They have found peace; they know who they are; they are joyfully thriving.

HOPE

HILDA, 65

CURRENTLY IN OUR SALON, WE have three "young ones" on our team. They are from the millennial generation, thus, our term for them, "the young ones." Sometime during her first month of working with us as an assistant, Stephanie, at the time 20 years old, asked me what I thought was a very mature question: "What advice would you give me at my age to help me in my career?" Frankly, in all of my years working with young people coming into our industry, none had ever asked me this question.

Taken by surprise, I answered quickly (their minds move swiftly as if texting or scrolling their smart phones, and they want answers now!) "I would stay focused on my career and not allow myself to get as distracted as I did. If I knew then what I know now, I would have paid more attention to it. Continue to educate and grow yourself, and it will reward you in ways that you can't even imagine at this time."

Afterwards and still to this day, I think of so much more that I could have answered. "I would make a plan and plan it out week by week and month by month and check and recheck my yearly numbers, bookings, accomplishments," and on and on, I still think I could have said. But the truth is there is one answer that stands out in my thoughts: "I would have unwavering hope for myself."

In his six books and 262 articles about the impact that hope can have on aspects of life, such as health, work, education, and personal meaning, C.R. Snider in *Hope Theory* writes that there are three main things that make up hopeful thinking: Goals—approaching life in a goal-oriented way; Pathways—finding different ways to achieve your goals, and Agency—believing that you can instigate change and achieve these goals.

He characterizes hopeful thinkers as people who are able to establish clear goals, imagine multiple workable pathways toward those goals, and persevere, even when obstacles get in their way. In her book *Rising Strong*, Brene Brown, quotes C.R. Snider and writes: *"Hope is not an emotion; it's a cognitive process."*

Of course, I would add that hope is a verb. It requires doing, as in setting goals to accomplish your dreams. Engage your physical body and keep it fed, exercised, and mindful to the process. Stay curious and invite adventure, all the while discovering ways to keep the passion alive and thriving. Forgive yourself when hope seems to wane, and give yourself reassuring praise when you accomplish another stage of confidence. Stay flexible, both physically and emotionally, like a tree in a storm; don't let the wind scare you from coming back up again. Refresh and hold close relationships with those who promote and empower you and release those who try to hold you back. And lastly, believe in you, believe in others who are good and honest and have earned your trust, and believe that you were created to be the magnificent you.

Unwavering hope for ourselves is the elixir of thriving all along the way to the finish. Consider that all the best-laid plans can go off course, and no matter how much planning and worry we call upon into our lives, what keeps us moving forward when times get rough is our hope, the state of mind that we cognitively decide to draw upon. It takes time and the progression of years until we become hopeful in all of our thinking. Thoughtful consideration of what we desire to experience and achieve in our lives is indeed the fountain of youthful living and living bravely.

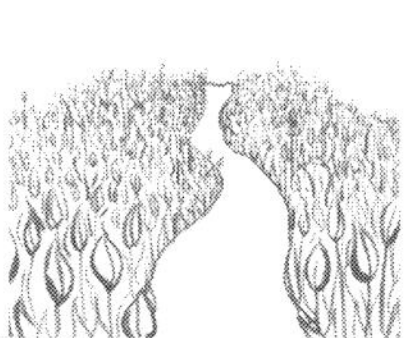

CONCLUSION

As I sit down to write the conclusion to *Living Brave*, I find myself hesitating to say, ". . . the end!"

I WOULD LIKE FOR THE book not to end. Instead, both Mary Beth and I would like to keep the voices of women pouring out and onto more pages.

As most plans have a tendency to change as they move forward, our plan for writing the book was altered and what we thought would be a resource for creating safety nets and finding the pathways to thriving, instead became a reminder, as Lory Fischler in her review stated, "...that we women are powerful. We are resilient. And we have each other. *Living Brave* reminds us of that. What a gift."

The book became a reminder that women are, in fact, powerful and resilient. Through their stories, we heard their voices. We read their thoughts. And we felt their emotions as they moved through our pages, some more painful than others, and yet at the end of each story, we knew that each woman was undeniably powerful and resilient because she found the authentic gift...herself.

In the introduction, I stated that what happens to one woman happens for the benefit of all women. I believe this with all my being and only wish that I had understood this principle in my younger years. But, like most of us, we all make mistakes and can only forgive ourselves and move forward to now take on the task of uplifting others along the path. Darn! I so wish that we didn't have to grovel with the chickens before flying with the mighty eagles. But, of course, the eagles have their own issues, and we have to be well-prepared before joining them up in the air. (Please don't anyone send me a message about belittling the chickens. I love chickens.) Nevertheless, reading a book about women's stories and their struggles and their reach for autonomy connects us and reminds us that we have each other, and we can ascend with each other.

No matter your age, whether 20, as is our youngest voice in the book or 91, our eldest, friendships with other women are, without a doubt, a gift. Lend yourself, stop the judgments, be kind and trustworthy, be a friend to keep a friend, and discover a plethora of companionship, safety nets, and enjoyment, as the women did in Chapter 11.

Many of the women who shared their stories have strong and loving marriages. We celebrate their unions and know that couples who grow strong together, stay together, and actually live longer lives. We went through a phase in the salon when we decided to count the number of good marriages that we witnessed through our clientele. (Everyone needs a little hope of coming attractions.) And we discovered that we had many who did. There is hope for our women who are still looking for that special relationship with a man. But don't give up your girlfriends. We need each other.

Endings are not always final—they can be the beginning of even greater experiences, as revealed in the book. In reading over the words that seem to stand out the most in the pages of the *Living Brave*, we came to the conclusion that words like living, sharing, thriving, hoping, and reinventing are all verbs that require a call to action. We invite you to take action in your lives and generate pathways for yourself to thrive...and bring others with you.

There is no ending, only another beginning.

Yours truly,

Hilda and Mary Beth